BASIC for Business for the PDP-11

Alan J. Parker
Associate Professor of Management
School of Business and Organizational Science
Florida International University
Miami, Florida

Val Silbey
Associate Professor of Management Science
Department of Management Science
Ball State University
Muncie, Indiana

Reston Publishing Company, Inc.
A Prentice-Hall Company
Reston, Virginia

PDP is a trademark of Digital Equipment Corporation.

Library of Congress Cataloging in Publication Data

Parker, Alan J
BASIC for business for the PDP-11.

Includes bibliographical references and index.
1. Basic (Computer program language)
I. Silbey, V., joint author. II. Title.
HF5548.5.B2P36 001.6′424 79-19156
ISBN 0-8359-0349-4

10 9 8 7 6

Printed in the United States of America

To our parents, David, Sally, Stan, and Ada
and to our wives, Ann and Margie

Contents

Read By

MID TERM

Preface

Courses in computer programming and management information systems are required in most collegiate business schools. Such courses teach the student to think logically and they provide an introduction to computer terminology. But a knowledge of the terminology is not enough to generate an understanding of computers, and logical thinking by itself does not unlock the power of computers. Computers are used to solve problems, and students must learn *how* computers can help them solve problems.

In this text we have presented problems from the business data processing environment as a reason for learning BASIC. Of course, not all facets of a problem can be explained at once, since different parts require different approaches and tools. But step by step, as we look at the many facets of a problem and introduce the necessary BASIC statements, the student will collect the tools needed to solve all these problems.

Because of the emphasis on problem-solving, the focus of this book is the point at which problem elements meet language capabilities. The BASIC language fundamentals, syntax and grammar, are not the dominant elements —they are subordinate to the problem requirements. So language capabilities that do not fit clearly into a problem context were omitted for the purposes of this text.

The programs were designed and run on the PDP-11 series of computers with BASIC-PLUS or BASIC-PLUS-TWO. In order to use computers in business, files are required. There are significant differences in the BASIC file instructions among various computer manufacturers. Since the programs used in the book were designed for the PDP-11, the PDP-11 file instructions are used.

We would like to express gratitude to our former students, Susan Clay and especially Manuel Castro, for their assistance. Professor Bruce DeSautel was extremely helpful, offering many suggestions to clarify explanations throughout the book. Our thanks goes also to Margaret Wickline and Becky White, who did an excellent job typing the manuscript.

A. J. Parker
V. Silbey

1 / Introduction

Performance Objectives

At the end of this chapter you should be able to:

- Understand the importance and impact of computer usage
- Sign-on and sign-off a terminal
- Understand how the computer system reacts to system commands

Everyone living in the United States today is affected by computers. The federal government uses computers in almost all of its departments. The Social Security Administration and the Internal Revenue Service are highly computerized. State and local governments use computers for tax collections and assessments. Businesses and utilities use computers for customer billing. Banks and other financial organizations use computers to handle customer accounts. Hospitals use computers for hospital administration and patient billing. Unless you live as a hermit in a cave, you are affected everyday in some way by computers.

THE IMPACT OF COMPUTERS ON SOCIETY

The computer revolution is approximately thirty years old. Since 1946 when the ENIAC (the first electronic digital computer) began operating, the changes that computers have wrought have been prodigious. All areas of our society have been, and are being, touched by computers. From the time we read the morning newspaper (typeset by computer) until we go to sleep watching television (computer allocated programs), we are constantly using computers either directly or indirectly.

The effect of the Computer Revolution can be compared to the Industrial Revolution, which also radically changed society. Both revolutions changed work and leisure activities. With respect to work, no occupations were left untouched by the Industrial Revolution, except artisan crafts (sculptors, painters, etc.). Now, approximately two hundred years after the beginning of the Industrial Revolution, there are no coopers (barrel makers), wainwrights (horse drivers), millers (flour makers) or weavers (cloth makers) in the old sense of those occupations. The products or services are still supplied, but the methods of production have been radically altered. Work hours at the beginning of the Industrial Revolution were dawn to dusk, six days a week, leaving limited time for leisure activities. Now leisure is available during long weekends and after working hours. The impact of the Industrial Revolution may aid us in imagining the breadth of changes that will result from the computer revolution.

Initially, the few digital computers available were used for numerical calculations ("number crunching") by an elite group of mathematicians, engineers and scientists. Since then, radical changes in the cost, design, and use of computers have occurred. Today, computers are no longer the exclusive tool of mathematicians and scientists. More computers are used in businesses, such as insurance, banking, retailing, utilities, manufacturing and hospitals, than are used in scientific organizations. Almost daily, television and newspapers report new uses of computers. The computer has taken the drudgery out of calculating and printing bills, invoices, paychecks and other record-keeping tasks, freeing people from many of the routine tasks of adding numbers together. With the shift of paperwork from people to computers, some significant implications have become apparent. For society the use of computers is considered by some people to be a mixed blessing. But blaming the computer for human failings is an error. The computer itself is a tool. It is simply a new technology and this technology will be used as society chooses. The first quarter century of the computer revolution has brought us

- Computer controlled air-defense and air traffic control systems
- The landing of men on the moon
- Large scale and inexpensive use of checking accounts
- Credit cards
- Integrated reservation systems for travel
- Computerized hospitals
- A new field of employment (data processing)
- Management Information Systems

But so far we can barely envision what the second quarter century will bring.

Impact of Computers on Management

The first computer dedicated to business applications was installed in 1954. Since that time business applications have become more sophisticated. Applications at first consisted of simple clerical functions: preparation of payroll, financial statements, and other bookkeeping tasks. Thousands of clerical jobs were replaced by computers. The computer could do these routine tasks faster, cheaper, and more accurately.

The next major step was the use of computers to make simple decisions, e.g., ordering to restock inventory when a low level has been reached. At the present time, computers are the tools used to implement Management Information Systems (MIS). Management Information Systems transcend routine business applications because attention is focused upon providing management with the proper information for decision making. In many organizations, it is common to see computer terminals in the offices of the president and other senior executives. And MIS will become more common in organizations as computers become less expensive and easier to use. The manager of the future will need some familiarity with computers in order to make use of the great potential of MIS.

WHY USE BASIC?

BASIC (Beginners All-purpose Symbolic Instruction Code) is a computer language. It was chosen for this text for numerous reasons. The first and most significant reason is that it is the simplest computer language that is widely available. The second reason is that the time required to learn BASIC is the shortest of all the common languages. Additionally, the extensions and enhancements made to BASIC have added power to the language, making BASIC comparable to other, more difficult languages.

A final reason for learning BASIC is that almost all of the manufacturers and vendors of microcomputers and minicomputers provide BASIC for their machines and systems; and these smaller computers are the fastest growing segment of the computer market. Radio Shack alone sold over 100,000 microcomputers in 1978; and every one of these small computers used BASIC for its higher-level language. Computers of this type are used by the hobbyist as well as by the largest organization.

Prerequisites

This text is written with an assumption that the student has some basic knowledge of business transactions such as payroll, invoicing, and customer statements. It is also helpful if the student has the ability to think logically. The computer is not affected by emotions. If the student is a disciple of Marshall McLuhan, beware: The computer is not!

It is *not* important, however, that you possess a mathematical background in order to learn BASIC. (A mathematical background, however, will not penalize a student.) On the basis of the successful completion of this text alone, the reader will probably *not* be able to find employment as a computer programmer or technician; but the student will understand the fundamentals of programming and be able to write programs of reasonable complexity.

HOW TO USE A COMPUTER

In business, one usually wishes to computerize a manual system or function. It is important to understand how the manual system operates in order to successfully perform this function on a computer. Throughout this text, the major example will be the payroll function. It will serve as a vehicle for the introduction of programming (instructing the computer to perform a function, in this case payroll). A payroll system consists of the collection and manipulation of data to pay people for their time spent working. An hourly payroll system will be analyzed and programmed.

The first step in computerizing a payroll is an analysis of the system and a clear definition of the system: The Silpar Company, Inc., has approximately 14 hourly employees used in the fabrication and assembly of computer components. All hourly wages are computed on the basis of hourly rate multiplied by the regular hours worked, plus time-and-a-half for overtime. The normal work week is 40 hours with one paid hour per day for lunch and coffee breaks. An employee may work a maximum of 20 overtime hours per week, if work is available. The payroll system should produce weekly paychecks and the necessary reports for tax and auditing purposes.

It should be obvious that all of the analysis and definition of the computerized payroll system has not been performed in the preceding paragraph. However, enough has been stated to begin the computerization of the payroll system. The first step consists of identifying the data necessary to produce all of the output (paychecks and reports). An examination of the manual system data will provide the answers to our first step.

In the manual system, each employee has a record that contains information such as employee number, social security number, address, marital status, number of dependents, hourly wages, wage payments made during the last year, federal income taxes withheld, FICA (Social Security) and other miscellaneous data. Each week, time cards are used to accumulate the regular and overtime hours worked by each employee. At the end of a pay period (weekly), the time cards are signed by the employee's supervisor and sent to the payroll department for processing. The payroll department computes the employee's pay for the week, the required deductions, issues a check for the employee's net pay (gross pay minus deductions), enters this information into the employee's record, and prepares a payroll register. A payroll register is a listing of the amounts paid to all employees, all deductions subtracted from their pay, and totals for all amounts.

In computerizing the payroll function or any other business application, it is very important to understand that files are used exactly as in the manual system. In the payroll, two files are used. The first is the employee *master file;* it consists of the *records* of all the employees. Each employee record contains data in *fields.* The fields are: employee number, name, hourly rate, etc. It is important to note that all records in one file must contain the same fields in the same order. Also, fields may contain data that is numeric, alphabetic, or both alphabetic and numeric (alphanumeric). The second file is the time *file;* it consists of a record for each employee and contains as fields the regular and overtime hours worked. With these two files and the appropriate program, a payroll register will be produced.

COMPUTER TERMINALS

Sometime in the not too distant future, we may communicate with computers by simply talking. In many science fiction films this is already the case. Unfortunately, technology has not taken us that far yet. As a consequence, we have to communicate with a computer through some sort of mechanical device. The common name for this device is a computer terminal or as it is simply known—a terminal. All terminals have many things in common. One important feature is a keyboard that is similar to a typewriter keyboard.

The terminal allows us to communicate with the computer. It takes the information that we transmit by pressing on the keys and transforms it into electronic signals that can be understood by the computer. Conversely, when the computer communicates with us, the terminal transforms the electronic signals from the computer into characters printed on paper or displayed on a video screen. A short way of referring to the screen is by the initials CRT, which stands for cathode ray tube. The way messages are written on a CRT is similar to the way pictures appear on a TV screen. (A television picture tube is a CRT, but no one calls it that, except technicians.)

You should not be timid about using computer terminals: The important thing to remember is that *you cannot damage* a computer or do any harm to it by typing *anything* on the terminal. The only way you can cause any damage is by banging on the terminal or spilling coffee on it; and that will *only affect the terminal* and not the computer. *You may type anything* on the terminal and *not harm or "break" the computer system.* Similarly, neither the terminal nor the computer can harm the user in any physical manner.

Sign-On Procedure (SON)

Every time you wish to use the computer, there is a very formal method of telling the computer that you: (a) wish to use it and (b) that you have authorization to use it. These steps are called the sign-on procedure (SON). Silly as it may sound, your first step, after sitting at the terminal, is to make sure it is on.

Once the terminal is on, type the word "HELLO." Then press the carriage return (CR) or transmit (T) key. The system will respond with a message. You always indicate by means of the *carriage return* or *transmit* key (CR or T) that you want to send a message to the computer. (Some systems require you to press CR to send a message; others require you to press T. In this book we will always use CR for this function.)

Next, type your account number (given to you by your instructor) and press the CR key. The system will respond with the word PASSWORD if your account number is valid and correctly entered. (**Note:** The number zero is a different character from the letter O.) If your account number was incorrectly entered, the system will respond with a message asking you to reenter your account number.

When the system responds with "PASSWORD," you should type your password and press the CR key. The system will respond with "READY."

It is *very* important to make sure that every time you sign-on, you use your correct account number and password. As the course progresses, you will be writing and saving programs. These will be stored under your account number and password (similar to a numbered *Swiss Bank* account). The only way you will be able to retrieve the information that you have stored is by using the same account number and password. Once you have signed-on, the computer reserves a "work area" for you; after you sign-off, your work area is erased. The concept is the same as being assigned a blackboard for a time period and at the end of that period, the blackboard is erased.

To recap:

1. Make sure the terminal is turned on.
2. Type HELLO (CR). (System responds with a message.)
3. Type your account number (CR). (System responds with PASSWORD.)
4. Type your password (CR). (System responds with READY.)

The word HELLO is a system command that indicates someone wishes to use the computer. The proper entry of the account number and password sets up an area within the computer system that will be yours as long as you remain at the terminal. This is called your "working area." Another area, where you may store information in the computer memory, will also be reserved for you. It is called your "save area." Your working area will vanish when you finish at the terminal. Your save area will remain and vary in size with the amount of information you ask the computer to retain.

Sign-Off Procedure (SOF)

When you are finished at the terminal type "BYE." The system responds with "CONFIRM." Next type "Y" (for yes) and hit CR. The system responds with a series of messages and disconnects the terminal from the computer.

Programming in BASIC

In order to write programs (instructions understood by the computer), the sign-on (SON) procedure must be used. At the beginning of each sample program in the next chapter, the letters "SON" will appear as a shorthand method of indicating a sign-on. The letters "SOF" will indicate a sign-off procedure. The program in BASIC is entered through the terminal after the SON.

The greatest problem that people have when first using a terminal is that they forget to press the carriage return (CR) or transmit (T) key after entering something on a line. The result is that nothing happens! The CR or T *must* be pressed to indicate the end of your message to the computer. Until it is pressed, the computer assumes that you have not finished whatever you are trying to tell it!

2 / Performing Simple Calculations

Performance Objectives

At the end of this chapter you should be able to:

- Write a program that will do simple calculations
- Enter a program into the computer and use simple BASIC commands (NEW, SAVE, LIST, RUN)
- Use BASIC instructions for data manipulation and calculations (assignment to data fields, addition, subtraction, multiplication, division, output of results, end of program)
- Modify an existing program using BASIC commands (OLD, RENAME, REPLACE)

The first uses of computers were computational. The power of the computer was used to perform engineering and scientific calculations. In business there are many instances where calculations have to be performed. Computers can perform these calculations very quickly. In this chapter we will show you how to program the computer to perform calculations and how to display the results of these calculations.

WRITING A PROGRAM

The first problem deals with payroll calculations. Starting with elementary calculations, this problem will be expanded to include more and more realistic elements. For the very first problem you are given the hourly rate and the number of hours worked. You are asked to calculate the gross pay for an employee.

Flowcharting The Logic of a Program

One way of showing what a program does is to diagram the general steps of a program. Such a diagram shows the order in which the various steps are performed. Conceptually the execution of a program flows from one instruction to another; hence, the name flowchart. Flowcharts are used throughout this book to illustrate the structure of programs. For simple programs a flowchart may not be necessary; however, for complex programs flowcharts are very helpful. The symbols used in program flowcharting are explained here.

The rectangle is used to describe all processing performed by a computer. The arrow shows the direction of flow in the flowchart. In general the flow is top to bottom and left to right on a page.

The diamond is used to indicate a decision point where the flow may go in one of two directions depending on the condition in the diamond. The parallelogram is used to indicate input of data to the computer or output of information from the computer. The oval is used for the beginning or end of the program.

Problem Summary

Input

Hourly rate: $3.00

Number of hours worked: 40

Processing

Multiply hourly rate times hours worked, giving gross pay.

Output

Gross pay

The paycheck calculation program has to perform the following steps:

1. Assign values to data fields.
2. Calculate the gross pay.
3. Output the gross pay amount.
4. End the program.

The flowchart and a BASIC computer program to perform these four steps is shown below:

```
10 REM PROGRAM TO COMPUTE PAY
100 LET R=3.00
110 LET H=40
120 LET P=R*H
130 PRINT P
140 STOP
32767 END
```

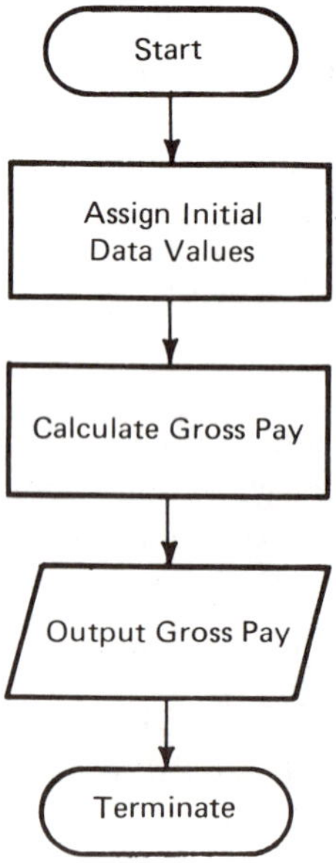

This program consists of seven lines. Each line starts with a number. This number, also called the statement number, is important because it tells the computer the sequence in which this program should be performed. The statement with the lowest number will be performed first, then the statement with the next lowest number, and so on until the end of the program is reached.

In this example the statement numbers go from 10 to 32767. However, any other sequence of numbers that keeps the same order could have been used. As long as the order of the lines is not changed, the lines could have been numbered from 10 to 16. These line numbers would have the same effect as the present numbers in the example program. Each line of the program is now explained:

The first line, 10 REM PROGRAM TO COMPUTE PAY, serves the programmer and not the computer. In fact, all "REM" statements are ignored by the computer. REM is short for remark. It is used to insert comments in a program as an aid to understanding the logic of the program.

The second line, 100 LET R = 3.00, states that the value 3.00 (the hourly rate of $3.00) is assigned to the field called R (for rate). The programmer identifies these fields by giving each a name. In BASIC, field names consist of one letter, or a letter followed by a single-digit number. Following are examples of field names with explanations of their validity.

Example	*Explanation*
A	Valid field name; one letter
AA	Invalid field name; two letters
A1	Valid field name; one letter followed by single-digit number
A11	Invalid field name; the letter can be followed by only one digit
B2	Valid; one letter and one digit
2B	Invalid; the first character has to be a letter
O0	Valid; letter "O" followed by zero "0" *(but not recommended since it is hard to see the difference)*
I1	Valid; letter "I" followed by number "1" *(also not recommended since it may be difficult to distinguish between I and 1)*

The third line, 110 LET H = 40, sets the value of H (H stands for hours worked) to 40. It is good practice to use field names that will help you to remember what is in that field. Such descriptive names are called mnemonic

—memory aids. Of course, with only one letter or a letter followed by a number, BASIC is limited in mnemonic capability.

The fourth line, 120 LET P = R * H, performs the calculations for gross pay. First the hourly rate (R) is multiplied by the number of hours worked (H). Then the result of this multiplication is placed in the field P. The asterisk (*) between R and H means multiply. Other arithmetic operations are + (plus) for addition, − (minus) for subtraction, / (slash) for division and ** (double asterisk) for raising to a power. Parentheses may be used to separate parts of an arithmetic statement.

The next line, 130 PRINT P, tells the system to display the value of field P. Whatever number has been placed into the field called P, will be typed, if you are working on a typewriter terminal, or it will be written on the screen, if you are working on a CRT.

The last two lines are used to terminate the program. The "STOP" tells the computer that the processing is finished. The "END", which must be the last statement of a program, tells the system that the program is finished. The STOP can be found almost anywhere in a program, but the END must be the last statement. That is why the END statement has the line number 32767; 32767 is the highest number available for a line in most BASIC systems.

RUNNING THE PROGRAM

The next step in the problem-solving process is the entry of the program into a computer system. First, sign-on the system using the procedure from the previous chapter. Once you are in BASIC, then type

NEW

Don't forget the CR or T! The command NEW tells the system that a new BASIC program will be entered. The system will ask for a program name. Type a program name; for example, PAY. (You can use up to six characters for a program name.) The system will respond by indicating

READY

Once this message is printed, the computer is ready to accept the program. At this time, type the program, one line at a time, ending each line with CR or T, depending on the terminal. The program that you enter will be held in the user work area.

```
10 REM PROGRAM TO COMPUTE PAY
100 LET R=3.00
110 LET H=40
120 LET P=R*H
130 PRINT P
140 STOP
32767 END
```

If a mistake is made in typing a line, the mistake can be corrected by retyping the line. Most errors in BASIC instructions will be caught by the computer and the system will display a message indicating that it did not understand. For example, if a line number is omitted, a message such as HUH? or WHAT? will appear. Do not worry, mistakes will occur; to err is human. Merely retype the line correctly. However, if, for example, you typed "130 PRINT Q" instead of "130 PRINT P", the system cannot detect this error because it is a logical error. To correct logical errors, you must also retype the line.

When the program has been entered into the system, type

SAVE

This command places a copy of the program into the user save area and stores it there under the program name. The program itself is also still in the user work area (only a copy of the program exists in the user save area). To see what is in the user work area type

LIST

This command will display the program in the user work area. Each line of the program is printed on the terminal or written on the screen. The command permits you to check that the program was entered correctly. Errors can be corrected by retyping incorrect lines. When a new line is typed with an old line number, the new line wipes out the old line and takes its place in the program sequence. To tell the computer to do what the program says (i.e., to execute or run the program) type the word

RUN

```
NEW PAY

Ready

10 REM PROGRAM TO COMPUTE PAY
100 LET R=3.00
110 LET H=40
120 LET P=R*H
130 PRINT P
140 STOP
32767 END
SAVE

Ready

LIST
PAY
10 REM PROGRAM TO COMPUTE PAY
100 LET R=3.00
110 LET H=40
120 LET P=R*H
130 PRINT P
140 STOP
32767 END

Ready

RUN
PAY
 120
Stop at line 140

Ready
```

Since the terminal session is now complete, sign-off.

When looking at the process that has occurred, some elements become apparent. First the problem has to be precisely specified. In this case the specification included a definition of starting values, hourly rate and hours worked; a statement of the desired output, gross pay; and a statement of how to get the output from the given inputs—multiply hourly rate by hours worked to get gross pay. Second, a program has to be written to perform the actions required to solve the problem. Third, the computer performs the instructions, one at a time in line number sequence. The BASIC instructions that tell the computer what to do were:

The LET statement, which assigns a value to a field
The PRINT statement, which displays the value of a field
The STOP statement, which tells the computer to stop executing
The END statement, which indicates the end of the program

These are all statements in the BASIC language. Furthermore, to work with a program, these BASIC commands were used:

NEW: To tell the system that a new program will be input from the keyboard

SAVE: To tell the system to keep a copy of the program in the user save area

LIST: To display the program currently in the user work area

RUN: To tell the system to perform (execute) the program

BASIC commands do not have line numbers; BASIC instructions (statements) must have line numbers. Only after the last command (RUN) is entered does the computer actually perform (execute) the instructions of a program.

Examples

Invoice Example: This example deals with invoice calculations. Initial data are the number of units sold and the price per unit for an item. The output desired is the dollar amount of the invoice.

Problem Summary

Input

Number of units sold: 50
Price per unit: $15

Processing

Multiply number of units sold by price per unit, giving dollar amount of invoice.

Output

Dollar amount of invoice

```
NEW INVCE

Ready

10 REM THIS PROGRAM COMPUTES INVOICE AMOUNT
100 LET U=50
110 LET P=15
120 LET D=U*P
130 PRINT D
140 STOP
32767 END
SAVE

Ready

RUN
INVCE
 750
Stop at line 140

Ready
```

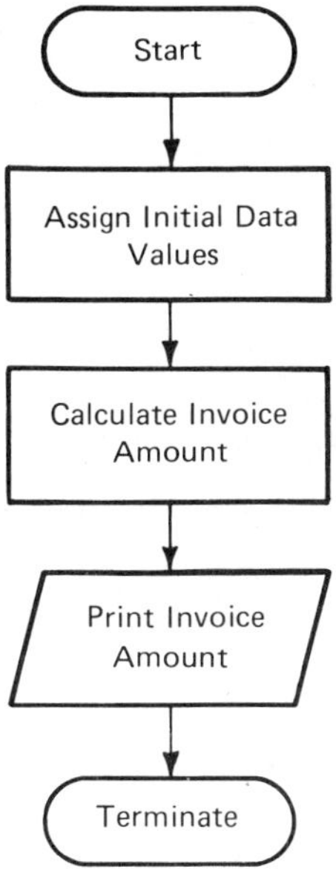

Inventory Example: This problem asks for the calculation of ending inventory. The number of units in beginning inventory, the number of units received into inventory and the number of units released from inventory are given.

Problem Summary

Input

Number of units in beginning inventory: 120
Number of units received into inventory: 40
Number of units released from inventory: 45

Processing

Add number of units received to inventory; then subtract number of units released, giving ending inventory.

Output

Number of units in ending inventory

```
NEW INVTY

Ready

10 REM THIS PROGRAM COMPUTES ENDING INVENTOR
100 LET B=120
110 LET R1=40
120 LET R2=45
130 LET E=B+R1-R2
140 PRINT E
150 STOP
32767 END
SAVE

Ready
```

```
RUN
INVTY
 115
Stop at line 150

Ready
```

Exercises

Note: Save all programs. These exercises will be modified in later problems.

Commission Exercise: Write a program to calculate the commission that a salesman has earned. The initial data are gross sales and the commission rate.

Problem Summary

Input

Gross sales: $12000

Commission rate: 0.05

Processing

Multiply gross sales by commission rate, giving dollar amount of commission.

Output

Dollar amount of commission

Program:

Run your program, and see if your output matches the following:

```
RUN
EX21
 600
Stop at line 150
```

Account Balance Exercise: Retail merchants have to update customer accounts. The update consists of adding new charges to an account balance and subtracting customer payments from an account balance. Write a program that will perform these tasks to arrive at an ending balance for the customer.

Problem Summary

Input

Starting balance: $60
Customer payments: $60
New charges: $45

Processing

Subtract customer payments from starting balance; then add customer charges to balance, giving ending balance.

Output

Ending balance

Program:

____

____

____

____

____

____

____

____

____

____

Run your program and check your ending balance with the following ending balance:

```
RUN
EX22
 45
Stop at line 150

Ready
```

MODIFYING THE PROGRAM

To change a program that has already been written requires the use of some new BASIC commands. For the payroll example, a modification is in order, if the problem is changed.

Assume that the output requirement is changed so that the words "GROSS PAY" as well as the amount of gross pay are displayed. This change requires that the print statement in the program be expanded for the output of alphabetic information. Printing aphabetic information is easy: Simply type "PRINT" followed by the alphabetic information enclosed in quotation marks as illustrated in line 125 below. Each PRINT causes one line of output. Therefore to display a line with "GROSS PAY", followed by a line with the amount of gross pay, the new program would look as follows:

```
10 REM PROGRAM TO COMPUTE PAY
100 LET R=3.00
110 LET H=40
120 LET P=R*H
125 PRINT "GROSS PAY"
130 PRINT P
140 STOP
32767 END
```

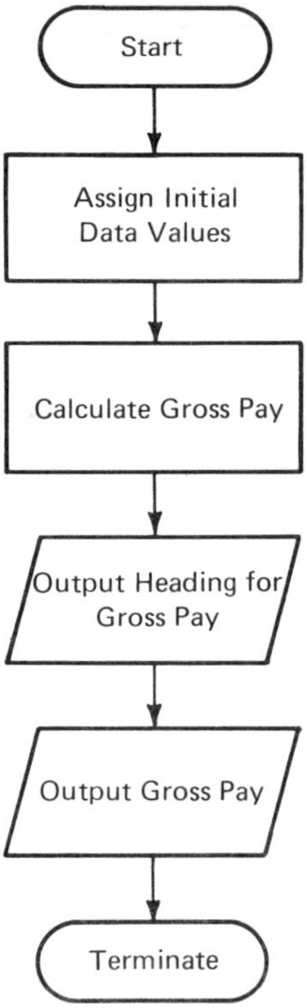

This new program has an extra line. To add this line to the existing program, it will be necessary to get the old program, and make the addition. This modification involves a series of steps.

First, sign-on the system. Next to get a copy of the program from the user save area, type the word

OLD

The system will ask for the old program name. Type

PAY

since that is the name under which the program was initially saved. If you cannot remember the program's name, type

CAT

"CAT" is short for Catalogue. The command CAT gives a list of the program names in the user save area.

Once the program is in your work area, list it to make sure that it is the correct program. If the old and the modified program are both to be retained, it will be necessary to change the program name, since two programs cannot be stored with the same name. To change the name of the program in your work area, type

RENAME PAY2

Save the program by typing SAVE. Now, if the CAT command is issued, it will show two programs in your save area: PAY and PAY2. The new line can now be inserted into the program. Type the additional line

125 PRINT "GROSS PAY"

The system will place the line in the proper sequence automatically. In order to provide space for program modifications, the line numbers were initially picked so that there was room for the insertion of additional lines. If the line numbers in the original program had run from 10 to 16, then no open space for program modifications would have been available. To place a copy of the modified program in your save area, the command

REPLACE

will have to be used. SAVE will not work, since the SAVE command is used only for the first entry of a program into the user save area. If the command SAVE was given by accident, the system would remind you by telling you that a program with that name had already been saved and that a RENAME or a REPLACE is in order.

After saving the modified program, LIST it; then RUN it. Following is a terminal session that performs these tasks.

```
OLD PAY

Ready

RENAME PAY2

Ready

SAVE

Ready

125 PRINT "GROSS PAY"
REPLACE

Ready
```

```
LIST
PAY2
10 REM PROGRAM TO COMPUTE PAY
100 LET R=3.00
110 LET H=40
120 LET P=R*H
125 PRINT "GROSS PAY"
130 PRINT P
140 STOP
32767 END

Ready

RUN
PAY2
GROSS PAY
 120
Stop at line 140
```

Review of Problem Modification Procedure

The problem modification procedure starts with a change in one of the problem specifications, either a change in initial data, or in the processing requirement, or in the desired output. In this example, the output was changed to include alphabetic information. Then the required changes are identified in the written program.

Next, on the terminal, the old program is retrieved from the save area and placed in the work area. The program is renamed and saved. The new line is added to the program in the work area. The changed program is then listed and executed.

Examples

Invoice Example: In this problem we want to have a heading for the invoice dollar amount. The remaining problem specifications are unchanged. The procedure for making this modification is given as follows:

```
OLD INVCE

Ready

RENAME INVCE2

Ready

SAVE

Ready

LIST
INVCE2
10 REM THIS PROGRAM COMPUTES INVOICE AMOUNT
100 LET U=50
110 LET P=15
120 LET D=U*P
130 PRINT D
140 STOP
32767 END

Ready

125 PRINT "INVOICE AMOUNT"
REPLACE

Ready

RUN
INVCE2
INVOICE AMOUNT
 750
Stop at line 140
```

'Sales Tax Example: Many states and municipalities require that a sales tax be added to the purchase price of an item. The initial data for this problem are a dollar amount of taxable sales and the tax rate. The desired output is the total amount of the sale that the customer has to pay.

Problem Summary

Input

Dollar amount of sale: $10.00

Tax rate: 4%

Processing

Multiply tax rate by dollar amount to get taxes. Add taxes to dollar amount, giving total amount of sale.

Output

Total sale

```
NEW TAX

Ready

10 REM THIS PROGRAM COMPUTES THE TOTAL SALE
100 LET S=10.00
110 LET R=.04
120 LET T=S*R
130 LET A=S+T
140 PRINT A
150 STOP
32767 END
SAVE

Ready

RUN
TAX
 10.4
Stop at line 150
```

It now becomes desirable to have additional output. Customers would like to see the tax separate from the total. Therefore, the desired output has been changed to include a printing of the sales amount and of the tax.

```
OLD TAX

Ready

135 PRINT S
137 PRINT T
REPLACE

Ready

LIST
TAX
10 REM THIS PROGRAM COMPUTES THE TOTAL SALE
100 LET S=10.00
110 LET R=.04
120 LET T=S*R
130 LET A=S+T
135 PRINT S
137 PRINT T
140 PRINT A
150 STOP
32767 END
```

```
Ready

RUN
TAX
 10
 .4
 10.4
Stop at line 150
```

Exercises

Account Balance Exercise: Change the account balance problem so that the title "ENDING BALANCE" will appear as part of the output. Your output should look similar to the output shown below:

```
RUN
EX23
ENDING BALANCE
 45
Stop at line 150
```

Sales Tax Exercise: Change the sales tax problem to calculate the total sales amount for a tax rate of 5%. The title "TOTAL SALE" should appear in the output. You can check your results with the output shown below.

```
RUN
EX24
TOTAL SALE
 10.5
Stop at line 150
```

PRINTING MANY VALUES ON A LINE

The PRINT instruction has already been used to display the value of one field as well as to display alphabetic information. This PRINT statement can also be used to output many field values. To output many fields with one PRINT statement, the fields are separated by commas. This capability is illustrated by taking the initial payroll example and changing the desired output to a display of the hours worked and the hourly rate in addition to the output of gross pay.

Problem Summary

Input

Hourly rate: $3.00
Hours worked: 40

Processing

Multiply hours worked by hourly rate, giving gross pay.

Output

Hourly rate, hours worked, and gross pay

This change would alter line 130 of the Pay program to

130 PRINT R, H, P

To make this change in the program, the required sequence of steps is:

1. Sign-on.
2. Get the old program (OLD PAY).
3. Type the new line (130 PRINT R, H, P).

4. Save the program (REPLACE).
5. List the program (LIST).
6. Execute the program (RUN).
7. Sign-off.

This sequence of steps would produce the following output.

```
OLD PAY

Ready

LIST
PAY
10 REM PROGRAM TO COMPUTE PAY
100 LET R=3.00
110 LET H=40
120 LET P=R*H
130 PRINT P
140 STOP
32767 END

Ready

130 PRINT R,H,P
REPLACE

Ready

LIST
PAY
10 REM PROGRAM TO COMPUTE PAY
100 LET R=3.00
110 LET H=40
120 LET P=R*H
130 PRINT R,H,P
140 STOP
32767 END

Ready

RUN
PAY
 3             40             120
Stop at line 140
```

Notice that with the new PRINT instructions, three numbers are printed on a line. Each of these field values starts at a column position that has been built into the system. The prespecified column positions are 1, 15, 30, 45 and 60. Therefore, five field values can be printed on one line. If the print instruction contains more than five fields, then another line is used to continue output.

With the prespecified columns, headings and associated data will always line up. As long as the alphabetic information has less than 14 characters, including blanks, any data displayed will fall directly under the headings. This alignment is shown in the revised payroll problem where headings are added to the output.

Problem Summary

Input
Unchanged

Processing
Unchanged

Output
Change output to include headings for hourly rate, hours worked, and gross pay.

This modification requires that a line of headings be added to the program. After sign-on, the steps are:

1. Get the old program.

```
OLD PAY

Ready
```

2. List the program to see where to make the modification.

```
LIST
PAY
10 REM PROGRAM TO COMPUTE PAY
100 LET R=3.00
110 LET H=40
120 LET P=R*H
130 PRINT R,H,P
140 STOP
32767 END

Ready
```

3. Make the change. In this example, the data are printed in line 130. Since the headings have to appear before the data, a line has to be added before line 130. The headings consist of the words "Hourly Rate", "Hours Worked", and "Gross Pay". It is good practice to keep headings and data together. Therefore, line number 125 is used to output the headings.

```
125 PRINT "HOURLY RATE","HOURS WORKED","GROSS PAY"
LIST
PAY
10 REM PROGRAM TO COMPUTE PAY
100 LET R=3.00
110 LET H=40
120 LET P=R*H
125 PRINT "HOURLY RATE","HOURS WORKED","GROSS PAY"
130 PRINT R,H,P
140 STOP
32767 END

Ready
```

4. Execute the program.

```
RUN
PAY
HOURLY RATE    HOURS WORKED   GROSS PAY
 3              40             120
Stop at line 140

Ready
```

5. Check the output. Although this aspect has not been discussed before, it should be remembered that errors can occur. Therefore, whenever you execute a program for the first time, make sure that the output is correct. If you are satisfied with the output, then the program can be RENAMED and SAVED or REPLACED to store it for future use in the current form.

```
RENAME PAY3

Ready

SAVE

Ready
```

6. If you are finished, sign-off.

HANDLING ALPHABETIC TITLES

The headings in the last example were all less than the number of positions available. However, what would happen if the headings were longer? For example, what would the output look like, if the alphabetic titles that you wanted were "Hourly Rate of Pay", "Hours Worked", and "Gross Pay"? To find out what a system would do if requirements change, there is only one valid test—try it. Make the change and execute the program to see what happens. For the payroll problem, the key steps are shown below:

```
OLD PAY3

Ready

125 PRINT "HOURLY RATE OF PAY","HOURS WORKED","GROSS PAY"
RUN
PAY3
HOURLY RATE OF PAY            HOURS WORKED   GROSS PAY
 3             40              120
Stop at line 140

Ready
```

Oops! The data do not line up. One way of handling this problem is to print the headings on two lines. The heading "HOURLY RATE OF PAY" is separated into two parts "HOURLY" and "RATE OF PAY". The two parts are then printed separately. The procedure for this change involves retyping line 125 as

125 PRINT "RATE OF PAY", "HOURS WORKED", "GROSS PAY"

and a new line is added as line number 123

123 PRINT "HOURLY"

Now the output from the program would look as follows:

```
125 PRINT "RATE OF PAY","HOURS WORKED","GROSS PAY"
123 PRINT "HOURLY"
RUN
PAY3
HOURLY
RATE OF PAY   HOURS WORKED   GROSS PAY
 3              40              120
Stop at line 140

Ready

SAVE
?File exists-RENAME/REPLACE

Ready

REPLACE

Ready
```

Example

Inventory Example: Inventory records typically show more than just the number of units in ending inventory. In this example we want to show the beginning inventory, the number received into inventory, the number issued from inventory, the number in ending inventory and the dollar amount of ending inventory. Furthermore, a general heading for the output is also worked.

Problem Summary

Input

Number of units at beginning: 120
Number received into inventory: 40
Number of units issued from inventory: 45
Cost per unit: $5.20

Processing

Add number received to beginning inventory and subtract number issued from inventory, giving ending inventory. Multiply ending inventory by cost per unit to get dollar amount of inventory.

Output

Heading of "Inventory Status", labels for each field of output "Beginning Inventory", "Receipts", "Issued", "Ending Inventory", and "Dollar Amount" followed by a line of field values.

Note: Five fields are printed. The heading "Inventory Status", should appear centered over the output. Therefore, to align the words "Inventory Status" over the third column, it is necessary to skip to the third built-in tab position. Printing two blank fields will skip to the third column. Similarly, two blank fields are inserted in the print line for "Receipts" and "Issued" since these titles do not have to be split over two print lines.

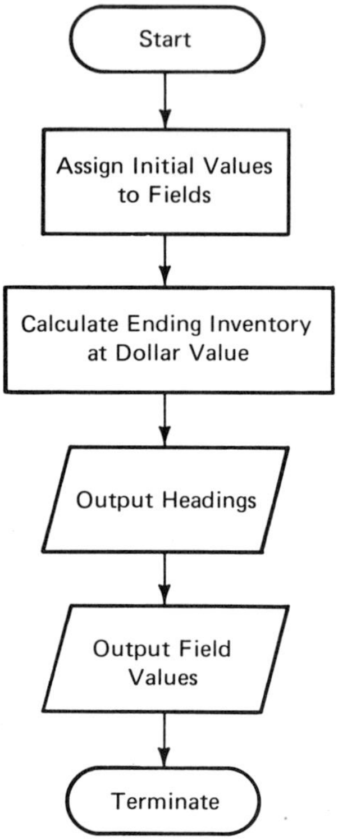


```
OLD INVTY

Ready

RENAME INV2

Ready

LIST
INV2
10 REM THIS PROGRAM COMPUTES ENDING INVENTORY
100 LET B=120
110 LET R1=40
120 LET R2=45
130 LET E=B+R1-R2
140 PRINT E
150 STOP
32767 END

Ready

132 LET C=5.20
134 LET D=E*C
136 PRINT " "," ","INVENTORY STATUS"
138 PRINT "BEGINNING"," "," ","ENDING","DOLLAR"
140 PRINT "INVENTORY","RECEIPTS","ISSUED","INVENTORY","AMOUNT"
142 PRINT B,R1,R2,E,D
REPLACE

Ready
```

```
LIST
INV2
10 REM THIS PROGRAM COMPUTES ENDING INVENTORY
100 LET B=120
110 LET R1=40
120 LET R2=45
130 LET E=B+R1-R2
132 LET C=5.20
134 LET D=E*C
136 PRINT " "," ","INVENTORY STATUS"
138 PRINT "BEGINNING"," "," ","ENDING","DOLLAR"
140 PRINT "INVENTORY","RECEIPTS","ISSUED","INVENTORY","AMOUNT"
142 PRINT B,R1,R2,E,D
150 STOP
32767 END

Ready

RUN
INV2
                              INVENTORY STATUS
BEGINNING                                    ENDING        DOLLAR
INVENTORY     RECEIPTS        ISSUED         INVENTORY     AMOUNT
 120           40              45             115           598
Stop at line 150
```

Exercises

Sales Tax Exercise: Change the output of the sales tax problem so that it will print the amount of sale, the tax, and the total with appropriate headings.

```
RUN.
EX25
SALE                          TOTAL
AMOUNT        TAX             SALE AMOUNT
 10            .5              10.5
Stop at line 150
```

Account Balance Exercise: Change the account balance problem so that the heading "Beginning Balance", "Payments", "New Charges" and "Ending Balance" will appear over their respective values.

```
RUN
EX26
BEGINNING                                               ENDING
BALANCE          CHARGES          PAYMENTS              BALANCE
 60               45               60                    45
Stop at line 150
```

SUMMARY

This chapter has shown you how to use the computer for simple calculations. The instructions of the BASIC language and the BASIC commands are listed below. BASIC commands are used to manipulate a program; they have no line numbers. BASIC instructions are used to manipulate data in a program; they do have line numbers.

Additionally, you have learned, not only how to write a program from scratch, but also ways of changing your program. The method of program modification will be continued throughout this book as the problem requirements and the BASIC capabilities are further developed.

BASIC Commands Introduced:

NEW — Tells the system that the operator is about to type in a new program. The system will ask for a program name.

LIST	Gives a printout (listing) of the program.
SAVE	Puts a copy of the program into the user save area under the current program name.
RUN	Executes a program, i.e., tells a computer to perform the program instructions.
OLD	Asks for a copy of a program from the user save area. The system will ask for the program name that should be retrieved.
RENAME	Gives a new name to the program that the user is working on.
REPLACE	Puts a copy of the program into the user save area under the program name. This is used when a copy of the program with the current program name already exists in the user save area.
CAT	Lists the names of programs in the user save area (catalogue).

BASIC Instructions Introduced:

Statement	*Explanation*
LET X = Y	Assigns the value of Y to the field X
PRINT X,Y	Displays the values of X and Y
PRINT "XYZ"	Displays the alphabetic information XYZ
STOP	Tells the system to stop
END	Indicates the physical end of a program
REM	Ignored by computer—remarks for programmer
Arithmetic operations	
X + Y	Add Y to X
X − Y	Subtract Y from X
X * Y	Multiply X by Y
X / Y	Divide X by Y
X * * Y	Raise X to the Y power
( )	Parentheses may be used to group parts of arithmetic statements

Definitions

Field Name:	A field is named by a letter (A – Z) or by a letter followed by a number (A – Z, 0 – 9)
Program Name:	A program name is six characters; the first character must be a letter

PROBLEMS

Write programs that will do the following:

1. Write your name.
2. Calculate the amount of a sale where 175 units are sold at $1.19 per unit.
3. Calculate the net amount of a sale where 47 units are sold at $4.56 per unit and a return is made for 3 units at $6.26 per unit.
4. Calculate the average sale for a day in which sales were made for $126.46, $276.19, $197.50 and $252.71. (**Note:** Average = the sum of daily sales divided by the number of sales.)
5. Modify Problem 3 above where the output is labelled Net Sale.
6. Modify Problem 4 above where the output is labelled Average Sale.
7. Modify the inventory program on page 31 so that the dollar amount is printed on a separate line.
8. Calculate the amount of interest that would be earned in one year on $527.26 at 4%, 5%, 6%, 6.5%, and 7% annual interest. Display the results on one line and place headings of the interest rate above the interest amounts. Also center the heading Interest Calculation in your output.
9. In economics, the concept of unit elasticity means that the price times the quantity is a constant. If a product is manufactured by a company whose revenue is $125,000, and output could be 10,000, 8,000, 7,000, or 6,000 units, what would the price be at the four levels of output? Put headings on your output and write the numeric output on one line. (**Note:** pq = r where p = price, q = quantity, r = revenue.)
10. The formula for compound interest is $A = P(1 + i)^n$ where p = principal amount, i = interest rate expressed as a decimal, n = the number of time periods, and A = total amount at the end of n periods. Determine and label the output for p = $1,250, i = .055, and the number of time periods is from 1 to 5.

3 / Data Entry

Performance Objectives

At the end of this chapter you should be able to:

- Write a program that will take data from a keyboard device
- Write a program that will process many records
- Test data for reasonableness

ENTERING DATA FROM A TERMINAL

In many cases the data values are unknown when the program is written. For example, payroll data change from week to week. Consequently, to use the program, the data assignments have to be changed. Quite often in business, the person who runs a program is not the person who wrote the program. Therefore making changes, such as changing the assignment statements, would be cumbersome and awkward. Isn't there a way to give a program to somebody to run so that the person using the program doesn't have to know programming? The answer is yes. There is a way for a program to get data from a terminal. In this chapter, we will show you how to enter data while a program is running, how to process many records at the same time, and how to check field values for reasonableness.

Problem Description

The payroll function must calculate the employee's gross pay and the employee's net pay, the amount of his paycheck. Gross pay is the wages for regular and overtime hours. Net pay is gross pay minus deductions. Deductions include federal income tax and social security contributions (also known as FICA–Federal Insurance Contribution Act). In the following problems you are given the tax rate and the social security withholding rate.

The program should be written so that the data for the hourly rate, the number of regular hours worked, and the number of overtime hours worked can be entered from a keyboard. The required outputs are gross pay, taxes, social security deductions, and net pay. Gross pay is calculated by adding regular wages to overtime wages. Regular wages are regular hours worked multiplied by the hourly rate. With time-and-a-half for overtime, overtime wages are calculated by multiplying overtime hours by 1.5 and then multiplying by the hourly rate. The deductions are calculated by multiplying gross pay by the appropriate rate. Net pay is calculated by subtracting the deductions from gross pay. The person is identified by name.

Problem Summary

Input

Social security withholding rate: 6.13% (.0613)
Federal income tax rate: 15% (.15)
Hourly rate: $3.00
Regular hours worked: 40
Overtime hours worked: 2

Processing

Multiply regular hours by hourly rate, giving regular wages. Multiply overtime hours times 1.5 and then multiply by hourly rate, giving overtime wages. Add regular wages to overtime wages, giving gross pay.

Multiply gross pay by income tax rate, giving federal income tax deduction. Multiply gross pay by social security rate, giving social security deduction. Subtract federal income tax and social security deductions from gross pay, giving net pay.

Output

Gross pay, payroll deductions, and net pay.

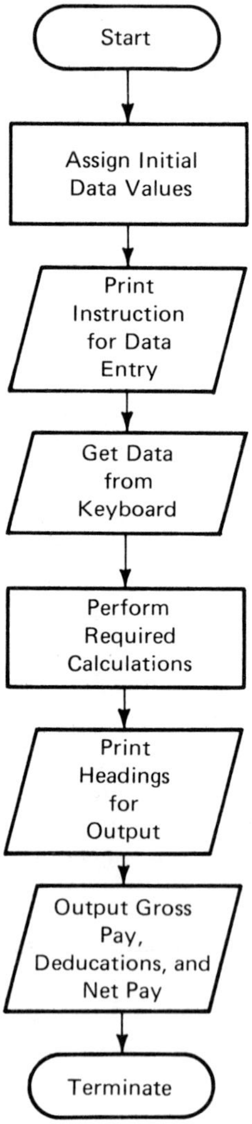


```
10 REM PROGRAM TO INPUT AND COMPUTE PAY
100 LET F1=.15
110 LET F2=.0613
120 PRINT "TYPE NAME,HOURLY RATE, REGULAR HOURS,OVERTIME HOURS"
```

```
130 INPUT N$,R,H1,H2
140 LET G=R*H1+R*H2*1.5
150 LET D1=G*F1
160 LET D2=G*F2
170 LET N=G-D1-D2
180 PRINT "NAME:",N$
190 PRINT "GROSS","F.I.T.","F.I.C.A.","NET"
200 PRINT "PAY","DEDUCTION","DEDUCTION","PAY"
210 PRINT G,D1,D2,N
220 STOP
32767 END
```

This program contains one new BASIC instruction. Line 130 contains the word "INPUT". This instruction tells the computer to ask for data from the keyboard. During program execution, a question mark (?) will be displayed on the terminal. Data values are typed, each field separated by a comma, after the question mark. One value has to be entered for each field of the INPUT statement. In this case, four values separated by commas have to be typed, one value each for name, hourly rate, regular hours and overtime hours. This program also contains a new type of field name (N$), for alphabetic information. In line 130, N$ is used to hold alphabetic information. In line 180 the name is printed. After this program is entered, it can be executed.

Note: When entering dollar amounts, do not use the dollar sign ($) and do not use commas to separate thousands. Commas are used to separate field values; and the "$" has a special meaning in BASIC. It is used to name a field that contains alphabetic or alphanumeric data. The definition of a field name remains the same, but a $ is added.

The arithmetic statement in line 140 computes gross pay. It also could have been written the following way:

140 LET G = (R*H1) + (R*H2*1.5)

The parentheses could have been added; but the computation in the program and the one above with parentheses give us exactly the same result. Arithmetic statements are performed in BASIC in the following sequence: First, exponentiation; next, division or multiplication; and last, subtraction or addition. In the program, G would be calculated in the following way: H2 is multiplied by 1.5, and this result is multiplied by R; H1 is multiplied by R, and this result is then added to the first result, giving us G.

```
RUN
PAY4
TYPE NAME,HOURLY RATE, REGULAR HOURS,OVERTIME HOURS
? JONES,3.00,40,2
NAME:          JONES
GROSS          F.I.T.         F.I.C.A.       NET
PAY            DEDUCTION      DEDUCTION      PAY
 129            19.35          7.9077         101.742
Stop at line 220

Ready
```

Notice that the name, the hourly rate, the regular hours, and the overtime hours have to be typed *in that order.* The program will take the first typed value and assign it to the first field in the input statement, assign the next value to the next field, and so on, until it has assigned a value to each field. With the capability of entering data during program execution, it is not necessary for you, the programmer, to know what the specific data values will be. You can write the logic of processing and use it for different data values. By this approach you achieve a generally more useful program, since changes in data values do not require changes in the program. However, the person who uses the program must know what the data values are and the order in which they must be entered.

Examples

Invoice Example: This example deals with invoice calculations. The data to be input during execution are the number of units sold and the price per unit for an item. The output desired is the dollar amount of the invoice.

Problem Summary

Input

Number of units sold: 50
Price per unit: $15

Processing

Multiply number of units sold by price per unit, giving dollar amount of invoice.

Output

Dollar amount of invoice

```
LISTNH
10 REM DETERMINE DOLLAR AMOUNT OF INVOICE
100 PRINT "TYPE NUMBER OF UNITS, PRICE PER UNIT"
110 INPUT U,P
120 LET D=U*P
130 PRINT "AMOUNT"
140 PRINT D
150 STOP
32767 END

Ready

RUN
INVCE3
TYPE NUMBER OF UNITS, PRICE PER UNIT
? 50,15.00
AMOUNT
 750
Stop at line 150
```

The flowchart to derive this program follows on the top of the next page.

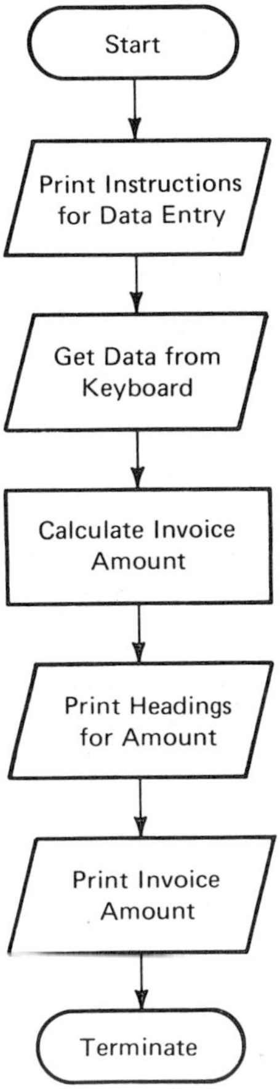

Inventory Example: This problem requires the calculation of ending inventory. The number of units in beginning inventory, the number of units received into inventory and the number of units released from inventory are given.

Problem Summary

Input

Number of units in beginning inventory: 120
Number of units received into inventory: 40
Number of units released from inventory: 45

Processing

Add number of units received to inventory; subtract number of units released, giving ending inventory.

Output

Number of units in ending inventory

```
10 REM CALCULATE ENDING INVENTORY
100 PRINT "TYPE BEGINNING UNITS, UNITS RECEIVED, UNITS RELEASED"
110 INPUT B,R1,R2
120 LET E=B+R1-R2
130 PRINT "ENDING INVENTORY"
140 PRINT E
150 STOP
32767 END

Ready

RUN
INV3
TYPE BEGINNING UNITS, UNITS RECEIVED, UNITS RELEASED
? 120,40,45
ENDING INVENTORY
 115
Stop at line 150
```

Exercises

Commission Exercise: Write a program to calculate the commission that a salesman has earned. The data are gross sales and the commission rate; both should be input during execution with instructions on the order of input. Label the output "Commission."

Problem Summary

Input

Gross sales: $12000

Commission rate: 0.05

Processing

Multiply gross sales by commission rate, giving dollar amount of commission.

Output

Dollar amount of commission

Program:

Run your program, and see if your output matches the following output.

```
TYPE GROSS SALES,COMMISSION RATE
? 12000,.05
COMMISSION
 600
Stop at line 150
```

Account Balance Exercise: Retail merchants have to update customer accounts. The update consists of adding new charges to the account balance and subtracting customer payments from the account balance. Write a program that will perform these tasks to arrive at an ending balance for the customer. The data should be input during execution. Label the output "Account Balance."

Problem Summary

Input

Starting balance: $60
Customer payments: $60
New charges: $45

Processing

Subtract customer payments from starting balance and add customer charges to balance, giving ending balance.

Output

Ending balance

Program:

Run your program and check your ending balance with the ending balance given on the next page.

```
TYPE STARTING BALANCE,CUSTOMER PAYMENT,NEW CHARGES
? 60,60,45
ACCOUNT BALANCE
 45
Stop at line 150
```

PROCESSING MANY RECORDS

Let's assume that you have collected the weekly payroll data. You have a stack of time cards, with each card containing the weekly data on a person. Depending on the size of the organization, the stack of time cards may contain anywhere from 20 to 2,000 records. Therefore, to do the calculations for the weekly payroll, you would have to run your payroll program 20 to 2,000 times. In this section we will show you how to write a program to process many records in one run.

The assignment for this problem is similar to the previous problem. But instead of data for only one person, the weekly time records of many people have to be processed. The data are listed in Table 3–1. A program for processing all the data in one run follows.

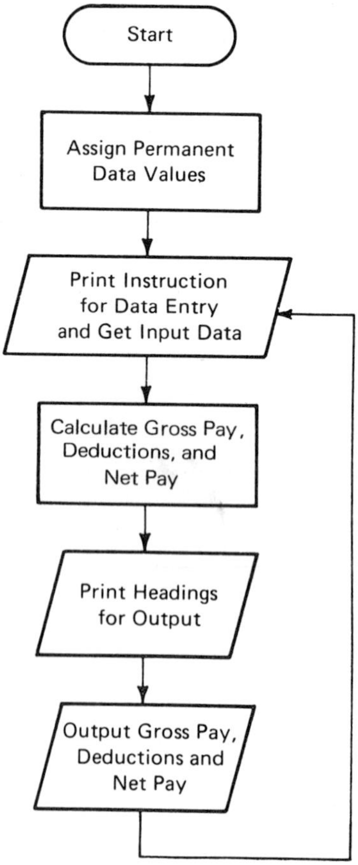

Table 3–1

Weekly Payroll Data

Name	*Hourly Rate*	*Regular Hours Worked*	*Overtime Hours Worked*
1. Adams	5.00	40	0
2. Baker	5.60	40	4
3. Cohen	6.25	38	0
4. Johnson	3.75	40	0
5. Tanner	4.25	36	0

```
10 REM PROGRAM TO INPUT AND COMPUTE PAY
100 LET F1=.15
110 LET F2=.0613
120 PRINT "TYPE NAME,HOURLY RATE, REGULAR HOURS,OVERTIME HOURS"
130 INPUT N$,R,H1,H2
140 LET G=R*H1+R*H2*1.5
150 LET D1=G*F1
160 LET D2=G*F2
170 LET N=G-D1-D2
180 PRINT "NAME:",N$
190 PRINT "GROSS","F.I.T.","F.I.C.A.","NET"
200 PRINT "PAY","DEDUCTION","DEDUCTION","PAY"
210 PRINT G,D1,D2,N
215 GO TO 120
220 STOP
32767 END
```

This program contains one new BASIC instruction,"GO TO 120," found in line 215. The instruction means exactly what it says: When the computer reaches line 215, it is instructed there to go back to line 120. When the program is run, the computer executes lines 100 to 210 in sequence; when it reaches line 215, it goes back to line 120 and executes from 120 onwards.

This repetition is shown in the flowchart by the arrow that takes the flow back to steps that have already been executed. Thus the computer effectively processes one payroll record, and, since more than one employee is involved, it goes back to get the next employee record. To stop the program, after the last employee record has been processed, type C while holding down the control key (CTRL) when asked for data by the input statement. The logical end of the program is therefore entered during execution—after the last piece of data has been processed and more data is requested.

Since this program is only a one line change from the previous program, the modification is accomplished speedily. The change and execution actions are shown as follows:

```
OLD PAY4

Ready

RENAME PAY5

Ready
```

```
215 GO TO 120
SAVE

Ready

RUN
PAY5
TYPE NAME,HOURLY RATE, REGULAR HOURS,OVERTIME HOURS
? ADAMS,5.00,40,0
NAME:           ADAMS
GROSS           F.I.T.          F.I.C.A.        NET
PAY             DEDUCTION       DEDUCTION       PAY
 200             30              12.26           157.74
TYPE NAME,HOURLY RATE, REGULAR HOURS,OVERTIME HOURS
? BAKER,5.60,40,4
NAME:           BAKER
GROSS           F.I.T.          F.I.C.A.        NET
PAY             DEDUCTION       DEDUCTION       PAY
 257.6           38.64           15.7909         203.169
TYPE NAME,HOURLY RATE, REGULAR HOURS,OVERTIME HOURS
? COHEN,6.25,38,0
NAME:           COHEN
GROSS           F.I.T.          F.I.C.A.        NET
PAY             DEDUCTION       DEDUCTION       PAY
 237.5           35.625          14.5588         187.316
TYPE NAME,HOURLY RATE, REGULAR HOURS,OVERTIME HOURS
? JOHNSON,3.75,40,0
NAME:           JOHNSON
GROSS           F.I.T.          F.I.C.A.        NET
PAY             DEDUCTION       DEDUCTION       PAY
 150             22.5            9.195           118.305
TYPE NAME,HOURLY RATE, REGULAR HOURS,OVERTIME HOURS
? TANNER,4.25,36,0
NAME:           TANNER
GROSS           F.I.T.          F.I.C.A.        NET
PAY             DEDUCTION       DEDUCTION       PAY
 153             22.95           9.3789          120.671
TYPE NAME,HOURLY RATE, REGULAR HOURS,OVERTIME HOURS
? ^C

Ready
```

Examples

Invoice Example: In this problem we want a heading for the invoice dollar amount and to process four records. The remaining problem specifications are unchanged. The procedure for making this modification is given below.

Problem Summary

Input

Units sold	*Price per unit*
50	$15.00
20	$14.00
120	$ 1.20
30	$ 6.00

Processing

Perform calculations for four records.

Output

Unchanged

```
OLD INVCE3

Ready

RENAME INVCE4

Ready

LIST
INVCE4
10 REM DETERMINE DOLLAR AMOUNT OF INVOICE
100 PRINT "TYPE NUMBER OF UNITS, PRICE PER UNIT"
110 INPUT U,P
120 LET D=U*P
130 PRINT "AMOUNT"
140 PRINT D
150 STOP
32767 END

Ready

145 GO TO 100
REPLACE

Ready

RUN
INVCE4
TYPE NUMBER OF UNITS, PRICE PER UNIT
? 50,15.00
AMOUNT
 750
TYPE NUMBER OF UNITS, PRICE PER UNIT
? 20,14.00
AMOUNT
 280
TYPE NUMBER OF UNITS, PRICE PER UNIT
? 120,1.2
AMOUNT
 144
TYPE NUMBER OF UNITS, PRICE PER UNIT
? 30,6
AMOUNT
 180
TYPE NUMBER OF UNITS, PRICE PER UNIT
? ^C
```

Sales Tax Example: Many states and municipalities require that a sales tax be added to the purchase price of an item. The initial data for this problem are a dollar amount of taxable sales and the tax rate. The desired output is the total amount of the sale that the customer has to pay. Six records should be processed.

Problem Summary

Input

Dollar amount of sale: $10.00, $42.00, $57.00, $2.50, $726.32, $9.27

Tax rate: 4%

Processing

Multiply tax rate by the dollar amount to get the taxes; add the taxes to dollar amount, giving the total amount of sale.

Output

Total sale

```
100 PRINT "TYPE AMOUNT OF SALE"
110 INPUT S
120 LET R=.04
130 LET T=R*S
140 LET A=S+T
150 PRINT "TOTAL SALE"
160 PRINT A
170 GO TO 100
180 STOP
32767 END

Ready

RUN
TAX2
TYPE AMOUNT OF SALE
? 10.00
TOTAL SALE
 10.4
TYPE AMOUNT OF SALE
? 42.00
TOTAL SALE
 43.68
TYPE AMOUNT OF SALE
? 57
TOTAL SALE
 59.28
TYPE AMOUNT OF SALE
? 2.50
TOTAL SALE
 2.6
TYPE AMOUNT OF SALE
? 726.32
TOTAL SALE
 755.373
TYPE AMOUNT OF SALE
? 9.27
TOTAL SALE
 9.6408
TYPE AMOUNT OF SALE
? ^C
```

Exercise

Account Balance Exercise: Change the Account Balance Problem so that five records are input.

Problem Summary

Input

Starting balance	60	130	59.95	22.50	37.62
Customer payment	60	120	59.95	22.50	0.00
New charges	45	60	39.75	0.00	42.97

Processing

Perform calculations for five records.

Output

Unchanged

```
TYPE STARTING BALANCE,CUSTOMER PAYMENT,NEW CHARGES
? 60,60,45
ACCOUNT BALANCE
 45
TYPE STARTING BALANCE,CUSTOMER PAYMENT,NEW CHARGES
? 130,120,60
ACCOUNT BALANCE
 70
TYPE STARTING BALANCE,CUSTOMER PAYMENT,NEW CHARGES
? 59.95,59.95,39.75
ACCOUNT BALANCE
 39.75
TYPE STARTING BALANCE,CUSTOMER PAYMENT,NEW CHARGES
? 22.50,22.50,0.00
ACCOUNT BALANCE
 0
TYPE STARTING BALANCE,CUSTOMER PAYMENT,NEW CHARGES
? 37.62,0,42.97
ACCOUNT BALANCE
 80.59
TYPE STARTING BALANCE,CUSTOMER PAYMENT,NEW CHARGES
? ^C

Ready
```

PROGRAM VERIFICATION

When a program is written, it is necessary to make sure it performs its intended function. In the examples given so far, the numbers have been sufficiently simple so that the calculations can be checked by hand. It is good practice to check all calculations of a program whenever possible.

Errors do occur in complex programs. Errors crop up in the specification of a problem: For example, if salesman commissions are defined as a percentage of gross margin (sales minus cost of goods sold), then a specification of commission on the basis of gross sales would be in error. Errors can happen when the program is first written: For example, if receipts were subtracted from rather than added to beginning inventory, then a design error would exist. Errors can happen when the program is entered into the computer: Hitting the wrong key on the keyboard can cause many problems. Some of these errors will be caught by the computer. If a wrong letter is typed for a BASIC command, then the system will output a message stating that it did not understand the command. These errors, called syntax errors, are caught when the program is first typed into the system. Other errors will be caught when the program tries to do something and can't. Logical errors like these will show up during execution.

But many errors, such as the erroneous calculation of inventories will not give any error messages. In those cases it is necessary to do the calculations by hand to make sure that the output is correct. However, even hand calculation will not catch problem specification errors. The salesman commission error—the calculation of commission on the basis of gross sales instead of gross margin—would require a comparison of the specifications with the actual operations of the company.

HOW TO CATCH SOME ERRORS IN DATA

Errors in programs, called "bugs", bedevil even experienced programmers. But the largest number of errors in data processing is caused by bad data. This source of errors has been immortalized by the phrase "garbage in, garbage out." In this section we show you how to catch some of the "garbage in." The concept is known as "range checking."

Range checking assumes that you know the permissible range of data values. Range checks make sure that data are not too high or too low. But range checking can not catch errors when the erroneous data is within the range. A transposition error (for example, $3.69 is entered incorrectly as $3.96) will not be caught by range checks if the erroneous data is within range. In the case of the payroll example, we know that regular hours worked cannot exceed 40 hours. Therefore, we can check to make sure that values for regular hours worked are not larger than 40. The permissible ranges for the data fields are:

Field	*Low Value*	*High Value*
Hourly rate	3.05	10.00
Regular hours	0	40
Overtime hours	0	20

Checking range values of input fields is only part of the task. Once an error has been found, it must be identified so that the keyboard operator can correct the mistake. By accident, such as misinterpreting handwritten numbers, or through carelessness, erroneous data may have been typed. Range checks help to catch input that is obviously wrong. But the operator also needs to be told that the input is wrong. Hence, appropriate error messages must be printed. Following are flowcharts (Figs. 3–1 and 3–2) and a program that perform these additional requirements:

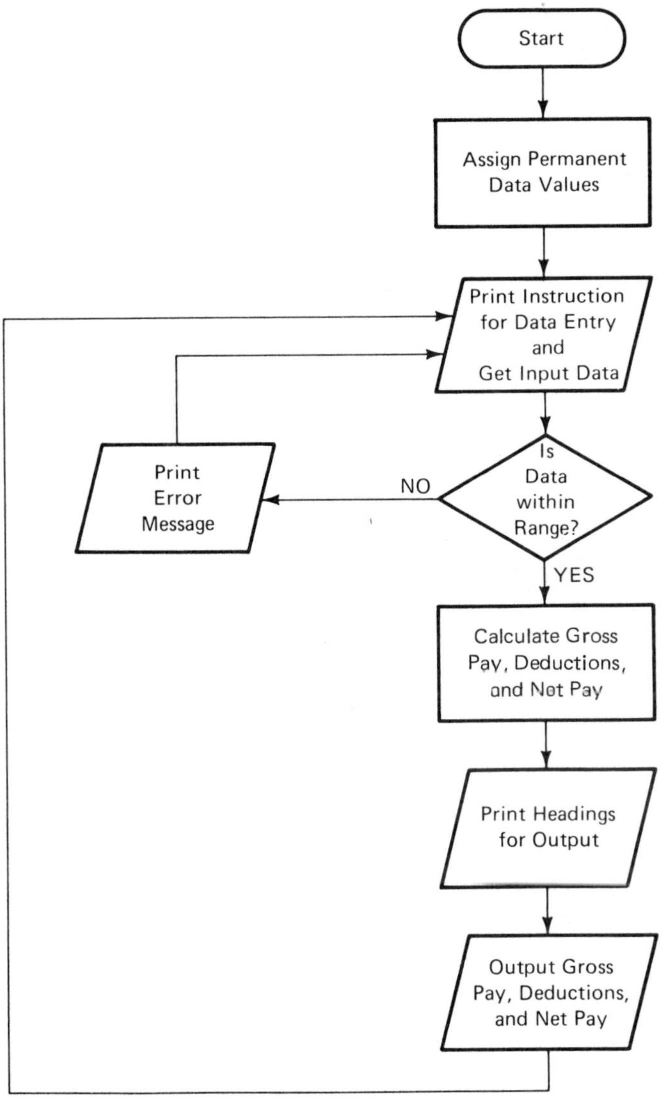

Flowchart of Range Test Program

Figure 3–1

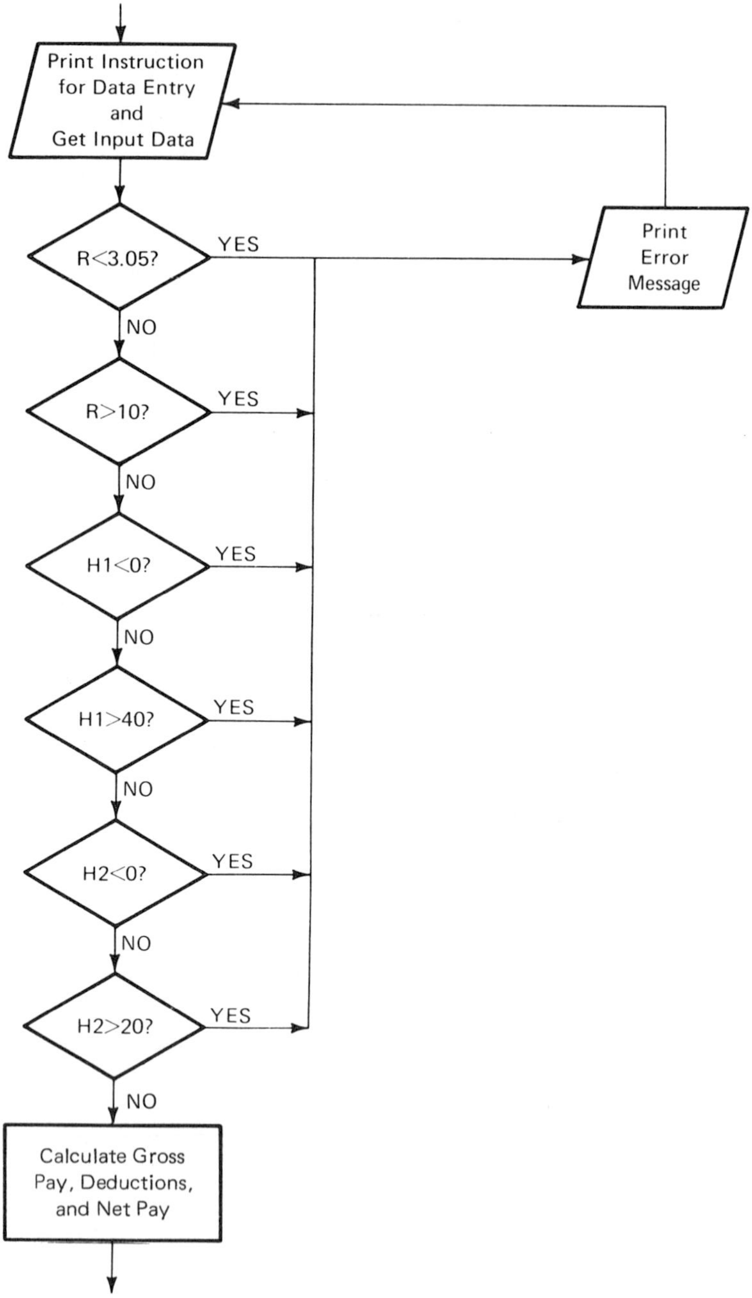

Figure 3–2 Range Tests:
Expansion of Decision—"Is Data Within Range?"

```
10 REM PROGRAM TO INPUT AND COMPUTE PAY
100 LET F1=.15
110 LET F2=.0613
120 PRINT "TYPE NAME,HOURLY RATE, REGULAR HOURS,OVERTIME HOURS"
130 INPUT N$,R,H1,H2
131 IF R<3.05 THEN 138
132 IF R>10  THEN 138
133 IF H1<0 THEN 138
134 IF H1>40 THEN 138
135 IF H2<0 THEN 138
136 IF H2>20 THEN 138
137 GO TO 140
138 PRINT "ERROR IN INPUT DATA"
139 GO TO 120
140 LET G=R*H1+R*H2*1.5
150 LET D1=G*F1
160 LET D2=G*F2
170 LET N=G-D1-D2
180 PRINT "NAME:",N$
190 PRINT "GROSS","F.I.T.","F.I.C.A.","NET"
200 PRINT "PAY","DEDUCTION","DEDUCTION","PAY"
210 PRINT G,D1,D2,N
215 GO TO 120
220 STOP
32767 END

Ready
```

The difference between this program and the previous program on page 47 is in lines 131 to 139. Here we test the data with a series of IF statements. An IF statement compares two values.

The six comparison operators are:

=	Equal
<	Less than
< =	Less than or equal
>	Greater than
> =	Greater than or equal
< >	Not equal

The comparison is followed by THEN and a line number. The "THEN line number" means GO TO the line number indicated if the comparison is true. If the comparison is not true, the next line is executed (see Fig. 3–2). Fields are compared with values or with other fields. Thus we can read line 131 as, "IF the hourly rate (R) is less than 3.05 THEN go to line 138." Similarly, line 132 means: "IF the hourly rate (R) is greater than 10 THEN go to line number 138." In line 138 an error message is printed. The error message is followed by a return to the instruction (line 120) for data entry.

Notice the GO TO 140 in line 137. This GO TO directs control to line 140 for the processing of valid data. When the computer reaches line 137, the data must be valid because it passed all the tests in lines 131 to 136. If line 137 did not exist, then valid records would also print the error message.

These changes to the old program are shown below:

```
OLD PAY5

Ready

RENAME PAY6

Ready

SAVE

Ready

131 IF R<3.05 THEN 138
132 IF R>10  THEN 138
133 IF H1<0 THEN 138
134 IF H1>40 THEN 138
135 IF H2<0 THEN 138
136 IF H2>20 THEN 138
137 GO TO 140
138 PRINT "ERROR IN INPUT DATA"
139 GO TO 120
REPLACE

Ready

LIST
PAY6
10 REM PROGRAM TO INPUT AND COMPUTE PAY
100 LET F1=.15
110 LET F2=.0613
120 PRINT "TYPE NAME,HOURLY RATE, REGULAR HOURS,OVERTIME HOURS"
130 INPUT N$,R,H1,H2
131 IF R<3.05 THEN 138
132 IF R>10  THEN 138
133 IF H1<0 THEN 138
134 IF H1>40 THEN 138
135 IF H2<0 THEN 138
136 IF H2>20 THEN 138
137 GO TO 140
138 PRINT "ERROR IN INPUT DATA"
139 GO TO 120
140 LET G=R*H1+R*H2*1.5
150 LET D1=G*F1
160 LET D2=G*F2
170 LET N=G-D1-D2
180 PRINT "NAME:",N$
190 PRINT "GROSS","F.I.T.","F.I.C.A.","NET"
200 PRINT "PAY","DEDUCTION","DEDUCTION","PAY"
210 PRINT G,D1,D2,N
215 GO TO 120
220 STOP
32767 END

Ready
```

Example

Inventory Example: We want to modify the inventory example in Chapter 2 to process three records and check the appropriateness of their values. The high values were determined by examining the capacity of the company to store and handle inventory. The low values cannot be negative, and the lowest cost of an item of inventory is $1.00.

Problem Summary

Input

Number of units at beginning:	120	20	60
Number received into inventory:	40	70	20
Number of units issued from inventory:	45	100	80
Cost per unit:	$5.00	$7.00	$3.25

Processing

Test the data for reasonableness.

Data Ranges

Field	Low Value	High Value
Units at Beginning	0	10,000
Units Received	0	3,000
Units Issued	0	*
Cost	$1.00	$10.00

*Number of Units in Inventory = Units at Beginning + Units Received.

Output

Unchanged

```
10 REM THIS PROGRAM CALCULATES ENDING INVENTORY VALUE
100 PRINT "TYPE BEGINNING UNITS, UNITS RECEIVED, UNITS RELEASED"
105 PRINT"AND COST, SEPARATED BY COMMAS"
110 INPUT B,R1,R2,C
111 IF B<0 THEN 120
112 IF B>10000 THEN 120
113 IF R1<0 THEN 120
114 IF R1>3000 THEN 120
115 IF R2<0 THEN 120
116 IF R2>(B+R1) THEN 120
117 IF C<1.00 THEN 120
118 IF C>10.00 THEN 120
119 GO TO 130
120 PRINT"ERROR IN INPUT DATA"
121 GO TO 100
130 LET E=B+R1-R2
134 LET D=C*E
136 PRINT " "," ","INVENTORY STATUS"
138 PRINT "BEGINNING"," "," ","ENDING","DOLLAR"
140 PRINT "INVENTORY","RECEIPTS","ISSUED","INVENTORY","VALUE"
142 PRINT B,R1,R2,E,D
143 GO TO 100
150 STOP
32767 END

Ready
```

```
RUN
INV4
TYPE BEGINNING UNITS, UNITS RECEIVED, UNITS RELEASED
AND COST, SEPARATED BY COMMAS
? 120,40,45,5.00
                                INVENTORY STATUS
BEGINNING                                    ENDING          DOLLAR
INVENTORY       RECEIPTS        ISSUED       INVENTORY       VALUE
 120            40              45           115             575
TYPE BEGINNING UNITS, UNITS RECEIVED, UNITS RELEASED
AND COST, SEPARATED BY COMMAS
? 20,70,100,7.00
ERROR IN INPUT DATA
TYPE BEGINNING UNITS, UNITS RECEIVED, UNITS RELEASED
AND COST, SEPARATED BY COMMAS
? 60,20,80,3.25
                                INVENTORY STATUS
BEGINNING                                    ENDING          DOLLAR
INVENTORY       RECEIPTS        ISSUED       INVENTORY       VALUE
 60             20              80           0               0
TYPE BEGINNING UNITS, UNITS RECEIVED, UNITS RELEASED
AND COST, SEPARATED BY COMMAS
? ^C
```

Review of Validity Check Operations and Deleting Obsolete Programs

This sequence of actions starts with the sign-on procedure. The old program is copied from the user save area and placed into the user work area with the command

OLD PAY5

When the system indicates that it is ready, the program name is changed and a copy of the program with its new name is placed in the user save area. These RENAME and SAVE actions are taken as security precautions. If anything should go wrong while you are working with the program PAY6 then you can recover by calling PAY5, and then repeat the modification steps.

After PAY6 has been saved, the new lines between 130 and 140 are typed. The REPLACE and LIST command, save a copy of the modified PAY6 and provide a display of the program so that you can visually verify your modifications. If an error has occurred, you can call the old PAY5 program and make the modifications again. This same sequence is used for the inventory example.

Note that only the program in the user work area is changed. The user save area is not affected unless you SAVE or REPLACE a program. SAVE and REPLACE copy a program from the user work area to the user save area. You can find out what programs are stored for you in the user save area by typing the BASIC command CATALOG or CAT for short.

You can also delete programs from the user save area with the UNSAVE command. Old programs that have been superseded by newer programs should be removed. Look at the catalog. See if you have programs that you no longer need. If there are obsolete programs in your catalog that you want to remove, then type UNSAVE followed by the program name.

When the system responds READY, the program has been deleted from the user save area.

SUMMARY

This chapter covered four new techniques:

- How to get data from a terminal
- How to process many records
- How to check records for reasonableness
- How to delete obsolete programs

All these techniques make your programs more realistic because they add generality and flexibility. No longer do you need to know specific data values when you write a program. The specific data can be entered when the program is used. No longer does a program have to be re-run for each record. A loop controlled by a GO TO can process many records in one run. And with range checks, some of the errors in input data will be caught. Therefore, programs written this way use the computer more flexibly and provide important assistance to the users.

BASIC Commands Introduced:

UNSAVE	Eliminating a program from user save area.

BASIC Instructions Introduced:

Statement	*Explanation*
INPUT X,Y	Takes numeric values for fields X and Y from the keyboard.
INPUT X$,Y$	Gets alphabetic values for fields X$ and Y$ from the keyboard.
GO TO nnn	Tells the system to go to line number nnn for the next instruction.
IF x THEN nnn	If x is true then go to line nnn for the next instruction, otherwise (if x is false) go to the next line in sequence.
Comparison operators	*Result of comparison*
X = Y	Result is true if X equals Y
X < Y	Result is true if X is strictly less than Y
X < = Y	Result is true if X is less than or equal to Y

X > Y	Result is true if X is strictly greater than Y
X > = Y	Result is true if X is greater than or equal to Y
X < > Y	Result is true if X is not equal to Y

Another way of stating the comparison as true or false is yes or no.

PROBLEMS

Write a program to do the following:

1. Modify the invoice problem in this chapter to check the value of the price per unit. The price should not be less than zero or more than $20. Data to be input at execution time

Units	20	12	34	27	100
Price	1.50	21.22	14.50	1.95	2.56

2. Modify the commission problem in this chapter to check the values of gross sales and commission rate. Gross sales may range from 0 to $100,000. The commission rate varies from 2% to 6%. Data to be input at execution time

Gross sales	2,476	29,650	400,000	97,727
Commission rate	4%	4.2%	2.1%	6.7%

Error messages should indicate whether the error detected is in gross sales or the commission rate.

3. Modify the payroll example on page 56 to output specific error messages such as "HOURLY RATE TOO HIGH", "HOURLY RATE TOO LOW", "HOURS TOO HIGH", "HOURS TOO LOW", "OVERTIME TOO HIGH", "OVERTIME TOO LOW". Use the following data:

Name	*Hourly Rate*	*Regular Hours*	*Overtime*
Able	$1.95	40	0
Baker	2.96	42	26
Charlie	11.65	−4	0
Fern	5.50	40	25
Graak	7.20	40	10

4. In Problem 3 above, a single error will result in not processing a person's data. Modify your program so that multiple errors in a person's data will be detected and result in appropriate error messages. Use the same data. **Note:** Process invalid records.

5. Modify the inventory example on page 57 to output specific error messages such as "BEGINNING INVENTORY TOO HIGH", "BEGINNING INVENTORY TOO LOW", "UNITS RECEIVED TOO HIGH", "UNITS RECEIVED TOO LOW", "UNITS ISSUED TOO HIGH", "UNITS ISSUED TOO LOW", "COST TOO HIGH", "COST TOO LOW". Use the following data:

Beginning Inventory	*Units Received*	*Units Issued*	*Cost*
100	20	60	$ 4.00
20	3,500	4,000	$ .75
500	200	600	$12.00
20	−40	60	$ 1.50
−100	200	700	$14.00

6. Modify your program in Problem 5 so that multiple errors in a data record (a line of input) will be indicated. Use the same data. **Note:** Process invalid records.

4 / Sequential Files

Performance Objectives

At the end of this chapter you should be able to:

- Use files to store data
- Write a program that will put data in a file
- Write a program that will read data from a file
- Find a record in a file

To use a computer, it is necessary to get data into the computer. In many cases when the amount of data is large, a computer file has to be set up to store the data. With files, the same data can be used again and again.

With files, entry of data is separated from the processing of data. Therefore, the data can be entered into a computer file at one time to be processed later.

But the files that a computer uses are different from the files used by people. Data is stored in a computer file in electromagnetic form. And people can't read electromagnetic data directly.

It is necessary to write a program to enter data into files and to write programs that read data from files. In this chapter, we will show you how to set up a file for computer processing. The type of file used is a sequential file. The file is called a sequential file because it is organized in a particular sequence, one record next to another. In a later chapter another type of file, a direct access file, will be discussed.

SETTING UP A FILE

The payroll problem will illustrate the capabilities of BASIC to handle files. In this case, we want to write a program that lets a terminal (data entry) operator enter data into a file. Later, we will use the data in the file for calculations and reports.

The payroll data for this problem consists of records with the following fields:

- Employee number
- Employment department number
- Employee name
- Hourly rate of pay
- Regular hours worked
- Overtime hours worked

The processing consists of entering data through a terminal and placing it in a file. For output, messages telling the operator what to do are necessary.

Problem Summary

Input	*Valid Range*
Employee number	100 to 999
Employee department number	1 to 20
Employee name	anything
Hourly rate	3.05 to 15.00
Regular hours worked	0 to 40
Overtime hours worked	0 to 20

Processing

Take data from a keyboard and place valid data in a file. Check the data for validity.

Output

Instructions for operator and data on a computer file.

Therefore the program has to be able to:

1. Set up a new file.
2. Get data from the terminal when an operator types it.
3. Write the data into a file that the computer can use.
4. Stop when all the data has been entered.

See the flowchart (Fig. 4–1) and program to do all of these actions below:

```
10 REM THIS PROGRAM TAKES DATA FROM THE KEYBOARD AND
20 REM         PLACES IT IN THE EMPLOY FILE
100 OPEN "EMPLOY" AS FILE #1
110 PRINT "TYPE EMPLOYEE NUMBER, DEPARTMENT NUMBER,EMPLOYEE NAME"
120 PRINT "HOURLY RATE, REGULAR  HOURS"
130 PRINT "OVERTIME HOURS,SEPARATED BY COMMAS"
140 PRINT "WHEN FINISHED TYPE 99,99,AA,99,99"
150 INPUT N,D,N$,H,R,V
160 IF N=99 THEN 400
170 IF N<100 THEN 290
180 IF N>999 THEN 290
190 IF D<1 THEN 290
200 IF D>20 THEN 290
210 IF H<3.05 THEN 290
220 IF H>15.00 THEN 290
230 IF R<0 THEN 290
240 IF R>40 THEN 290
250 IF V<0 THEN 290
260 IF V>20 THEN 290
270 PRINT #1 N;",";D;",";N$;",";H;",";R;",";V
280 GO TO 110
290 PRINT "ERROR IN INPUT DATA,PLEASE RETYPE"
300 GO TO 110
400 CLOSE #1
32767 END
```

This program contains three new statements:

- Line 100 opens a file.
- Line 270 writes data into a file.
- Line 400 closes a file.

Let's look closely at these three statements.

Open a file: Line 100 is OPEN "EMPLOY" AS FILE #1. This statement is used to open a file for either input or output. If we do not have a file, then the computer creates one. The statement says to open a file and that

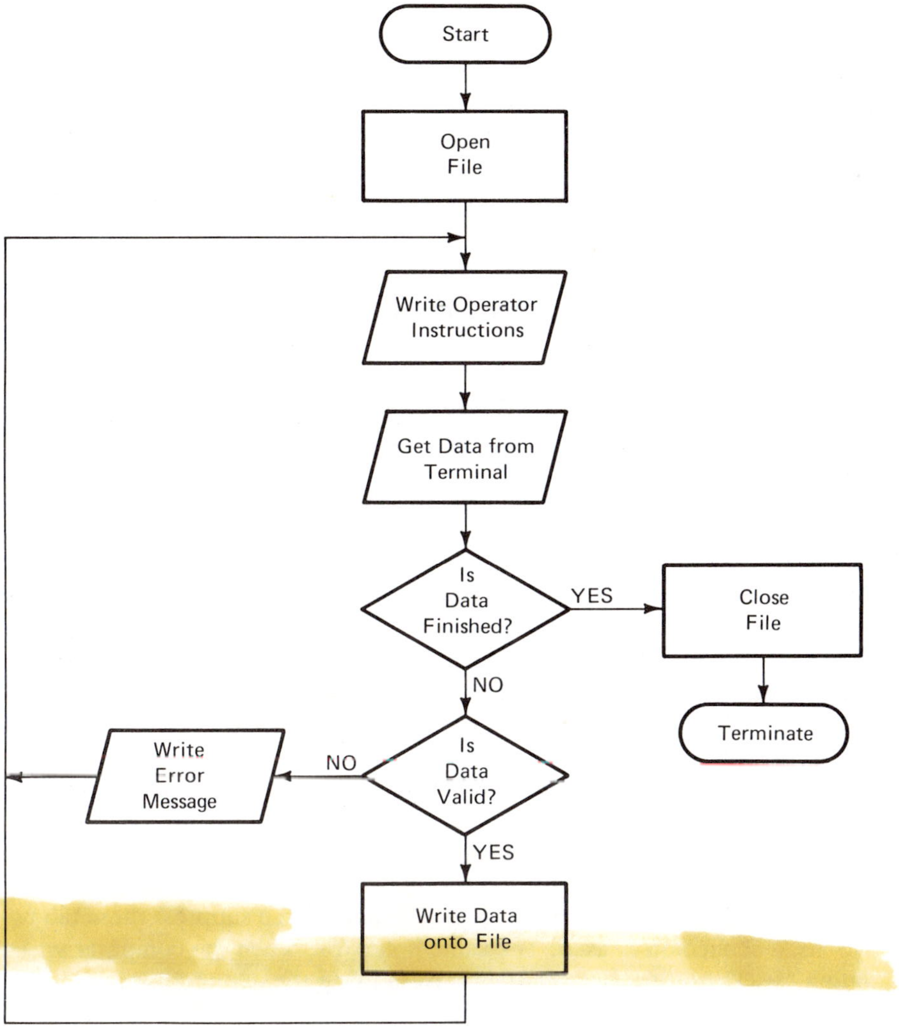

Flowchart for Setting Up a File

Figure 4–1

this file will be called file number 1. "EMPLOY" is the file name that the computer will use.

The file name is limited to six alphanumeric characters. Examples of valid and invalid file names are shown in the following list. (**Note:** The rules for filenames are the same as the rules for program names!)

Example	*Explanation*
A	Valid file name. You can use up to six characters, but you don't have to use all six.

A1	Valid file name. Numbers are also alphanumeric characters. The file names A and A1 are not recommended since they may be confused with field names.
LIST	Valid file name; but not recommended since it is a BASIC command and therefore a possibility of confusion exists.
ACCREC	Valid file name. Good choice of a name since ACCREC for Accounts Receivable has mnemonic (helps you remember) characteristics.
PAYROLL	Invalid file name. File names are limited to six alphanumeric characters.

The file number is necessary inside the program to identify the file. The statement in line 100, therefore, links the computer file name with the file number. At the end of this program you will find that your catalog contains not only programs but also the data file "EMPLOY".

Write into a file: Line 270 uses the file number, one (1) in this case, preceded by a "#" symbol. The # symbol means that the number following it is a file identifier number. A file number is used for brevity–it is shorter to use a file number than to refer to a file by its name ("EMPLOY" in this case). Valid file numbers are 1 to 12.

The PRINT in line 270 tells the computer to write. The "#1" tells it where to write. And the list of fields tells it what to write.

The fields N, D, N$, H, R, and V in line 270 are separated from each other by ;",". The semicolons tell the computer not to use tab positions.

In Chapter 2 we used the predefined tab positions. We wrote on the terminal the values of different fields and they came out in these predefined tab positions–starting in column 1, 15, 30, 45, and 60. To suppress these tab positions, a semicolon is used. The same holds true when the computer writes into a file. The semicolon prevents it from using the tab positions.

The other item in this print line is the ",". This inserts a comma between the field values in the record. That way, with the ;"," the PRINT on file #1 will look like the input data for line 150.

Therefore, line 270 writes the field values for N, D, N$, H, R, and V into file number 1, the "EMPLOY" file, separated by commas.

Close a file: Line 400 closes a file. That tells the computer that it can now store the file. Storing a file in this case means that the file is placed into your catalog in the user save area. That way the file will be available to you for processing. It will remain there until you decide that you no longer need the file. Until then, you can always gain access to it with an OPEN statement.

One last explanation before you try this program. In line 140 the operator is instructed to type "99,99,AA,99,99,99" when no more data has to be entered. This entry generates a last record. In effect, we have a dummy record. It is used to indicate that the data input to the file is finished.

But the computer doesn't know that you have chosen a record with 99's and an AA in each field to end the data. This record is called a dummy record since it does not contain usable payroll data. To the machine, it looks like any other record. We know that this record indicates the end of data because that's what we told the operator to do in line 140 in order to end data input. We could have told the operator to enter any other values in line 140 to indicate the end of data. But whatever we told the operator, we have to pick carefully. The dummy record should be invalid so that it stands out. It should be the same every time so that when the data changes, we don't have to rewrite the program.

The instruction to type 99's and AA serves to end the data for the payroll problem. When such a record is reached, we know that it is time to close the file since data entry is finished. The end of data is tested in line 160. If N, the field for employee number, has a 99 then we assume that no more data will be forthcoming, and we go to line 400 to close the file.

Sign-on the system and type the program. Once you have finished typing the program and given the RUN command, enter the payroll data shown below in Table 4–1.

Payroll Data

Table 4–1

Employee Number	*Department Number*	*Employee Name*	*Hourly Rate*	*Regular Hours*	*Overtime Hours*
101	1	Adams	$5.00	40	0
103	12	Baker	5.60	40	4
104	17	Bravo	4.00	40	2
108	16	Cohen	6.25	38	0
172	2	Johnson	3.75	40	0
198	1	Tanner	4.25	36	0
202	16	Wilson	4.00	40	0
206	7	Lester	5.25	40	0
255	12	Schmidt	5.60	40	4
281	12	Miller	6.00	40	0
313	7	Smith	4.25	40	4
347	12	Gray	6.00	38	0
368	1	Weaver	3.50	40	2
422	1	Williams	4.00	40	0

Better yet, write the program and talk somebody else into entering the data from a terminal. By having somebody else enter the data, you have a closer approximation to how things are actually done in organizations. If an error occurs during data entry, then you must stop the program and run it again from the beginning. So be careful. In the last section of this chapter you will learn how to correct records in a data file.

Example

Inventory Example: Create a file called "INV" with five fields per record.

Problem Summary

Input

Part Number	*Beginning Units*	*Units Received*	*Units Issued*	*Cost*
101	120	40	45	$5.00
210	20	70	100	7.00
219	60	60	80	3.25
226	5	110	90	2.95
235	100	0	50	6.20
347	0	50	20	4.60

Data ranges remain the same as in Chapter 3.

Processing

Take data from keyboard and place valid records in a file named "INV".

Output

Instructions for data entry and a file named "INV".

```
100 REM THIS PROGRAM PUTS DATA INTO THE INV FILE
110 OPEN "INV" AS FILE #1
120 PRINT "TYPE PART NUMBER,BEGINNING UNITS,UNITS RECEIVED,UNITS ISSUED,
"
130 PRINT "AND COST, WITH COMMAS IN BETWEEN"
140 PRINT "WHEN FINISHED TYPE 1,1,1,1,99"
150 INPUT P,B,R,I,C
160 IF C=99 THEN 350
170 IF B<0 THEN 270
180 IF B>1000 THEN 270
190 IF R<0 THEN 290
200 IF R>3000 THEN 290
210 IF I<0 THEN 310
220 IF I>B+R THEN 310
230 IF C<1 THEN 330
240 IF C>10 THEN 330
250 PRINT #1 P;",";B;",";R;",";I;",";C
260 GO TO 120
270 PRINT "ERROR IN BEGINNING UNITS-RETYPE"
280 GO TO 120
290 PRINT "ERROR IN UNITS RECIEVED-RETYPE"
300 GO TO 120
310 PRINT "ERROR IN UNITS ISSUED-RETYPE"
320 GO TO 120
330 PRINT "ERROR IN COST-RETYPE"
340 GO TO 120
350 CLOSE #1
360 STOP
32767 END

Ready
```

```
RUN
INV5
TYPE PART NUMBER,BEGINNING UNITS,UNITS RECEIVED,UNITS ISSUED,
AND COST, WITH COMMAS IN BETWEEN
WHEN FINISHED TYPE 1,1,1,1,99
? 101,120,40,45,5.00
TYPE PART NUMBER,BEGINNING UNITS,UNITS RECEIVED,UNITS ISSUED,
AND COST, WITH COMMAS IN BETWEEN
WHEN FINISHED TYPE 1,1,1,1,99
? 210,20,70,100,7.00
ERROR IN UNITS ISSUED-RETYPE
TYPE PART NUMBER,BEGINNING UNITS,UNITS RECEIVED,UNITS ISSUED,
AND COST, WITH COMMAS IN BETWEEN
WHEN FINISHED TYPE 1,1,1,1,99
? 219,60,60,80,3.25
TYPE PART NUMBER,BEGINNING UNITS,UNITS RECEIVED,UNITS ISSUED,
AND COST, WITH COMMAS IN BETWEEN
WHEN FINISHED TYPE 1,1,1,1,99
? 226,5,110,90,2.95
TYPE PART NUMBER,BEGINNING UNITS,UNITS RECEIVED,UNITS ISSUED,
AND COST, WITH COMMAS IN BETWEEN
WHEN FINISHED TYPE 1,1,1,1,99
? 235,100,0,50,6.20
TYPE PART NUMBER,BEGINNING UNITS,UNITS RECEIVED,UNITS ISSUED,
AND COST, WITH COMMAS IN BETWEEN
WHEN FINISHED TYPE 1,1,1,1,99
? 347,0,50,20,4.60
TYPE PART NUMBER,BEGINNING UNITS,UNITS RECEIVED,UNITS ISSUED,
AND COST, WITH COMMAS IN BETWEEN
WHEN FINISHED TYPE 1,1,1,1,99
? 1,1,1,1,99
Stop at line 350
```

Exercises

Account Balance Exercise: Set up a customer statement file ("CUST") with six records that contains the data specified below.

Problem Summary

Input

Customer Number	*Customer Name*	*Balance*	*Payments*	*Charges*
2741	Fernwood	120	120	40
2937	Blakey	0	0	90
3246	Grey	250	130	170
3359	Phillips	90	40	100
3426	Bird	180	180	200
3527	Lombard	100	100	250

Processing

Take data from keyboard and place it in a file named "CUST".

Output

Instructions for data entry and a file named "CUST".

Sales Commission Exercise: Set up a sales file called "SALES" that contains seven records with the data specified below.

Problem Summary

Input

Sales Territory	*Salesman*	*Gross Sales*	*Commission Rate*
1	Bill	$12,050	.05
1	Joe	5,270	.045
2	Tom	6,940	.04
2	Phil	11,200	.055
3	Clyde	7,340	.04
3	Harry	9,460	.045
3	Bob	14,690	.05

Processing

Take data from keyboard and place it in a file named "SALES".

Output

Instructions for data entry and a file named "SALES".

READING A FILE

In the previous section, you learned how to set up a computer file. To know what is in a computer file, it is necessary to write a program. The program will read a file and print its contents.

The processing for this program consists of reading a file, record by record, and then printing the records. The program continues reading and printing records until there are no more records in the file.

A program to do that is shown below:

```
10 REM THIS PROGRAM READS AND PRINTS THE "EMPLOY" FILE #1
100 OPEN "EMPLOY" AS FILE #1
110 INPUT #1 N,D,N$,H,R,V
120 PRINT N,D,N$,H,R,V
130 GO TO 110
250 CLOSE #1
500 STOP
32767 END
```

This program contains one new instruction. Line 110 tells the computer to input field values from file number 1. The input statement for a file is identical to the input from a terminal except for the specification of the file number.

When we run this program, the content of the file is printed:

```
101           1             ADAMS          5              40
0
103           12            BAKER          5.6            40
4
104           17            BRAVO          4              40
2
108           16            COHEN          6.25           38
0
172           2             JOHNSON        3.75           40
0
198           1             TANNER         4.25           36
0
202           16            WILSON         4              40
0
206           7             LESTER         5.25           40
0
255           12            SCHMIDT        5.6            40
4
281           12            MILLER         6              40
0
313           7             SMITH          4.25           40
4
347           12            GRAY           6              38
0
368           1             WEAVER         3.5            40
2
422           1             WILLIAMS       4              40
0
?End of file on device at line 110
```

As you can see, it takes two lines to print each record. The first five fields are in one line. The sixth is in the following line. Line 120 asked the computer to PRINT N, D, N$, H, R, V. The fields are separated by commas, which means that the pre-defined tab positions (in columns 1, 15, 30, 45 and 60) should be used. But there are only five tab positions and each record has six fields. Therefore, the sixth field starts a new line.

You'll also note that, at the end of the file, a message is printed stating that the end of file has been reached at line 110. We'll tackle these two problems in succession.

The first problem—output on two lines—is easy to correct. We'll use a semicolon to separate the first two fields in the PRINT command.

```
120 PRINT N; D, N$, H, R, V
```

Now when we run the program the output looks as follows:

```
101  1        ADAMS         5              40             0
103  12       BAKER         5.6            40             4
104  17       BRAVO         4              40             2
108  16       COHEN         6.25           38             0
172  2        JOHNSON       3.75           40             0
198  1        TANNER        4.25           36             0
202  16       WILSON        4              40             0
206  7        LESTER        5.25           40             0
255  12       SCHMIDT       5.6            40             4
281  12       MILLER        6              40             0
313  7        SMITH         4.25           40             4
347  12       GRAY          6              38             0
368  1        WEAVER        3.5            40             2
422  1        WILLIAMS      4              40             0
?End of file on device at line 110
```

This corrects the first problem. For the error message, some more new statements are needed. We need to specify what to do in case of error. And we need to identify what error has occurred. Adding the following four statements to the program will remove the "end of file" message.

```
20 ON ERROR GO TO 200
200 REM ***ERROR CHECKING ROUTINE
210 IF ERR=11 THEN RESUME 250
220 PRINT "UNUSUAL ERROR CONDITION",ERR
250 CLOSE #1
```

This segment contains two new statements. Line 20 tells the computer where to go if an error crops up. And line 210 checks which error has occurred. If the error number is 11 (IF ERR = 11) then the error condition is caused by an attempt to read beyond the end of the file. (A listing of all error numbers and their messages is Appendix C.) If the error is error number 11, then processing resumes with line 250.

Below you have a listing of the program and its output.

```
10 REM THIS PROGRAM READS AND PRINTS THE "EMPLOY" FILE #1
20 ON ERROR GO TO 200
100 OPEN "EMPLOY" AS FILE #1
110 INPUT #1 N,D,N$,H,R,V
120 PRINT N;D,N$,H,R,V
130 GO TO 110
200 REM ***ERROR CHECKING ROUTINE
210 IF ERR=11 THEN RESUME 250
220 PRINT "UNUSUAL ERROR CONDITION",ERR
250 CLOSE #1
500 STOP
32767 END

Ready

RUN
PAY8
 101  1        ADAMS          5           40          0
 103  12       BAKER          5.6         40          4
 104  17       BRAVO          4           40          2
 108  16       COHEN          6.25        38          0
 172  2        JOHNSON        3.75        40          0
 198  1        TANNER         4.25        36          0
 202  16       WILSON         4           40          0
 206  7        LESTER         5.25        40          0
 255  12       SCHMIDT        5.6         40          4
 281  12       MILLER         6           40          0
 313  7        SMITH          4.25        40          4
 347  12       GRAY           6           38          0
 368  1        WEAVER         3.5         40          2
 422  1        WILLIAMS       4           40          0
Stop at line 500
```

Inventory Example: Read the file "INV" and print each record in that file. Example

```
10 REM THIS PROGRAM READS "INV" FILE AND PRINTS IT
20 ON ERROR GO TO 200
100 OPEN "INV" AS FILE #1
110 INPUT #1 P,B,R,I,C
120 PRINT P,B,R,I,C
130 GO TO 110
200 REM *** ERROR CHECKING ROUTINE
```

```
210 IF ERR=11 THEN RESUME 250
220 PRINT "UNUSUAL ERROR CONDITION",ERR
250 CLOSE #1
500 STOP
32767 END

Ready

RUN
INV6
 101          120          40          45          5
 219          60           60          80          3.25
 226          5            110         90          2.95
 235          100          0           50          6.2
 347          0            50          20          4.6
Stop at line 500
```

Exercises

Account Balance Exercise: Read the customer statement file "CUST" and print each record.

Sales Commission Exercise: Read the sales file "SALES" and print each record.

FINDING A RECORD IN A FILE

A file of data is created for some purpose. Files are not created to be placed on a shelf in the corner to collect dust. Files are used to hold data until there is a need for it. When there is a need for data, we must be able to go to a file and pull data, with the desired characteristics, out of the file.

Suppose that Smith, employee number 313, wanted to know how many hours of overtime he had worked. Smith is one of the people in the file "EMPLOY". To answer his question, we need to write a program that will locate his record and print it out. But to locate his record in a sequential file, all preceding records will have to be read.

Problem Summary

Input

The file "EMPLOY" with each record having six fields:

- Employee identification number
- Department number
- Employee name
- Hourly rate
- Regular hours worked
- Overtime hours worked

Processing

Search the file until the record with employee number 313 is found. Print that record and stop.

Output

If the search is successful, the desired record is printed. If the search is not successful (the record is not in the file) then a "RECORD NOT FOUND" message is printed.

The logic of the program for finding a record in a sequential file is:

1. Link to the file.
2. Read a record.
3. If it is the record we want, then print it; otherwise, read the next record.
4. Stop when the search is finished.

A flowchart (Fig. 4–2) and program to do these tasks are shown below:

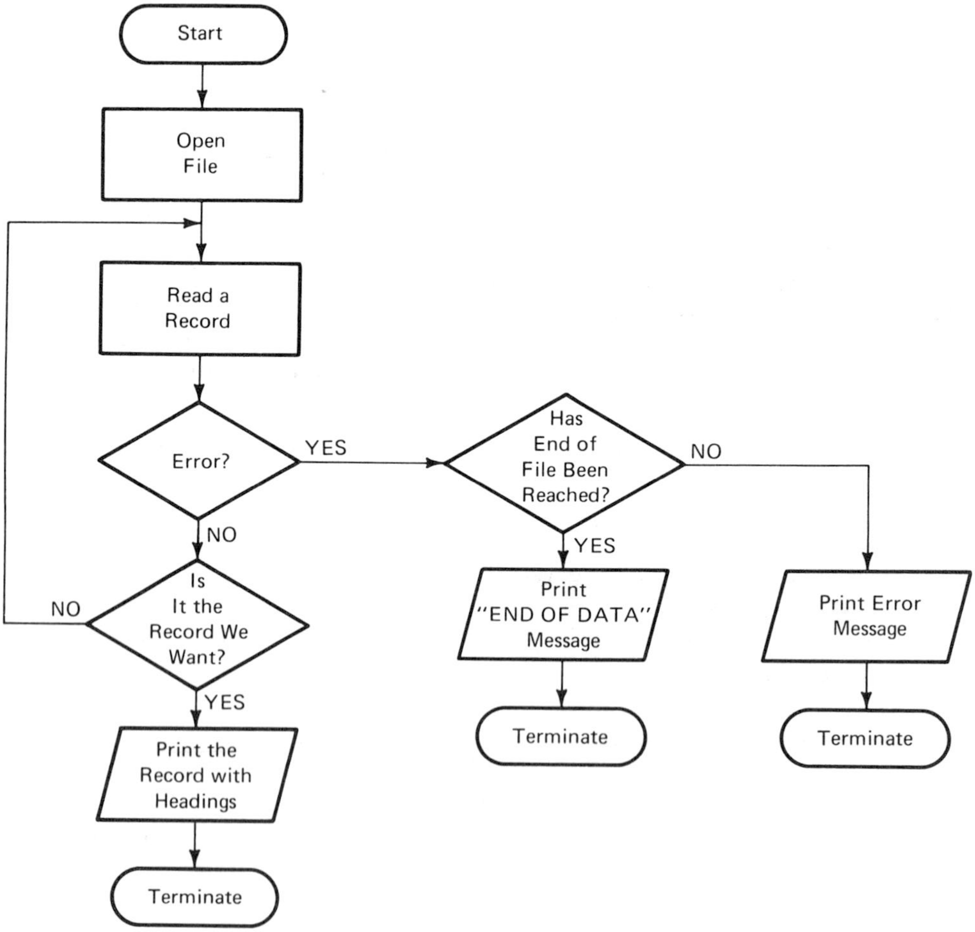

Figure 4–2 Flowchart of Finding a Record

```
100 REM PROGRAM TO FIND AN EMPLOYEE RECORD
110 OPEN "EMPLOY" AS FILE #1
120 ON ERROR GO TO 230
130 INPUT #1 N,D,N$,H,R,V
140 IF N=313 THEN 170
150 GO TO 130
160 REM PRINT THE RECORD FOUND
170 PRINT "EMPLOYEE","EMPLOYEE","HOURLY", "REGULAR","OVERTIME"
180 PRINT "NUMBER","NAME","RATE","HOURS","HOURS"
190 PRINT N,N$,H,R,V
200 CLOSE #1
210 STOP
220 REM ERROR CHECKING ROUTINE
230 IF ERR=11 THEN RESUME 280
240 PRINT "UNUSUAL ERROR CONDITION",ERR
250 CLOSE #1
260 STOP
270 REM RECORD NOT IN FILE
280 PRINT "END OF DATA-RECORD NOT FOUND"
290 CLOSE #1
300 STOP
32767 END

Ready

RUN
PAY9
EMPLOYEE        EMPLOYEE        HOURLY          REGULAR         OVERTIME
NUMBER          NAME            RATE            HOURS           HOURS
 313            SMITH            4.25            40              4
Stop at line 210
```

The key to the search program lies in statement 140. Here the employee number of the record that was read from the file is compared to 313, Smith's employee number. If there is a match (i.e., the value of N, the employee number, is 313), then we know that the desired record has been found and can be printed in lines 170–190. Or, if the employee number is not 313, the next record in the file is read and the check for a match is repeated.

But notice that we also need to consider the possibility that Smith is not in the file. Maybe he was on vacation or sick leave and did not work that week. Or maybe his time card was lost and not entered into the file. Hence, we must include instructions telling the computer what to do if the end of file is reached. The ON ERROR condition in line 120 and the statements following line 220 take care of that possibility.

No matter the result, whether the desired record is found, or the desired record is not in the file, or the program "bombs" (fails), the file must be closed and the program must be terminated.

We have repeated this same logic in the next example. Look it over, and try the exercises that follow.

Example

Inventory Example: Read the file "INV", find and print out the record for part number 235 with suitable headings.

```
100 REM TO FIND INVENTORY RECORD
110 OPEN "INV" AS FILE #1
120 ON ERROR GO TO 230
130 INPUT #1 P,B,R,I,C
140 IF P=235 THEN 170
150 GO TO 130
160 REM PRINT THE RECORD FOUND
```

```
170 PRINT "PART NUMBER","BEG. UNITS","UNITS REC."
175 PRINT P,B,R
177 PRINT
178 PRINT
180 PRINT "UNITS ISSUED","COST"
185 PRINT I,C
190 PRINT
200 CLOSE #1
205 PRINT
206 PRINT
210 STOP
220 REM ERROR CHECKING ROUTINE
230 IF ERR=11 THEN RESUME 280
240 PRINT "UNUSUAL ERROR",ERR
250 CLOSE #1
260 STOP
270 REM RECORD NOT IN FILE
280 PRINT "END OF DATA-RECORD NOT FOUND"
290 CLOSE #1
300 STOP
32767 END

Ready

PART NUMBER   BEG. UNITS    UNITS REC.
 235           100           0


UNITS ISSUED  COST
 50            6.2


Stop at line 210
```

Exercises

Account Balance Exercise: Read the customer statement file "CUST", find and print out the record for customer number 2741 with suitable headings.

Sales Commission Exercise: Read the sales file, "SALES", find and print out the record for salesman Clyde with suitable headings.

CORRECTING RECORDS IN A FILE

Once a file has been created it is good practice to check it by writing a program that reads and prints the file. Then you can look at what is in the file to see that all records have been entered correctly. Although the range checks will catch some errors in data entry, they do not catch errors if the incorrect value entered is within the range specified. These errors can be caught by comparing the records in a file with what the data should have been. To correct them, a program has to be written.

Assume that the "EMPLOY" file had an error: for some reason the regular hours for Gray, employee number 347, was entered as 38 when it should have been 40. A program to correct that error is shown below:

```
100 REM PROGRAM TO CORRECT THE HOURS WORKED FOR GRAY
110 REM
120 REM   LINK TO FILES
130 REM
140 OPEN "EMPLOY" AS FILE #1
150 OPEN "EMPLCR" AS FILE #2
160 REM
170 REM   READ THE RECORDS FROM EMPLOY
180 REM
190 ON ERROR GO TO 380
200 INPUT #1 N,D,N$,H,R,V
210 REM
220 REM DETERMINE WHETHER ITS THE RECORD FOR GRAY
230 REM
240 IF N<>347 THEN 330
250 REM
260 REM  IT IS THE RECORD FOR GRAY, EMPLOYEE NUMBER 347,
270 REM  THEREFORE ASSIGN THE CORRECT HOURS WORKED
280 REM
290 R=40
```

```
300 REM
310 REM PUT RECORD INTO EMPLCR -- THE CORRECT FILE
320 REM
330 PRINT #2 N;",";D;",";N$;",";H;",";R;",";V
340 GO TO 200
350 REM
360 REM *** ERROR CHECKING ROUTINE ***
370 REM
380 IF ERR=11 THEN RESUME 410
390 PRINT "UNUSUAL ERROR",ERR
400 STOP
410 CLOSE #1
420 CLOSE #2
430 STOP
32767 END

Ready

RUN
PAY10
Stop at line 430
```

If you now change the program that prints the "EMPLOY" file in line 100 to

100 OPEN "EMPLCR" AS FILE #1

and run it, you can list the "EMPLCR" file as follows:

101	1	ADAMS	5	40	0
103	12	BAKER	5.6	40	4
104	17	BRAVO	4	40	2
108	16	COHEN	6.25	38	0
172	2	JOHNSON	3.75	40	0
198	1	TANNER	4.25	36	0
202	16	WILSON	4	40	0
206	7	LESTER	5.25	40	0
255	12	SCHMIDT	5.6	40	4
281	12	MILLER	6	40	0
313	7	SMITH	4.25	40	4
347	12	GRAY	6	40	0
368	1	WEAVER	3.5	40	2
422	1	WILLIAMS	4	40	0

```
Stop at line 500
```

The logic for this program is illustrated in Fig. 4–3 (next page). This program is designed to find a specific record, employee number 347, and to change the value of the regular hours in that record. When you look at the program two differences from earlier programs emerge:

1. Two files are opened.

2. A LET seems to be missing in line 290.

The program runs despite the apparent error in line 290. It runs because the LET is optional. Many computer systems permit you to assign values to a field without the keyword LET. A few systems do not. Find out whether your system requires the LET in an assignment or whether it is optional. If the LET is optional, you do not have to use it, and by this omission you can save time, and energy, not to mention the added possibility of making typographical errors. In all subsequent programs we have omitted the LET.

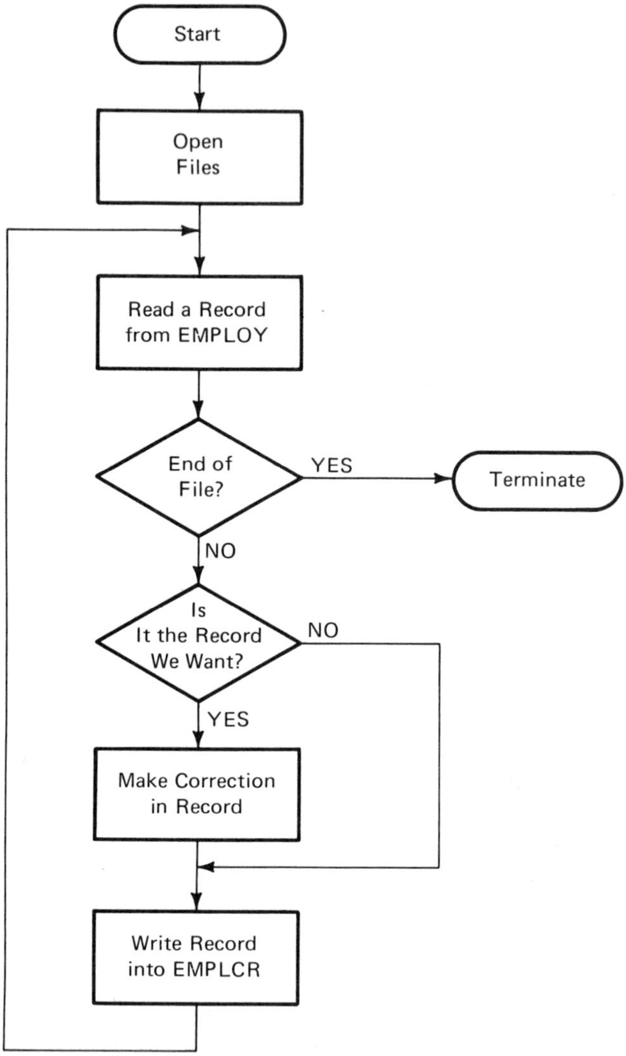

Figure 4–3 Flowchart for Correcting Records in a File

Two files are necessary because sequential files can only be used for input to the program or for output from the program, but not both. Therefore to correct an error, we need to read the old file and place the correct data in a new file.

In this program, lines 140 and 150 open the two files. You can open up to 12 files in a program (using file numbers 1 through 12), but each file must be unique (a filename should appear only once) and each file ID number must be unique (you cannot open two files with the same number—that would confuse the computer). At the end, both files are closed.

The logic of this program takes a record from "EMPLOY". Line 240 checks whether it is the record with an error. If it is, the error is corrected; the statement in line 290 assigns the correct value to R thereby erasing the old, incorrect value of R. And correct records are written into "EMPLCR". The process continues until all records have been read from "EMPLOY" and written into "EMPLCR".

After this program has been run, both files will appear in your catalog—"EMPLOY" with its error, and "EMPLCR" with only correct records. In effect we have copied the "EMPLOY" file.

A more general error correction program is the next example.

Example

Inventory Example: It has been discovered that when the file "INV" was initially created, two errors were made. The units received for part number 219 should have been 160 instead of 60; and the beginning units for part number 235 should have been 90 instead of 100. These records must be corrected. Part numbers to be corrected should be entered in ascending order.

Problem Summary

Input

The file "INV" where each record has five fields:

- Part number
- Beginning units
- Units received
- Units issued
- Unit cost

Correct field values for erroneous records.

Processing

Get the identification number for incorrect records from the terminal. Search the file until the desired record has been found. Get correct data for incorrect records from the terminal. Place correct records into file "INVCR".

Output

Instructions for data entry and the file "INVCR" with correct inventory records.

```
100 REM THIS PROGRAM TO CORRECT ERRORS IN THE INV FILE
110 REM
120 REM LINK TO FILES
130 REM
140 OPEN "INV"AS FILE #2
150 OPEN "INVCR" AS FILE #4
160 REM
170 REM GET PART NUMBER OF RECORD TO BE CORRECTED
180 REM
190 PRINT "TYPE PART NUMBER OF RECORD TO BE CORRECTED"
200 PRINT "WHEN FINISHED --TYPE 99"
```

```
210 INPUT N
220 REM
230 REM CHECK IF ERROR CORRECTIONS ARE FINISHED
240 REM
250 IF N=99 THEN 550
260 REM
270 REM GET A RECORD FROM INV
280 REM
290 INPUT #2 P,B,R1,R2,C
300 ON ERROR GO TO 610
310 REM
320 REM CHECK IF THE RECORD NEEDS TO BE CORRECTED
330 REM
340 IF P=N THEN 420
350 REM
360 REM WRITE RECORD INTO THE INVCR FILE
370 REM
380 PRINT #4 P;",";B;",";R1;",";R2;",";C
390 GO TO 290
400 REM
410 REM
420 PRINT "FOR PART NUMBER";P
430 PRINT "ENTER BEGINNING UNITS,UNITS RECEIVED"
440 PRINT "UNITS ISSUED, AND COST"
450 INPUT B,R1,R2,C
460 PRINT #4 P;",";B;",";R1;",";R2;",";C
470 REM
480 REM GET PART NUMBER OF NEXT RECORD TO BE CORRECTED
490 REM
500 GO TO 190
510 REM
520 REM CORRECTIONS FINISHED,COPY REMAINING RECORDS
530 REM FROM INV TO INVCR
540 REM
550 INPUT #2 P,B,R1,R2,C
560 PRINT #4 P;",";B;",";R1;",";R2;",";C
570 GO TO 550
580 REM
590 REM ERROR CHECKING ROUTINE
600 REM
610 IF ERR=11 THEN RESUME 670
620 PRINT "UNUSUAL ERROR",ERR
630 STOP
640 REM
650 REM TERMINATE
660 REM
670 CLOSE #2
680 CLOSE #4
690 STOP
32767 END
```

```
TYPE PART NUMBER OF RECORD TO BE CORRECTED
WHEN FINISHED --TYPE 99
? 219
FOR PART NUMBER 219
ENTER BEGINNING UNITS,UNITS RECEIVED
UNITS ISSUED, AND COST
? 60,160,80,3.25
TYPE PART NUMBER OF RECORD TO BE CORRECTED
WHEN FINISHED --TYPE 99
? 235
FOR PART NUMBER 235
ENTER BEGINNING UNITS,UNITS RECEIVED
UNITS ISSUED, AND COST
? 90,0,50,6.20
TYPE PART NUMBER OF RECORD TO BE CORRECTED
WHEN FINISHED --TYPE 99
? 99
Stop at line 690
```

If the old program to list the "INV" file is changed as follows:

```
100 OPEN "INVCR" AS FILE #1
```

and run, the "INVCR" file is printed as follows:

```
101          120          40          45          5
219          60           160         80          3.25
226          5            110         90          2.95
235          90           0           50          6.2
347          0            50          20          4.6
Stop at line 500
```

This program can correct any number of erroneous records. No matter which records are wrong or which fields have false values, the program can correct them. However, the operator must know in which records the errors have occurred and what the correct field values are. Both items have to be entered by the operator from the terminal.

The program finds a record specified by the operator by searching through the file. As it searches, records that have a lower identification number are placed in the new file. When the record to be corrected has been found, the operator is instructed to enter the data for that record. The data received from the terminal is then placed into the new file. This cycle is repeated until there are no more records to be corrected. At that time any records still remaining in the old file are copied into the new file.

COPYING A FILE

At times it is necessary to make a copy of a file for back up. Then if the first file is accidentally destroyed the copy can be retrieved and used. In the previous section, where errors in records were corrected, a revised version of a file was created.

The general approach to error corrections is also appropriate to copying a file:

- Link to the desired files
- Read data from one file
- Write the data into the other file
- When no more data remains in the first file, then close both files and terminate.

These steps are included in both examples and in both exercises of the previous section. They are particularly obvious in lines 550–570 of the last program (page 86) where the records remaining in file "INV" are copied to file "INVCR".

SUMMARY

This chapter introduces you to sequential files. Sequential files are very economical when large volumes of data have to be processed. You have seen how to set up files and how to enter data into a file. Next the data file was read and printed. Finding a record in a file is an elementary operation that has uses in many applications. In this chapter finding a record was used to correct erroneous data. The chapter concluded by pointing out that error correction has to copy a file. Copying a file is necessary in error correction because sequential files can only be read or written, not both.

BASIC Instructions Introduced:

OPEN "filename" as FILE #n	Opens the file identified by the filename and gives it an identifying number. The filename can be from 1 to 6 characters. The file number can be from 1 to 12.
INPUT #n fieldname1, fieldname2, etc.	Reads a record from file number n. The file is identified by its file number. Records are specified by their fieldnames.
PRINT #n fieldname1;","; fieldname2;","; etc.	Writes a record on file n. The fields of the record will be separated by commas.
CLOSE #n	Closes file n and stores it in the user save area.
ON ERROR GO TO line number	Tells the computer to go to *line number* when an error is encountered.
IF ERR = n THEN RESUME line number	Tells the computer that if the error encountered is n, then processing should resume at the line number given.

PROBLEMS

1. Set up a file called "XKl" and enter the following data:

I.D. Number	*Time 1*	*Time 2*
101	40	0
103	40	4
104	40	2
108	38	0
172	40	0
198	36	0
202	40	0
281	40	0
347	38	0
422	40	0

2. Print out the contents of file XKl.
3. Write a simple program that will set up a file "TOP" with the input data (below) and print out the file.

I.D.	*Name*
247	Farnsworth
262	Lowell
264	Fergerson
275	Fong

4. Read the sales file, "SALES". Find and print out the record for salesman Joe with suitable headings.
5. Read the inventory file. Find and print out the records for part numbers 219 and 347 with suitable headings. The END OF DATA–RECORD NOT FOUND message will be printed.
6. Read the "XKl" file from Problem 1, above. Find and print out the record for I.D. number 172 with suitable headings.

For problems 7–10 below, write an additional program to read and print the file:

7. Write a program that will read the customer statement file "CUST" and place that data in a new file "CUST1" so that you have two files with exactly the same data. Verify by printing "CUST1".
8. Write a program that will read the customer statement file "CUST" and place only customer data that have customer numbers from 3000 to 4000 into a new file "CUST2". Verify by printing "CUST2".

9. Write a program that will read the sales commission file "SALES" and place the name and gross sales data into a new file "SALE1". However, the company has instituted a new sales policy so that the commission rate for all salesmen will be 6%. Verify by printing "SALES1".

10. Write a program that will read the payroll file "EMPLOY" and place the following data fields into a new file "EMPL1": Employee number, department number, name, hourly rate.

5 / Writing Reports from Sequential Files

Performance Objectives

At the end of this chapter you should be able to:

- Calculate totals and subtotals for a file
- Produce reports that are clear and legible

Data is the lifeblood of a business. Without data, a business could not operate. For example, customer orders tell a firm what items to ship to a customer. They also tell a business who to bill and how much the customer owes the business. Data, such as customer orders, direct the operations of a business.

There are many other items of data that have the same characteristic, i.e. they support business operations. Production orders, inventory transactions, vendor invoices, time cards, and the like all serve to direct the activities of the firm.

But data is also used to support management decision making. From a management perspective, it is not enough to know that one customer has ordered one item. For decision making it is necessary to keep track of all customers. It is necessary to look at inventories as a whole. It is necessary to judge and evaluate all products. It is necessary to plan and control the operations of the firm as a whole.

Data to support management decisions has to be collected and processed. The processed data has to be presented to management as information in a report that will help management keep track of the activities of a firm. For example, a customer report allows management to determine their best customers. A product-line sales summary would tell management which products are selling well and which products are selling poorly.

This chapter shows you how sequential files are processed to produce reports. It will show you how to accumulate totals for the whole file and how to calculate subtotals for parts of the file. And it will show you how to use additional PRINT capabilities to make your reports neat and orderly.

HOW TO ACCUMULATE TOTALS

In order to understand the programming involved in accumulating totals, the following example illustrates what is required.

Problem Summary

Input

"EMPLOY" file

Processing

Accumulate the total number of regular hours worked for all employees.

Output

Total regular hours worked with an appropriate heading.

See the flowchart (Fig. 5–1) and program to do this on the next page.

```
10 REM PROGRAM TO TOTAL REGULAR HOURS WORKED FOR
11 REM ALL EMPLOYEES; R1 WILL BE THE ACCUMULATION
12 REM OF REGULAR HOURS
100 OPEN "EMPLOY" AS FILE #1
110 R1=0
120 INPUT #1 N,D,N$,H,R,V
130 ON ERROR GO TO 160
140 R1=R1+R
150 GO TO 120
160 IF ERR=11 THEN RESUME 190
170 PRINT "UNUSUAL ERROR CONDITION",ERR
180 STOP
190 CLOSE #1
200 PRINT "TOTAL REGULAR HOURS",R1
210 STOP
32767 END
```

This program is very similar to the last payroll program with the exception of lines 110 and 140.

110 R1 = 0

Line 110 sets the value of R1 to zero. This is called initializing an accumulation. Most computer systems will do this automatically, however some systems will not. Therefore it is worth the slight additional effort to put in an initialization statement. The choice of the name, R1 in this case, is up to the programmer. Any name could be used provided it is not used to define any other field. R1 seems a reasonable choice since R is the name assigned to the regular hours field.

140 R1 = R1 + R

This statement looks strange until you remember that the equal sign (=) is not an equal sign in algebraic terms. This statement looks the same as the algebra statement a = a + b; however, it is different. The equal sign in BASIC is an assignment. Line 140, if translated into English means take the value that you found in field R, add its value to the current value of R1, and assign the sum to R1. If we look at the first four records in EMPLOY the values of R are: 40 for Adams, 40 for Baker, 40 for Bravo, and 38 for Cohen.

When the computer executes line 110 it sets the value of R1 to 0, at line 120 the value of R for Adams is 40. At line 140 the values to the right of the equal sign are 0 and 40 which sum to 40. The value 40 is now assigned to R1; after line 140 has been executed, R1 has the new value of 40. The program then directs that the next record be input (Baker). Again at 120 the value of R for Baker is 40. In line 140 R1 is 40 and R is 40. When they are summed, the new value of R1 is 40 + 40 which is 80. The program directs that the next record be input (Bravo). At line 120 the value of R for Bravo is 40. At line 140, R1 is now 80 and R is 40. These values are summed and the new value of R1 is assigned as 120. The next record is input (Cohen). The value of R is 38, R1 is 120. The new value of R1 is assigned as 158.

This process repeats until the end of the file is reached and ERR = 11 is detected. Then the file is closed and the following output is produced:

```
PAY12
TOTAL REGULAR HOURS           552
Stop at line 210

Ready
```

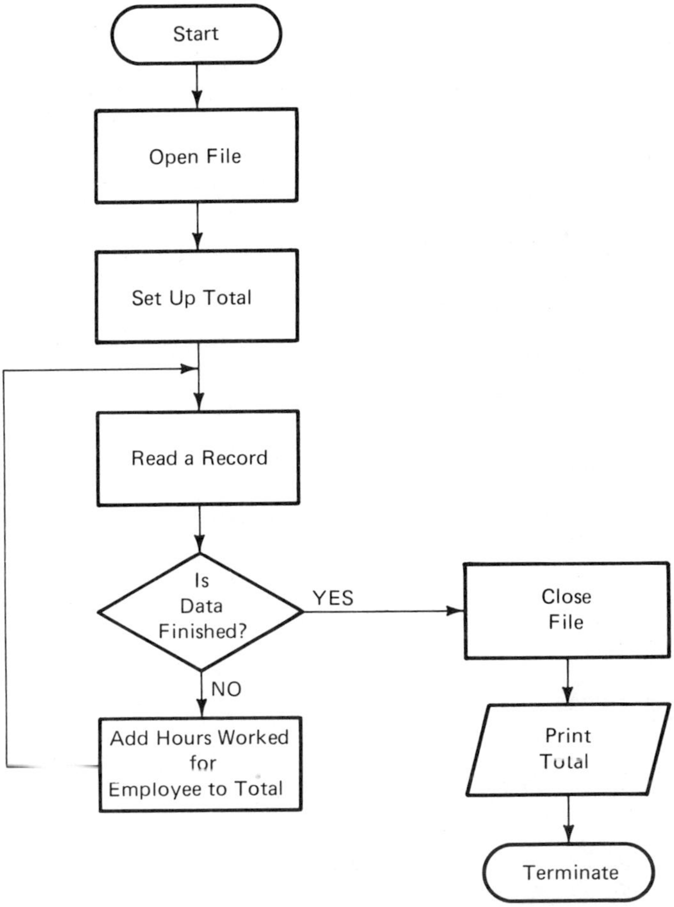

Flowchart for Accumulating Totals

Figure 5–1

As a second example, let us increase the number of totals. For this case, we want to calculate the total hours worked (both regular and overtime) and the total wages earned by everyone. The "EMPLOY" file will again be used. Now, we need to add the regular and overtime hours worked by each employee to get their totals, also we need to add the wages earned by each employee to get the total wages earned.

Problem Summary

Input

"EMPLOY" file

Processing

Accumulate regular hours worked, overtime hours worked, and wages earned by each employee to get totals.

Output

Totals for regular hours worked, overtime hours worked, and wages earned with appropriate headings.

The program therefore has to:

1. Link to the "EMPLOY" file.
2. Set up fields for the totals.
3. Read the records in the file.
4. Accumulate totals.
5. Print the totals with appropriate headings.

The program to perform these steps is shown below:

```
10 REM THIS PROGRAM TO ACCUMULATE TOTALS FOR REGULAR HOURS
11 REM OVERTIME HOURS,AND TOTAL WAGES EARNED IN THE "EMPLOY"FILE
100 OPEN "EMPLOY" AS FILE #1
120 R1=0
130 V1=0
140 W1=0
150 INPUT #1 N,D,N$,H,R,V
160 ON ERROR GO TO 220
170 R1=R1+R
180 V1=V1+V
190 W1=W1+H*R+1.5*H*V
200 GO TO 150
210 REM ERROR CHECKING ROUTINE
220 IF ERR=11 THEN RESUME 250
230 PRINT "UNUSUAL ERROR CONDITION",ERR
240 STOP
250 CLOSE #1
260 PRINT "TOTAL REGULAR HOURS WORKED",R1
270 PRINT "TOTAL OVERTIME HOURS WORKED",V1
280 PRINT "TOTAL WAGES EARNED BY ALL EMPLOYEES",W1
290 STOP
32767 END

Ready

RUN
PAY13
TOTAL REGULAR HOURS WORKED    552
TOTAL OVERTIME HOURS WORKED   16
TOTAL WAGES EARNED BY ALL EMPLOYEES          2771.7
Stop at line 290
```

The first group of statements, lines 120, 130, and 140, sets the fields called R1, V1, and W1 to zero. R1 will be used to accumulate regular hours. V1 will be used to accumulate overtime hours. And W1 is used, later in the program, to accumulate the wages earned. Again, as in the preceding example, before you read a record, you have to initialize these fields to zero anywhere before the loop.

The second group of statements performs the accumulation of totals. As each record is read, the data from the record is added to the fields that are used to hold the accumulation. Remember the = symbol is an assignment symbol and not an equal sign! What line 170 tells the computer to do is: Take the value that is currently in R1, add to this the value that is currently in R, and place the sum back into R1.

A similar operation occurs in lines 180 and 190. In line 180, the current contents of V1 is added to the current contents of V; and the result is placed into V1. In line 190, a somewhat more complicated procedure is involved:

First, the regular wages are computed when the hourly rate is multiplied by the hours worked (H*R).

Next, the computer calculates overtime wages when it multiplies the overtime hours (V) by one-and-a-half times the hourly rate (1.5*H).

Then, the regular wages and the overtime wages are added to the current wage total (W1).

Finally, that sum is stored again in W1.

In this way, the wages of all employees are accumulated, but only one at a time.

The third group of statements, in lines 260–280, prints what has been accumulated in R1, V1, and W1, with appropriate headings, of course.

To further illuminate this process, here is another example. To highlight how the accumulation procedure works, let's take a simple data file and generate the totals of that file.

Assume you have a file called "SALORD", that contains sales orders. Further assume that each sales order has just two fields—order number and dollar amount of order. The file of data could look like this:

Sales Order Number	*Dollar Amount of Sale*
20473	1800.00
20474	450.00
20475	600.00
20476	150.00
20477	500.00

Of course, a *real* sales order would have many more fields. For example, a sales order would have to identify the customer, the customer address, the salesman who made the sale (for commission calculation if needed), where to ship the items, who to bill for the sale, and so on. And obviously, a *real* sales order file would contain many more records than the five that are shown. For our simple example, this file will be adequate.

Now, what we need to do is write a program that will accumulate the total dollar amount of sales, and then print out this total. But let's also print the value of sales and the value for the total as we are accumulating.

A program to perform this task is given below:

```
100 REM PROGRAM TO TOTAL SALES ORDERS
110 OPEN "SALORD" AS FILE #1
120 T = 0
130 INPUT #1 N,S
140 ON ERROR GO TO 180
150 T = T + S
160 PRINT "S=";S,"T=";T
170 GO TO 130
180 IF ERR=11 THEN RESUME 210
190 PRINT "UNUSUAL ERROR",ERR
200 STOP
210 CLOSE #1
220 PRINT"THE TOTAL DOLLAR SALES ARE:";T
230 STOP
32767 END
```

If you now type RUN, the program will give the following output.

```
S= 1800        T= 1800
S= 450         T= 2250
S= 600         T= 2850
S= 150         T= 3000
S= 500         T= 3500
THE TOTAL DOLLAR SALES ARE: 3500
Stop at line 230
```

Look again at the program. We'll go over the steps that it performs one by one, and we'll trace what happens to the fields labelled N, S, and T.

After opening the file, line 120 sets the field T to zero. So, picture a box called T and put a zero into it.

T [0]

Line 130 reads two values from the file and puts these values into N and S. Thus:

N [20473]   S [1800]

Line 150 (we skipped 140 because it's not yet pertinent) then takes the value of field T. Look at the box called T above. It contains a zero—right? So, it takes the zero and adds to it the content of the box called S. S contains 1800. So, 1800 is added to zero and now T would look like:

T [1800]

In line 160, we print the contents of S and T. And line 170 gets us back to line 130. At line 130, the next set of values is placed into the fields N and S:

N [20474]   S [450]

Line 140 then adds what is in T (the 1800) to the contents of S (the 450).

And the result (2250) is placed into the field T.

T = 2250

Line 160 outputs S and T before line 170 takes us back for another cycle.

You can now repeat these steps on your own. Use the boxes below for the third, fourth and fifth records.

					ending
3rd	starting T	2250	N ____	S ____	T ____
4th			N ____	S ____	T ____
5th			N ____	S ____	T ____

Note the pattern that is followed in accumulating a total. Start by setting a field to zero. Then, add one item at a time to that field until you are out of data. When you next PRINT that field, the grand total is output.

Example

Problem Summary

Input

"SALES" file

Processing

Accumulate the total sales commissions that must be paid to the salesmen.

Output

Total of all the commissions suitably labelled.

```
10 REM THIS PROGRAM TO ACCUMULATE IN THE VARIABLE C1
11 REM THE TOTAL COMMISSION PAID TO ALL SALESMEN
12 REM IN THE FILE "SALES"
100 OPEN "SALES" AS FILE #4
110 C1=0
120 INPUT #4 D,S$,S,C
130 ON ERROR GO TO 200
140 C1=C1+S*C
150 GO TO 120
180 REM ERROR CHECKING ROUTINE
200 IF ERR=11 THEN RESUME 250
210 PRINT "UNUSUAL ERROR CONDITION",ERR
230 STOP
250 CLOSE #4
260 PRINT "TOTAL COMMISSION PAID",C1
270 STOP
32767 END

Ready

RUN
TOTCOM
TOTAL COMMISSION PAID          3187.05
Stop at line 270
```

Exercises

Inventory Value Exercise:

Problem Summary

Input

"INV" file

Processing

Accumulate the beginning units, units received, and units issued; calculate the total inventory value at the beginning of the period.

Output

Totals for beginning units, units received, units issued, and beginning inventory value, with appropriate headings.

```
TOTAL BEGINNING UNITS         305
TOTAL UNITS RECEIVED          330
TOTAL UNITS ISSUED            385
TOTAL VALUE OF THE BEGINNING INVENTORY      1569.75
Stop at line 300
```

Account Balance Exercise:

Problem Summary

Input data

"CUST" file

Processsing

Accumulate balances, payments, charges, and new balances for the file.

Output

Totals for balances, payments, charges and new balances, with appropriate headings.

```
TOTAL BEGINNING BALANCES     740
TOTAL PAYMENTS               570
TOTAL CHARGES  850
TOTAL NEW BALANCES           1020
Stop at line 300
```

HOW TO CALCULATE SUBTOTALS

In many cases, summaries of the file as a whole are too gross to make any decisions. A more refined breakdown of the data is needed. But the detail is not at the individual record level. Instead of totals for the file as a whole or detail at the individual record level, we need an intermediary categorization of the data. Subtotals provide such intermediary categorizations.

Again, we look to the payroll problem for an illustrative example. Look at the payroll data file. It contains values for employee number, department number, employee name, etc. For our example, we need a summary of employee wages by department.

Departmental subtotals furnish an intermediary breakdown of the data. They are not as aggregate as file totals, neither are they as detailed as the earnings by individual employee. Instead, they fit someplace between the employee level detail and the all encompassing aggregation of file totals.

But before subtotals can be calculated with sequential files, the data has to be reorganized. Table 5–1 shows how the EMPLOY file would look once it's been placed into department number sequence.

Table 5–1

Employee File Sorted by Department Number

Dept. Number	*Employee Number*	*Employee Name*	*Hourly Rate*	*Regular Hours*	*Overtime Hours*
1	422	Williams	$4.00	40	0
1	368	Weaver	3.50	40	2
1	198	Tanner	4.25	36	0
1	101	Adams	5.00	40	0
2	172	Johnson	3.75	40	0
7	313	Smith	4.25	40	4
7	206	Lester	5.25	40	0
12	347	Gray	6.00	38	0
12	281	Miller	6.00	40	0
12	255	Schmidt	5.60	40	4
12	103	Baker	5.60	40	4
16	202	Wilson	4.00	40	0
16	108	Cohen	6.25	38	0
17	104	Bravo	4.00	40	2

The process used to order the data in a particular sequence is called sorting. (Sorting is a complex subject, so we will not cover the logic of sorting a data file. Instead, Appendix B contains a set of sort programs with instructions on how to use them. Alternatively, you can use the sort utilities provided by the manufacturer of your computer. We will indicate where a sort is needed, but sorting itself is left to your discretion.)

Problem Summary

Input

"EMPLOY" file in department number sequence, which will be called "EMPLDP".

Processing

Accumulate regular hours worked, overtime hours worked, and wages earned by department and for the file as a whole.

Output

Subtotals and totals accumulated.

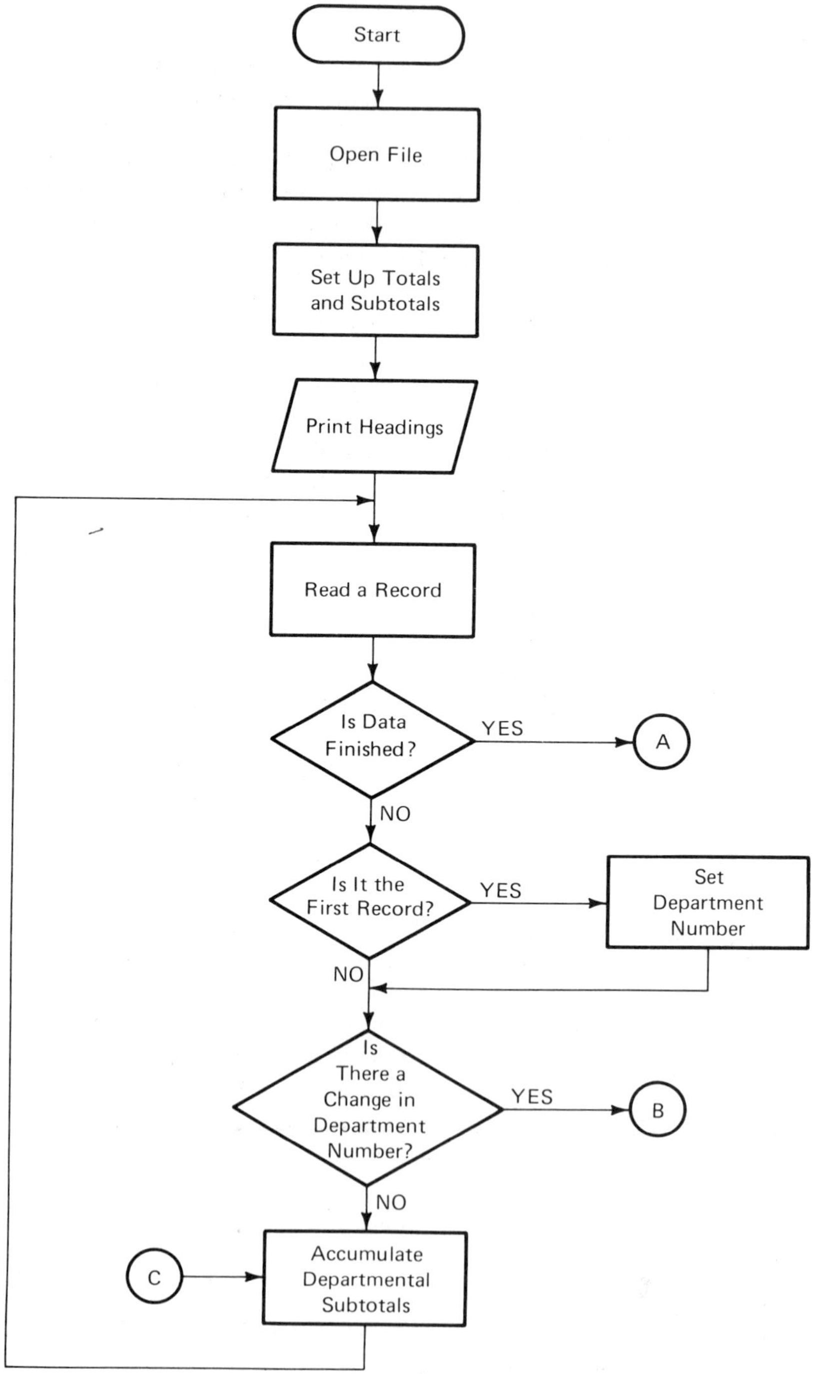

Figure 5–2 Flowchart for Program DEPSUB.

The program will have to:

1. Link to the "EMPLDP" file.
2. Set up fields for subtotals and totals.
3. Read the records in the file.
4. Accumulate subtotals by department.
5. Print the subtotals.
6. Accumulate totals for the file.
7. Print the totals.
8. Terminate.

The flowchart for the program is shown in Figure 5–2. A program to do these steps is shown on page 106.

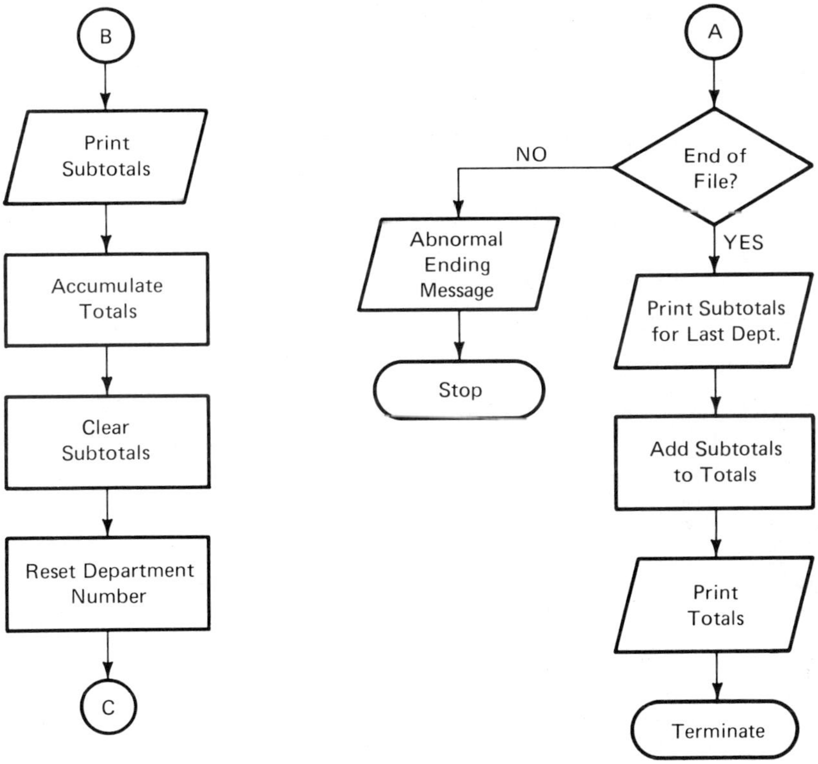

Flowchart for Program DEPSUB (Cont'd.) Figure 5–2

```
10 REM PROGRAM TO ACCUMULATE SUBTOTALS FOR THE
11 REM PAYROLL PROBLEM AND TO ACCUMULATE TOTALS
12 REM OF THE SUBTOTALS
130 OPEN "EMPLDP" AS FILE #1
140  R1=0
150 V1=0
160 W1=0
170 R2=0
180 V2=0
190 W2=0
200 D1=0
210 PRINT "DEPARTMENT","REGULAR","OVERTIME","WAGES"
220 PRINT "NUMBER","HOURS","HOURS","EARNED"
230 PRINT "------","-----","-----","------"
240 REM READ THE DATA IN THE FILE
250 INPUT #1 N,D,N$,H,R,V
260 ON ERROR GO TO 480
265 REM SET UP FOR THE FIRST DEPARTMENT
270 IF D1>0 GO TO 280
275 D1=D
280 IF D1<D THEN 350
290 REM THEN DEPARTMENT THE SAME AS FOR THE PREVIOUS RECORD
300 REM THEFORE ACCUMULATE SUBTOTALS FOR THE DEPARTMENT
310 R1=R1+R
320 V1=V1+V
330 W1=W1+H*R+1.5*H*V
331 REM READ THE NEXT RECORD
340 GO TO 250
341 REM PRINT DEPARTMENT SUBTOTALS
350 PRINT D1,R1,V1,W1
360 REM ADD SUBTOTALS TO TOTALS
370 R2=R2+R1
380 V2=V2+V1
390 W2=W2+W1
400 REM SET SUBTOTALS TO ZERO FOR THE NEXT DEPARTMENT
410 R1=0
420 V1=0
430 W1=0
440 REM SET DEPARTMENT TO CURRENT DEPARTMENT
450 D1=D
460 GO TO 310
470 REM ERROR CHECKING ROUTINE
480 IF ERR=11 THEN RESUME 520
490 PRINT "UNUSUAL ERROR CONDITION",ERR
500 STOP
510 REM PRINT SUBTOTALS FOR THE LAST DEPARTMENT
520 PRINT D1,R1,V1,W1
530 REM ADD SUBTOTALS FOR THE LAST DEPARTMENT  TO TOTALS
540 R2=R2+R1
550 V2=V2+V1
560 W2=W2+W1
570 REM PRINT THE TOTALS
580 PRINT "TOTAL",R2,V2,W2
590 REM TERMINATE THE PROGRAM
600 CLOSE #1
610 STOP
32767 END

RUN
DEPSUB
DEPARTMENT     REGULAR        OVERTIME       WAGES
NUMBER         HOURS          HOURS          EARNED
------         -----          -----          ------
 1              156            2              663.5
 2              40             0              150
 7              80             4              405.5
 12             158            8              983.2
 16             78             0              397.5
 17             40             2              172
TOTAL           552            16             2771.7
Stop at line 610
```

We can trace the logic of this program to see what it does. You'll note the same elements that existed in the process of getting totals.

First, the fields that are used to hold the subtotals (as well as those for the totals) are set to zero in lines 140–160. Next, they are used to accumulate the running totals in lines 310–330. Then they are printed in line 350; used in the accumulation of totals in lines 370–390; and set to zero for the accumulation of subtotals for the next department.

As you can see, calculating subtotals is identical to the process used to calculate totals. They key difficulty lies in determining when to start and when to stop accumulating for one department.

How do we know we have finished with a department? Look at Table 5–1, the employee file sorted by department number. Cover up the table (with a sheet of paper or your hand) except for the titles. Now look at the first record. Move your sheet of paper down the table one record at a time (because that is the way the computer does it—the computer sees the whole file, but only one record at a time). And herein lies the clue for determining the end of a department. We are finished with one department when we arrive at the next department.

Try it again. Look at Table 5–1, one record at a time. Look only at the department number. We start with department number 1. Remember that number. Look at the next record. It is still department 1. And the next one. Still 1. Look at the fourth record. Department number is 1. Read the next record. The department number is no longer one. Therefore, we know that we are finished with department one.

Now let's look at the program DEPSUB. The process that you have just gone through is in lines 250, 270, 275, 280, and 450. The statement in line 250 reads a record. Line 280 compares the department number of the record just read with a prior department number. The prior department number is defined in lines 270 and 275 for the first record read, and it is set in line 450 after each department break. (A "break" in this context refers to the point where a number changes from one value to another.)

So, D1 "remembers" the previous department number. And when in line 280 a different department number (D) is encountered (D1 not equal to D) then the accumulated values in R1, V1, and W1 represent the subtotals for the previous department. Hence, the logic flows to line 350 where the subtotals are printed.

One more item needs to be mentioned: printing the last department. We know we have finished accumulating the subtotals for the last department when we run out of data. But at that point, while the accumulation is complete, the answer resides in the computer. To get it out, it has to be printed. But a print different from line 350 has to be used. (If we did go to line 350, then the end of data would be ignored.) Hence, the "GO TO 480" to check on the error before printing the last set of subtotals.

Look over the inventory example and then try the exercises.

Example

Inventory Example: In the "INV" file, assume that part numbers 100–199 belong to department one (1), numbers 200–299 belong to department two (2), and numbers 300–399 belong to department three (3). Calculate the dollar value of the beginning and ending inventory for each department and print these values as well as their grand totals. We want to write a program that will calculate the departmental subtotals for the value of the beginning and ending inventory values, as well as the grand totals.

Problem Summary

Input

"INV" file

Processing

Accumulate beginning and ending inventory dollar values by department for the file.

Output

Departmental subtotals and grand totals suitably labelled.

The steps in this program are the same as in the previous payroll program in that the program will have to:

1. Link to the INV file.
2. Set up fields for subtotals and totals.
3. Read the records in the file.
4. Accumulate subtotals by department.
5. Print the subtotals.
6. Accumulate totals for the file.
7. Print the totals.
8. Terminate.

```
10 REM THIS PROGRAM TO ACCUMULATE SUBTOTALS FOR BEGINNING
11 REM AND ENDING INVENTORY VALUES BY DEPARTMENT
12 REM AND TO ACCUMULATE TOTALS FOR THE FILE
100 OPEN "INV" AS FILE #2
110 B1=0
120 E1=0
130 B2=0
140 E2=0
145 D1=0
150 PRINT "DEPARTMENT","BEGINNING","ENDING"
160 PRINT "NUMBER","INVENTORY","INVENTORY"
170 PRINT "------","---------","---------"
180 REM READ DATA IN THE FILE
210 INPUT #2 N,B,R1,R2,C
220 ON ERROR GO TO 430
225 N=INT(N/100)
230 IF D1>0 GO TO 260
250 D1=N
260 IF D1<N GO TO 330
```

```
270 REM DEPARTMENT NUMBER IS THE SAME AS THE PREVIOUS RECORD
280 REM THEREFORE ACCUMULATE THE SUBTOTALS
290 B1=B1+B*C
300 E1=E1+B*C+R1*C-R2*C
305 REM READ THE NEXT RECORD
310 GO TO 210
320 REM PRINT DEPARTMENT SUBTOTALS
330 PRINT D1,B1,E1
340 REM ADD THE SUBS TO THE TOTALS
350 E2=E2+E1
360 B2=B2+B1
370 REM SET SUBS TO ZERO FOR THE NEXT DEPARTMENT
380 B1=0
390 E1=0
400 REM SET D1 EQUAL TO THE NEXT DEPARTMENT NUMBER
410 D1=N
420 GO TO 290
430 REM ERROR CHECKING ROUTINE
440 IF ERR=11 THEN RESUME 470
450 PRINT "UNUSUAL ERROR" ERR
460 STOP
470 REM END OF FILE REACHED--PRINT SUBTOTALS FOR LAST DEPARTMENT
480 PRINT D1,B1,E1
490 REM ADD SUBTOTALS FROM THE LAST DEPARTMENT TO TOTALS
500 E2=E2+E1
510 B2=B2+B1
520 REM PRINT TOTALS FOR THE FILE
530 PRINT "TOTAL BEGINNING AND ENDING INVENTORIES",B2,E2
540 CLOSE #2
32767 END
```

```
RUN
INV10
DEPARTMENT     BEGINNING      ENDING
NUMBER         INVENTORY      INVENTORY
------         ---------      ---------
 1              600            575
 2              829.75         513.75
 3              0              138
TOTAL BEGINNING AND ENDING INVENTORIES      1429.75        1226.75
```

The only difference in logic between this program and the previous payroll program is the test for a new department. Before, department numbers were given in a field; in this example, the department number is determined from the part number. The instruction in line 225 does this. The statement

$$N = INT(N/100)$$

illustrates the use of a new type of BASIC statement. INT is called a function. It makes an integer (whole number) out of what appears in parenthesis after it, by dropping anything after the decimal point. For example, if we had the number 2.73 appearing in the parenthesis after INT, that is, if we had INT(2.73), the resulting value would be 2. In the particular case of the expression in this program, when the first record is input, N is equal to 101. INT(N/100) divides the value 101 by 100, giving 1.01, and the integer function makes an integer (1) out of this value.

So D1 has the value 1. In this way all parts with values 100–199 will be accumulated. When the second record with part number 219 is input, at line 250 D1 is equal to 1 so that we go to line 330 where departmental subtotals (for one) are printed. Then in line 410 D1 has the value of 2 and the program continues to accumulate the subtotals for department two. Similarly, when the last record with part number 347 is input, N in line 250 will have the value of 3. The department subtotals (for two) will be printed and D1 in line 410 will have the value 3. The subtotals for department 3 will be calculated and the next record (EOF) read. Since there are no more records, the end of file (ERR = 11) occurs and the subtotals for department 3 as well as the grand totals are printed.

Exercises

Sales Commission Exercise:

Problem Summary

Input

"SALES" file

Processing

Accumulate sales and commissions by sales territory and for the file as a whole.

Output

Territory subtotals and grand totals suitably labelled.

(Attach additional paper to complete your program.)

```
TERRITORY      TERRITORY      COMMISSIONS
NUMBER         SALES          PAID
------         -----          ----
 1              17320          839.65
 2              18140          893.6
```

Account Balance Exercise: The department is indicated by the first digit of the customer number.

Problem Summary

Input

"CUST" file

Processing

Accumulate initial balances and final balances by department and for the file as a whole.

Output

Department subtotals and grand totals suitably labelled.

(Attach additional paper to complete your program.)

```
DEPARTMENT      BEGINNING       ENDING
NUMBER          BALANCE         BALANCE
------          -------         -------
 2               120             130
 3               620             890
TOTAL BEGINNING AND ENDING BALANCES        740          1020
Stop at line 510
```

REPORT WRITING BY COMPUTER

So far the output of all the programs has been labelled in a manner that identifies it. The output of the programs up to now has been brief and satisfactory for programmer purposes. The output would be unsatisfactory for management purposes because it is too brief and is not self-explanatory to a manager. Managers do not read programs. It is important that the output be self-explanatory with appropriate headings and follow general business formats.

The output to the second payroll example consists of the following:

```
TOTAL REGULAR HOURS WORKED    552
TOTAL OVERTIME HOURS WORKED   16
TOTAL WAGES EARNED BY ALL EMPLOYEES        2771.7
Stop at line 290
```

The program can be modified so that the function of the program can be made clear in the output. The supporting data that resulted in that output can also be printed. The report that we want to produce is usually called a payroll report.

Problem Summary

Input

"EMPLOY" file

Processing

Accumulate regular hours, overtime hours, and wages for the company.

Output

An easily readable and understandable payroll report.

```
100 REM THIS PROGRAM TO ACCUMULATE TOTALS FOR REGULAR HOURS
110 REM OVERTIME HOURS,AND TOTAL WAGES EARNED IN THE "EMPLOY"FILE
120 PRINT
130 PRINT
140 PRINT "                              PAYROLL REPORT"
150 PRINT
160 PRINT
170 PRINT"EMPLOYEE  DEPT       NAME      HOURLY     REGULAR    OVERTIME   GR
OSS"
180 PRINT"NUMBER    NUMBER               RATE       HOURS      HOURS       PA
Y"
190  PRINT"-------------------------------------------------------------
-------"
200 OPEN "EMPLOY" AS FILE #1
210 R1=0
220 V1=0
230 W1=0
240 INPUT #1 N,D,N$,H,R,V
250 ON ERROR GO TO 330
260 R1=R1+R
270 V1=V1+V
280 W1=W1+H*R+1.5*H*V
290 W=H*R+(1.5*H*V)
300 PRINT USING"   ###       ##       \        \#.##        ##         ##
    ###.##"N,D,N$,H,R,V,W
310 GO TO 240
320 REM ERROR CHECKING ROUTINE
```

```
330 IF ERR=11 GO TO 360
340 PRINT "UNUSUAL ERROR",ERR
350 STOP
360 CLOSE #1
370 PRINT"******************************************************************
******"
380 PRINT USING"\       \                                    ###        ###
  #,###.##""TOTALS",R1,V1,W1
32767 END
```

```
                              PAYROLL REPORT

EMPLOYEE   DEPT        NAME        HOURLY     REGULAR    OVERTIME   GROSS
NUMBER     NUMBER                  RATE       HOURS      HOURS      PAY
-------------------------------------------------------------------------
   101        1        ADAMS       5.00         40          0       200.00
   103       12        BAKER       5.60         40          4       257.60
   104       17        BRAVO       4.00         40          2       172.00
   108       16        COHEN       6.25         38          0       237.50
   172        2        JOHNSON     3.75         40          0       150.00
   198        1        TANNER      4.25         36          0       153.00
   202       16        WILSON      4.00         40          0       160.00
   206        7        LESTER      5.25         40          0       210.00
   255       12        SCHMIDT     5.60         40          4       257.60
   281       12        MILLER      6.00         40          0       240.00
   313        7        SMITH       4.25         40          4       195.50
   347       12        GRAY        6.00         38          0       228.00
   368        1        WEAVER      3.50         40          2       150.50
   422        1        WILLIAMS    4.00         40          0       160.00
*************************************************************************
TOTALS                                         552         16     2,771.70
```

The only new BASIC instruction in this program is PRINT USING. It is similar to the PRINT instruction, but it allows us to align numbers in columns and print zeroes after decimal points. It also can be used for putting commas (,) in large numbers for thousands, millions, etc. The rules for PRINT USING are as follows:

1. After the words PRINT USING a pair of double quotation marks enclose what is to be printed on a line. Remember, a terminal can print a maximum of 72 characters on a line.

2. To indicate a numeric field use the sharp (#). Its length is determined by the number of sharps.

3. To print a decimal point in a number use a period (.). Its position is determined by its placement between sharps (#). The value printed will be rounded to the nearest decimal.

4. To print commas in long numbers use a comma (,). Its position may be determined by its placement between sharps (#).

5. To indicate an alphabetic field use a backward slash (\). Its length is determined by a pair of slashes and the space between.

6. After the second quotation mark, a list of the field names to be printed on the line, separated by commas, must appear.

7. If the number of characters in a field to be printed is larger than the number of characters in the PRINT USING statement, a percent (%) will be printed.

Assume for the examples the following values:

N = 101
N$ = ADAMS
H = 5.0
P = 200.0
T = 2476.436

The symbol "b̸" means a space or blank; it is used on this page to assist you in counting spaces, it is never used in a program.

Examples	*Printing Columns* 1	2	3	4	5	6	7	8	9
10 PRINT USING "# # #"N	1	0	1						
10 PRINT USING "b̸b̸b̸# # #"N				1	0	1			
10 PRINT USING "b̸# #.# #"H			5	.	0	0			
10 PRINT USING "b̸b̸# # #.# #"P			2	0	0	.	0	0	
10 PRINT USING "b̸#,# # #.# #"T		2	,	4	7	6	.	4	4
10 PRINT USING "b̸# # #b̸#.# #"N,H		1	0	1		5	.	0	0
10 PRINT USING "b̸b̸ \b̸b̸b̸ \"N$			A	D	A	M	S		
10 PRINT USING "b̸\ b̸b̸b̸\ b̸b̸"N$		A	D	A	M	S			
10 PRINT USING "# # #b̸\ b̸b̸b̸ \"N, N$	1	0	1		A	D	A	M	S

In the program the PRINT USING statement appears in line 300.

```
300 PRINT USING"   ###      ##      \        \#.##       ##        ##       
    ###.##"N,D,N$,H,R,V,W
```

The first field, N, will be printed in columns 4, 5, and 6. The three sharps indicate that it is three digits long. The three spaces after the quotation mark print blanks as the first three characters. The second field, D, is printed in columns 13 and 14. Its length is two digits. The third field, N$, is ten characters long. It is alphabetic and the name will be printed in columns 21 through 30. It is ten characters long because there are eight spaces between the slashes. The slashes are also counted in determining the length of the printed field. The fourth field, H, is four digits with a decimal point between the second and third numbers. It is printed in columns 31 through 34. Fields R and V are each two digits long and start in columns 42 and 52, respectively. The last field, W, is printed in columns 61 through 66 and will appear with a decimal point.

The second PRINT USING statement appears in line 380. It follows all of the rules given above, with one extension. The word "TOTALS" is to be printed in the first six columns of the total row. To do this, insert a pair of backward slashes to define the position and the length of the alphabetic information to be printed. Then indicate the alphabetic information in double quotations where fields are normally listed at the end of the statement.

The program does not have a STOP instruction before the END. This STOP instruction was removed after the program was tested so that the message STOP AT LINE 390 would not appear on the report. You may remove the final STOP instruction after you run the program and it is correct. Then run the program a final time and the message will not appear at the bottom of the report.

It is very important to make sure that you know the maximum length of a field in order to specify its length in a PRINT USING instruction. If you specify a numeric field larger than its maximum value, the numbers will be right justified. (Numeric fields are printed using the far right positions first.) Alphabetic fields are printed using the far left positions first (left justified). As a result of this, your printed output will line up in columns that are easily readable.

The preceding program is one example of how a report may be printed so that it is easily readable and understandable. Columns of numbers can be made neat with the PRINT USING instruction.

SUMMARY

In this chapter you have been shown how to accumulate subtotals and totals for a file. A use of the BASIC instruction INT has been explained for cases where department numbers are part of some identification number. Finally you have seen how to produce reports for management that are easily readable and understandable with the PRINT USING instruction.

BASIC Instructions Introduced:

INT(X)	The value X is made into an integer (whole number).
PRINT USING	Prints columns of data in a manner that they may be easily read.

PROBLEMS

1. Use the "XK1" file from the first problem in Chapter 4 (page 89) to accumulate the totals from Time 1 and Time 2. Output these totals suitably labelled.

2. Use the "XK1" file to accumulate departmental subtotals from Time 1 and Time 2 assuming that departments are defined as follows:

Department	*I.D. Number*
1	100–199
2	200–299
3	300–399
4	400–499

   Output these totals suitably labelled.

3. Use the "INV" file to accumulate department subtotals and grand totals for units received. Assume department one has part numbers 100–199, department two has part numbers 200–299, department three has part numbers 300–399. Output the totals suitably labelled.

4. Modify your program that produces sales and commission department subtotals and grand totals from the "SALES" file so that it may be read by management. Title it: Sales and Commission Report.

5. Modify your program that produces initial balances and final balances by department and grand totals from the "CUST" file so that it may be read by management. Title it: Customer Sales Report.

6. Modify the program that produces beginning and ending inventory value by department and grand totals from the "INV" file so that it may be read by management. Title it: Inventory Value Report.

7. Modify your program in Problem 3 above so that you produce a management report. Title it: Units Issued by Departments.

6 / Adding and Deleting Records

Performance Objectives

At the end of this chapter you should be able to:

- Add records to sequential files
- Delete records from sequential files

Files are not static. The contents of files change as the business changes. In the payroll example, employees are hired and new employee records are added to the files. People also leave or retire, and the old employee records have to be dropped from the file. Customers are acquired and new customer records have to be inserted into a file. Or a product becomes obsolete and it must be deleted from the file.

In this chapter we will show you how to add and delete records using sequential files.

ADDING RECORDS TO A FILE

An accidental omission has occured. When the data for the employee payroll (Table 4–1, Chapter 4) was given, two records were lost. Now they have been found. Fortunately, the payroll has not been prepared. But these two records have to be added to the file before the payroll program can be run.

This hypothetical situation (it would never occur in real life, would it?) serves as the basis for showing you how to add records to a file. Let's assume that the two missing records are the following:

Employee Number	*Department Number*	*Employee Name*	*Hourly Rate*	*Regular Hours*	*Overtime Hours*
425	17	Jones	4.80	40	2
426	17	Cooper	4.25	38	0

As you can see, Jones and Cooper belong at the end of the "EMPLOY" file. So we need to find the end of the file and add the records at that point.

But here we run into a limitation of sequential files. We can either read from a file or print into a file, but we cannot both read and print the *same* sequential file. Therefore, to add records to a file, we need to read from one file and print into another file.

The problem has two sets of input data. First, the payroll file with its records of six fields:

- Employee number
- Department number
- Employee name
- Hourly rate of pay
- Regular hours worked
- Overtime hours worked

Secondly, the two omitted records with the same fields (which must be added from the keyboard). For output the problem requires a complete file as well as messages to the keyboard operator.

The processing consists of reading the records in the old file and writing them into a new file. When the end of data has been reached in the old file, then records are entered from the keyboard and added to the new file.

Problem Summary

Input Data

1. "EMPLOY" file with six fields per record:
   - Employee number
   - Employee department number
   - Employee name
   - Hourly rate
   - Regular hours
   - Overtime hours

   No validity checks necessary since all fields have already been checked.
2. New records to be added to the file, each record consisting of six fields.

Field name	*Valid Range*
Employee number	100 to 999
Employee department number	1 to 20
Employee name	–
Hourly rate	3.05 to 15.00
Regular hours worked	0 to 40
Overtime hours worked	0 to 20

Processing

Take data from the old file and write into new file until end of data is reached. Then take data from keyboard and place valid records into new file.

Output

Instructions for operator and complete payroll data file.

The program, therefore, has to be able to:

1. Link to the file "EMPLOY".
2. Set up a new file.
3. Read from the old file and write into new file until end of data is reached.
4. Get data from terminal and check it for valid range.
5. Write valid records into new file.
6. Stop when new records have been added.

The flowchart for the program is given in Figure 6–1.

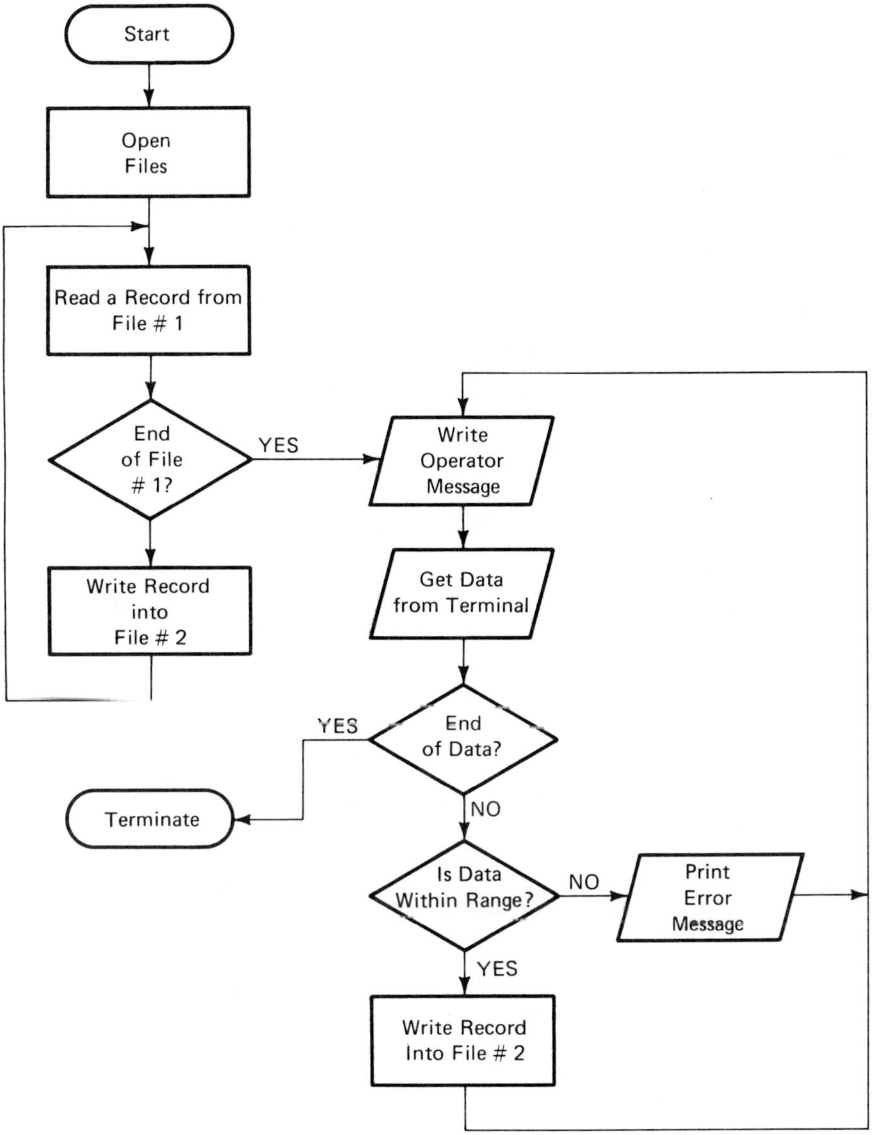

Flowchart for Adding Records to the End of a File

Figure 6–1

```
100 REM THIS PROGRAM APPENDS RECORDS TO A FILE
110 REM
120 REM OPEN FILES FOR INPUT AND OUTPUT
130 OPEN "EMPLOY" FOR INPUT AS FILE #1
140 OPEN "EMPLO2" FOR OUTPUT AS FILE #2
150 REM
160 REM READ THE FILE "EMPLOY"
170 REM CHECK FOR END OF FILE
180 REM AND PRINT INTO THE FILE "EMPLO2"
190 REM
200 INPUT #1 ,N,D,N$,H,R,V
210 ON ERROR GO TO 250
220 PRINT #2 N;",";D;",";N$;",";H;",";R;",";V
230 GO TO 200
250 IF ERR=11 THEN RESUME 300
260 PRINT "UNUSUAL ERROR CONDITION",ERR
270 GO TO 590
280 REM READ DATA FROM THE KEYBOARD AND
290 REM ADD IT TO FILE EMPLO2
300 PRINT"TYPE EMPLOYEE NUMBER, DEPARTMENT NUMBER"
310 PRINT "EMPLOYEE NAME,HOURLY RATE,REGULAR HOURS,
320 PRINT"AND OVERTIME HOURS--SEPARATED BY COMMAS"
330 PRINT "WHEN FINISHED TYPE 99,99,AA,99,99,99"
340 INPUT N,D,N$,H,R,V
350 REM
360 REM CHECK FOR END OF DATA
380 IF N=99 THEN 590
390 REM
400 REM CHECK THE DATA FOR VALIDITY
410 REM
420 IF N<100 THEN 540
430 IF N>999 THEN 540
440 IF D<1 THEN 540
450 IF D>20 THEN 540
460 IF H<3.05 THEN 540
470 IF H>15.00 THEN 540
480 IF R<0 THEN 540
490 IF R>40 THEN 540
500 IF V<0 THEN 540
510 IF V>20 THEN 540
520 PRINT #2 N;",";D;",";N$;",";H;",";R;",";V
530 GO TO 300
540 PRINT "***ERROR IN INPUT DATA--PLEASE RETYPE"
550 GO TO 300
560 REM
570 REM TERMINATE PROGRAM
580 REM
590 CLOSE #1,#2
600 STOP
32767 END
```

```
TYPE EMPLOYEE NUMBER, DEPARTMENT NUMBER
EMPLOYEE NAME,HOURLY RATE,REGULAR HOURS,
AND OVERTIME HOURS--SEPARATED BY COMMAS
WHEN FINISHED TYPE 99,99,AA,99,99,99
? 425,17,JONES,4.80,40,2
TYPE EMPLOYEE NUMBER, DEPARTMENT NUMBER
EMPLOYEE NAME,HOURLY RATE,REGULAR HOURS,
AND OVERTIME HOURS--SEPARATED BY COMMAS
WHEN FINISHED TYPE 99,99,AA,99,99,99
? 426,17,COOPER,4.25,38,0
TYPE EMPLOYEE NUMBER, DEPARTMENT NUMBER
EMPLOYEE NAME,HOURLY RATE,REGULAR HOURS,
AND OVERTIME HOURS--SEPARATED BY COMMAS
WHEN FINISHED TYPE 99,99,AA,99,99,99
? 99,99,AA,99,99,99
Stop at line 600
```

In order to determine whether the program worked, print the "EMPLO2" file with the following program.

```
20 ON ERROR GO TO 200
100 OPEN "EMPLO2" AS FILE #1
110 INPUT #1 N,D,N$,H,R,V
120 PRINT N;D,N$,H,R,V
130 GO TO 110
200 REM ***ERROR CHECKING ROUTINE
210 IF ERR=11 THEN RESUME 250
220 PRINT "UNUSUAL ERROR CONDITION",ERR
250 CLOSE #1
500 STOP
32767 END
```

```
 101  1     ADAMS      5      40    0
 103  12    BAKER      5.6    40    4
 104  17    BRAVO      4      40    2
 108  16    COHEN      6.25   38    0
 172  2     JOHNSON    3.75   40    0
 198  1     TANNER     4.25   36    0
 202  16    WILSON     4      40    0
 206  7     LESTER     5.25   40    0
 255  12    SCHMIDT    5.6    40    4
 281  12    MILLER     6      40    0
 313  7     SMITH      4.25   40    4
 347  12    GRAY       6      38    0
 368  1     WEAVER     3.5    40    2
 422  1     WILLIAMS   4      40    0
 425  17    JONES      4.8    40    2
 426  17    COOPER     4.25   38    0
Stop at line 500
```

This program contains no new statements. However, the OPEN instruction has been extended and *one* CLOSE instruction is used to close *two* files.

When we state that a file should be OPENED FOR INPUT, then the computer looks for an existing file and opens it. If it can't find a file with the specified name, it prints an error message. When a file is OPENED FOR OUTPUT, any existing file by that name is deleted and a new file is then created.

Look again at the program. As you can see, it transfers all of the records from the old file to the new file before it gets any data from the terminal. But what if the employees Jones and Cooper had employee numbers 154 and 232 respectively? Then the program would still place their records at the end of the file, but at the end of the file, their records would be out of sequence by employee number.

We must change the program so that new records fit into the middle of the new file. The location of these records is determined by the sequence of identification numbers, in this case employee number. Records to be added fit into the file after records with lower numbers, and before records with higher numbers.

However, the computer cannot see the whole file. It operates on the file *one record at a time.* It will know where to insert a record only after it has read a record from the old file with a *higher* identifying number.

Let's look at an example to illustrate this point. Below you have the employee numbers of a section of the payroll file. And the employee numbers of the records to be added.

Employee Number in File	*New Employee Numbers of Records to be Added*
104	154
108	232
172	
198	
202	
206	
255	
282	

Now look at the first number in each column. Remember, the employee number stands for the complete record. With the first number in each column you have the whole record. You can see that record 154 belongs after record 104. Hence 104 is transferred to the new file.

Now read the next record in the file—108. Again, since it is less than the record to be added—154, it gets transferred to the new file. When you now read the next record, we have the following position.

Record to be Added	*Record from Old File*	*Records in New File*
154	172	104
		108

Here the record from the old file is greater than the record to be added. Therefore the record to be added is placed into the new file. The new file now consists of three records in sequential (ascending) order—104, 108 and 154.

Since we do not know where the next record will fit, until we have read it, a new record to be added is obtained and the comparison is repeated. In our example, the record to be added is 232. But it could just as easily have been record 155 or 163 or 171. In that case, the record also should be placed prior to record 172.

Think your way through the process of placing record 232 into the new file. Read the old file, one record at a time. Move all records with lower employee numbers to the new file. Once you read a record with a higher ID number, then place the record to be added into the new file.

You have been playing "computer" when you think through a problem in this excruciatingly detailed way. And very simple thinking also; but that is the way the simple-minded computer works: one elementary operation at a time on small amounts of data.

The general pattern of record insertion hinges on two things:

1. The old records are in ascending order.
2. The program must find a record that is larger than the one that has to be inserted into the sequence.

The program therefore has to transfer all records with lower employee numbers to the new file. Then the record to be added can be written into the new file. *Then* the record with a higher employee number is written into the new file. Finally, another record to be added is input and the process continued.

A program to add records to a file is shown below. The range checks of the records to be added have been removed for brevity and to highlight the program logic.

Problem Summary

Input

"EMPLOY" file in employee number sequence. Records to be added, also in employee number sequence.

Processing

Place records to be added into their proper location in the file.

Output

Data entry operator instructions and complete file of payroll records.

Here is the program and flowchart (Fig. 6–2) for placing records in the middle of a file:

```
10 REM THIS PROGRAM ADDS RECORDS TO THE MIDDLE OF THE FILE
100 REM OPEN THE FILES
110 REM
130 OPEN "EMPLOY" FOR INPUT AS FILE #1
140 OPEN "EMPLO3" FOR OUTPUT AS FILE #2
150 REM GET A RECORD FROM THE TERMINAL
160 REM
170 REM
180 PRINT "TYPE EMPLOYEE NUMBER,DEPARTMENT NUMBER,EMPLOYEE NAME"
190 PRINT "HOURLY RATE,REGULAR HOURS, OVERTIME HOURS"
200 PRINT "SEPARATE BY COMMAS"
210 PRINT "WHEN FINISHED TYPE 99,99,AA,99,99,99"
220 INPUT N1,D1,N1$,H1,R1,V1
230 REM
240 REM CHECK FOR END OF DATA FROM TERMINAL
250 REM
260 IF N1=99 GO TO 670
270 REM
280 REM SEARCH THE FILE FOR NUMBER SEQUENCE
290 REM
300 INPUT #1 N,D,N$,H,R,V
310 ON ERROR GO TO 650
320 IF N1<N THEN 420
330 REM
340 REM RECORD FROM FILE LESS THAN RECORD FROM TERMINAL
350 REM
360 PRINT #2 N;",";D;",";N$;",";H;",";R;",";V
370 GO TO 300
```

```
380 REM
390 REM RECORD FROM TERMINAL IS LOWER THAN THE ONE IN THE FILE
400 REM PRINT THE RECORD IN THE NEW FILE
410 REM
420 PRINT #2 N1;",";D1;",";N1$;",";H1;",";R1;",";V1
430 REM
440 REM GET ANOTHER RECORD FROM THE TERMINAL
460 REM
470 PRINT "TYPE EMPLOYEE NUMBER,DEPARTMENT NUMBER,EMPLOYEE"
480 PRINT "NAME,HOURLY RATE,REGULAR HOURS,OVERTIME HOURS"
490 PRINT "WHEN FINISHED TYPE 99,99,AA,99,99,99"
510 INPUT N1,D1,N1$,H1,R1,V1
520 IF N1=99 GO TO 580
530 GO TO 320
540 REM
550 REM NO MORE RECORDS TO BE ADDED
560 REM TRANSFER REMAINING RECORDS TO THE NEW FILE
570 REM
580 PRINT #2 N;",";D;",";N$;",";H;",";R;",";V
590 INPUT #1 N,D,N$,H,R,V
610 GO TO 580
620 REM
640 REM
650 IF ERR=11 THEN RESUME 670
660 PRINT "UNUSUAL ERROR",ERR
670 CLOSE #1,#2
700 STOP
32767 END
```

```
TYPE EMPLOYEE NUMBER,DEPARTMENT NUMBER,EMPLOYEE NAME
HOURLY RATE,REGULAR HOURS, OVERTIME HOURS
SEPARATE BY COMMAS
WHEN FINISHED TYPE 99,99,AA,99,99,99
? 154,17,JONES,4.80,40,2
TYPE EMPLOYEE NUMBER,DEPARTMENT NUMBER,EMPLOYEE
NAME,HOURLY RATE,REGULAR HOURS,OVERTIME HOURS
WHEN FINISHED TYPE 99,99,AA,99,99,99
? 232,17,COOPER,4.25,38,0
TYPE EMPLOYEE NUMBER,DEPARTMENT NUMBER,EMPLOYEE
NAME,HOURLY RATE,REGULAR HOURS,OVERTIME HOURS
WHEN FINISHED TYPE 99,99,AA,99,99,99
? 99,99,AA,99,99,99
Stop at line 700
```

To determine whether the program worked, print the "EMPLO3" file. This may be done by modifying your program that prints the "EMPLOY" file. The change necessary is

100 OPEN "EMPLO3" AS FILE #1

Then run the changed program.

```
 101  1    ADAMS      5      40    0
 103  12   BAKER      5.6    40    4
 104  17   BRAVO      4      40    2
 108  16   COHEN      6.25   38    0
 154  17   JONES      4.8    40    2
 172  2    JOHNSON    3.75   40    0
 198  1    TANNER     4.25   36    0
 202  16   WILSON     4      40    0
 206  7    LESTER     5.25   40    0
 232  17   COOPER     4.25   38    0
 255  12   SCHMIDT    5.6    40    4
 281  12   MILLER     6      40    0
 313  7    SMITH      4.25   40    4
 347  12   GRAY       6      38    0
 368  1    WEAVER     3.5    40    2
 422  1    WILLIAMS   4      40    0
Stop at line 500
```

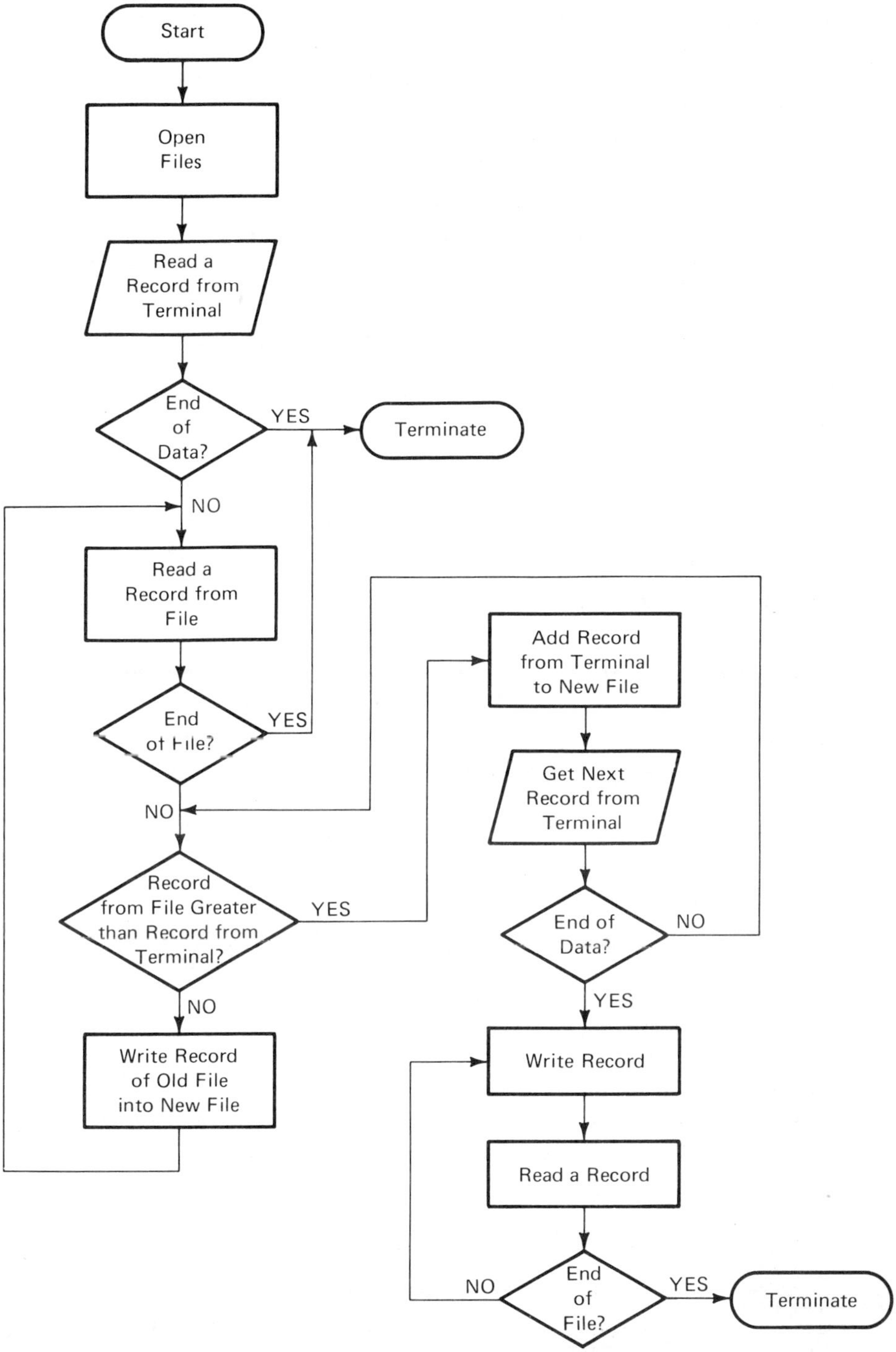

Flowchart for Adding a Record into the Middle of a File Figure 6–2

Let's take another look at this program. Notice how the end of file (EOF) for the old file and the end of data from the terminal (EOD) decisions appear a number of times. The program is made complicated by having to consider all possibilities:

1. There are no records to be added.
2. The file is empty when more records have to be added. (In our example, the program merely terminated when that happened; see line 310 and the RESUME 670. The extension of handling such records is left as an exercise for you.)
3. No more records have to be added while there are still records in the file.
4. The file is empty and no records need to be added.

For all four cases the program has to provide a means of reaching a satisfactory conclusion. In our example, the program merely terminates without telling the operator what has happened. Maybe you can think of some way to modify the program so that a message appears that would identify why the program stopped.

Example

Inventory Example: To the inventory file ("INV"), add the following two records.

Problem Summary

Input

	Part Number	*Beginning Units*	*Units Received*	*Units Issued*	*Cost*
Record 1	112	0	50	10	8.25
Record 2	300	0	150	70	6.85

"INV" file

Processing

Place records to be added into their proper sequence in the file.

Output

Data entry operator instructions
New file "INVl"
Print the file "INVl"

```
100 REM PROGRAM TO ADD INVENTORY RECORDS TO THE MIDDLE OF THE INV FILE
110 REM
120 REM LINK TO FILES
130 REM
140 OPEN "INV" FOR INPUT AS FILE #1
150 OPEN "INV1" FOR OUTPUT AS FILE #2
160 REM
170 REM GET RECORD TO BE ADDED FROM TERMINAL
180 REM
190 PRINT"ENTER PART NUMBER,BEGINNING UNITS, UNITS RECEIVED,"
200 PRINT"UNITS ISSUED,AND UNIT COST -- SEPARATED BY COMMAS"
210 PRINT"WHEN FINISHED -- TYPE  99  FOR EACH FIELD"
220 INPUT P9,B9,R9,I9,C9
```

```
230 REM
240 REM  CHECK FOR END OF DATA FROM TERMINAL
250 REM
260 IF P9=99 THEN 1130
270 REM
280 REM SEARCH FILE FOR PLACE TO ADD NEW RECORDS
290 REM
300 ON ERROR GO TO 990
310 T = 1
320 INPUT #1,P,B,R1,R2,C
330 IF P9<P THEN 440
340 REM
350 REM RECORD FROM TERMINAL GREATER THAN RECORD FROM FILE
360 REM THEREFORE PLACE RECORD FROM FILE INTO INV1
370 REM
380 PRINT#2 P;",";B;",";R1;",";R2;",";C
390 GO TO 320
400 REM
410 REM RECORD FROM TERMINAL LESS THAN RECORD FROM FILE
420 REM THEREFORE PLACE RECORD FROM TERMINAL INTO INV1
430 REM
440 PRINT #2 P9;",";B9;",";R9;",";I9;",";C9
450 REM
460 REM GET ANOTHER RECORD FROM TERMINAL
470 REM
480 PRINT"ENTER PART NUMBER, BEGINNING UNITS, UNITS RECEIVED,"
490 PRINT"UNITS ISSUED, AND UNIT COST -- SEPARATED BY COMMAS"
500 PRINT"WHEN FINISHED -- TYPE  99  FOR EACH FIELD"
510 INPUT P9,B9,R9,I9,C9
520 REM
530 REM  CHECK FOR END OF DATA ENTRY
540 REM
550 IF P9=99 THEN 620
560 GO TO 330
570 REM
580 REM NO MORE RECORDS TO BE ADDED, BUT RECORDS STILL IN INV
590 REM TRANSFER REMAINING RECORDS FROM OLD FILE (INV)
600 REM INTO NEW FILE (INV1)
610 REM
620 T = 2
630 PRINT #2 P;",";B;",";R1;",";R2;",";C
640 INPUT #1 P,B,R1,R2,C
650 GO TO 630
660 REM
780 REM
790 REM  NEW FILE HAS BEEN GENERATED,  SO PRINT IT OUT
800 REM
810 CLOSE #1, #2
820 OPEN "INV1" FOR INPUT AS FILE #1
830 REM
840 REM  PRINT HEADINGS
850 REM
860 PRINT
870 PRINT
880 PRINT
890 PRINT "PART","BEGINNING","UNITS","UNITS","UNIT"
900 PRINT"NUMBER","UNITS","RECEIVED","ISSUED","COST"
910 PRINT"------","---------","--------","------","----"
920 T=3
930 INPUT #1 P,B,R1,R2,C
940 PRINT P,B,R1,R2,C
950 GO TO 930
960 REM ********************************
970 REM *** ERROR CHECKING ROUTINES ***
980 REM ********************************
990 IF ERR=11 THEN RESUME 1080
1000 PRINT "UNUSUAL ERROR",ERR
1010 STOP
1020 REM
1030 REM  CHECK WHERE END OF FILE WAS ENCOUNTERED
```

```
1040 REM IF  T=1 THEN INV IS EMPTY BUT ADD MORE DATA
1050 REM IF  T=2 THEN INV IS EMPTY AND DATA ENTRY FINISHED
1060 REM IF  T=3 THEN NEW FILE INV1 HAS BEEN WRITTEN
1070 REM
1080 IF T=1 THEN 480
1090 IF T=2 THEN 810
1100 REM
1110 REM  T MUST BE 3 -- TERMINATE PROGRAM
1120 REM
1130 CLOSE #1
1140 STOP
32767 END
```

```
ENTER PART NUMBER,BEGINNING UNITS, UNITS RECEIVED,
UNITS ISSUED,AND UNIT COST -- SEPARATED BY COMMAS
WHEN FINISHED -- TYPE  99  FOR EACH FIELD
? 112,0,50,10,8.25
ENTER PART NUMBER, BEGINNING UNITS, UNITS RECEIVED,
UNITS ISSUED, AND UNIT COST -- SEPARATED BY COMMAS
WHEN FINISHED -- TYPE  99  FOR EACH FIELD
? 300,0,150,70,6.85
ENTER PART NUMBER, BEGINNING UNITS, UNITS RECEIVED,
UNITS ISSUED, AND UNIT COST -- SEPARATED BY COMMAS
WHEN FINISHED -- TYPE  99  FOR EACH FIELD
? 99,99,99,99,99
```

```
PART        BEGINNING    UNITS       UNITS      UNIT
NUMBER      UNITS        RECEIVED    ISSUED     COST
------      ---------    --------    ------     ----
 101        120          40          45         5
 112        0            50          10         8.25
 219        60           60          80         3.25
 226        5            110         90         2.95
 235        100          0           50         6.2
 300        0            150         70         6.85
 347        0            50          20         4.6
Stop at line 1140
```

This example contains two new features:

- A file is opened, closed, and reopened.
- A test value is used to determine where an error (end of file) occurs.

In line 150 the file "INVI" was opened for output, therefore the program can write into the file. However, the problem summary specifies that the file should also be printed. Therefore "INVI" must be opened for input, as shown in line 820. But before a file can be changed from output to input, it must be closed as in line 810.

It is perfectly legal for a program to open a file first for output, close it, and then open it again for input. When it is opened again, the records are read starting at the beginning of the file.

The second feature, the use of a test value, is necessary because the program hinges on where the error was encountered. The ON ERROR in line 300 tells the computer to go to line 990 if an error occurs. If we focus only on the end-of-file error (ERR = 11), then three locations in the program are possible.

1. The EOF was encountered in line 320.
2. The EOF was encountered in line 640.
3. The EOF was encountered in line 930.

If the culprit is line 320, then we have run out of data in "INV", but there are more records to be added. If line 640 was the cause of the error, then we have run out of data in the file "INV" and no more records have to be added. If line 930 caused the error, then the program was printing out the new file "INVl".

In the first case, error caused by line 320, the program should get more records from the terminal and add them to "INVl". In the second case, error caused by line 640, data entry is finished and the program should close the files and start to print out "INVl". In the third case error caused by line 930, the program is finished and it should terminate.

To distinguish between these three possible EOF conditions a test value is used. T is set to 1 in line 310 to indicate the first condition. T is set to 2 in 620 to indicate the second condition. It is set a last time to 3 in line 920.

When any error occurs, the computer goes to line 990. If it is an EOF error (ERR = 11) then it checks the T value in lines 1080 and 1090 to determine which action has to be taken. Depending on the value of T, the program directs the computer to

- Line 480 to get more data from the terminal
- Line 810 to close the files and print "INVl"
- Next line in succession (line 1130) if T is neither 1 nor 2, to terminate the program

With this logic the program can add records to the middle of a file.

Exercises

Account Balance Exercise: The firm has acquired two new customers. Write a program to add their records to the customer file.

Problem Summary

Input

	Customer Number	*Name*	*Balance*	*Payments*	*Charges*
Record 1	2995	Jones	0	0	50
Record 2	3370	Moats	0	0	75

Old "CUST" file

Processing

Get new customer data from the terminal and place it at the end of the "CUST1" file.

Output

Instructions for data entry
New customer file "CUST1"
Print the "CUST1" file

(Attach additional paper to complete your program.)

```
TYPE CUSTOMER NUMBER, CUSTOMER NAME, BALANCE
PAYMENTS, CHARGES --- SEPARATED BY COMMAS
WHEN FINISHED TYPE 999,AAA,999,999,999
? 2995,JONES,0,0,50
TYPE CUSTOMER NUMBER, CUSTOMER NAME, BALANCE
PAYMENTS, CHARGES --- SEPARATED BY COMMAS
WHEN FINISHED TYPE 999,AAA,999,999,999
? 3370,MOATS,0,0,75
TYPE CUSTOMER NUMBER, CUSTOMER NAME, BALANCE
PAYMENTS, CHARGES --- SEPARATED BY COMMAS
WHEN FINISHED TYPE 999,AAA,999,999,999
? 999,AAA,999,999,999


CUSTOMER       CUSTOMER
NUMBER         NAME           BALANCE       PAYMENTS      CHARGES
------         ----           -------       --------      -------
 2741          FERNWOOD        120           120           40
 2937          BLAKEY          0             0             90
 2995          JONES           0             0             50
 3246          GREY            250           130           170
 3359          PHILLIPS        90            40            100
 3370          MOATS           0             0             75
 3426          BIRD            180           180           200
 3527          LOMBARD         100           100           250
Stop at line 1050

Ready
```

Sales Commission Exercise: The firm has added two salesmen. Add their records to the file.

Problem Summary

Input

	Sales Territory	*Salesman*	*Gross Sales*	*Commission Rate*
Record 1	1	Kevin	2500	.045
Record 2	2	Jack	500	.05

"SALES" file

Processing

Get the data from the terminal and place it in the file ("SALES1") by sales territory.

Output

Instructions for data entry
New "SALES1" file
Print the "SALES1" file

(Attach additional paper to complete your program.)

```
TYPE  SALES TERRITORY,SALESMAN, GROSS
SALES, AND COMMISSION RATE.--SEPARATE WITH COMMAS
WHEN FINISHED TYPE 0,AA,0,0.
? 1,KEVIN,2500,.045
TYPE SALES TERRITORY,SALESMAN,GROSS SALES
COMMISSION RATE--SEPARATED BY COMMAS
WHEN FINISHED TYPE 0,AA,0,0
? 2,JACK,500,.05
TYPE SALES TERRITORY,SALESMAN,GROSS SALES
COMMISSION RATE--SEPARATED BY COMMAS
WHEN FINISHED TYPE 0,AA,0,0
? 0,AA,0,0


SALES                                GROSS           COMMISSION
TERRITORY        SALESMAN            SALES           RATE
---------        --------            -----           ----
  1              BILL                 12050            .05
  1              JOE                  5270             .045
  1              KEVIN                2500             .045
  2              TOM                  6940             .04
  2              PHIL                 11200            .055
  2              JACK                 500              .05
  3              CLYDE                7340             .04
  3              HARRY                9460             .045
  3              BOB                  14690            .05
Stop at line 1140
```

DELETING RECORDS FROM A FILE

Sometimes it is necessary to delete records from sequential files. Employees quit or retire. Occasionally an employee may be fired. Items in inventory become obsolete. Suppliers may be dropped. Old customers may shift their buying elsewhere. There are many instances when files need to be purged of records that are no longer needed.

In such cases it is necessary to find the records and delete them. Here again the nature of computer files places a burden on the programmer. Reading a record does not remove it from a file.

Therefore to delete a record, we have to read all of the records in a sequential file, and write all of the records into a new file—*except* those records that should be deleted.

Another aspect to consider is that sequential files are in sequence—and you can't go back. Once a record has been processed, it can only be found again if we start from the beginning of the file.

Therefore if there is more than one record that has to be deleted, they also must be in sequence. Otherwise, the whole file has to be read for each record to be removed.

So let's assume that we have to delete some records from our payroll file, for example, records with employee numbers 104 and 202. A flowchart (Fig. 6–3) and program to do this follow:

```
100 REM PROGRAM TO DELETE RECORDS FROM A FILE
110 REM
120 REM OPEN FILES
130 REM
140 OPEN "EMPLOY"FOR INPUT AS FILE #1
```

```
150 OPEN "EMPLO4" FOR OUTPUT AS FILE #2
160 REM
170 REM GET THE ID NUMBER OF THE RECORD TO BE DELETED
180 REM
190 PRINT
200 PRINT
210 PRINT "TYPE THE ID NUMBER OF THE RECORD TO BE DELETED"
220 PRINT "IF FINISHED--TYPE 99"
230 INPUT N1
240 IF N1=99 THEN 570
250 REM
260 REM READ A RECORD FROM THE EXISTING FILE
270 REM
280 INPUT #1 N,D,N$,H,R,V
290 REM
300 REM TEST FOR END OF FILE
310 REM
320 ON ERROR GO TO 500
330 REM
340 REM CHECK IF RECORD SHOULD BE DELETED
350 REM
360 IF N1=N THEN 450
370 REM
380 REM SINCE ID NUMBERS ARE NOT EQUAL THE RECORD REMAINS
390 REM
400 PRINT #2 N;",";D;",";N$;",";H;",";R;",";V
410 GO TO 280
420 REM
430 REM ID NUMBERS EQUAL; RECORD IS REMOVED
440 REM
450 PRINT "RECORD REMOVED";N;D,N$,H,R;V
460 GO TO 190
470 REM
480 REM END OF FILE REACHED WITH THE RECORD NOT FOUND
490 REM
500 PRINT "END OF FILE REACHED"
510 PRINT "RECORD",N1,"NOT FOUND"
520 GO TO 640
530 REM
540 REM NO MORE RECORDS TO BE DELETED,TRANSFER REMAINING
550 REM RECORDS FROM THE OLD FILE TO THE NEW FILE
560 REM
570 ON ERROR GO TO 640
580 INPUT #1 N,D,N$,H,R,V
590 PRINT #2 N;",";D;",";N$;",";H;",";R",";V
600 GO TO 580
610 REM
620 REM END OF PROGRAM
630 REM
640 CLOSE #1,#2
650 STOP
32767 END

TYPE THE ID NUMBER OF THE RECORD TO BE DELETED
IF FINISHED--TYPE 99
? 104
RECORD REMOVED 104  17      BRAVO          4              40  2


TYPE THE ID NUMBER OF THE RECORD TO BE DELETED
IF FINISHED--TYPE 99
? 202
RECORD REMOVED 202  16      WILSON         4              40  0


TYPE THE ID NUMBER OF THE RECORD TO BE DELETED
IF FINISHED--TYPE 99
? 99
Stop at line 650
```

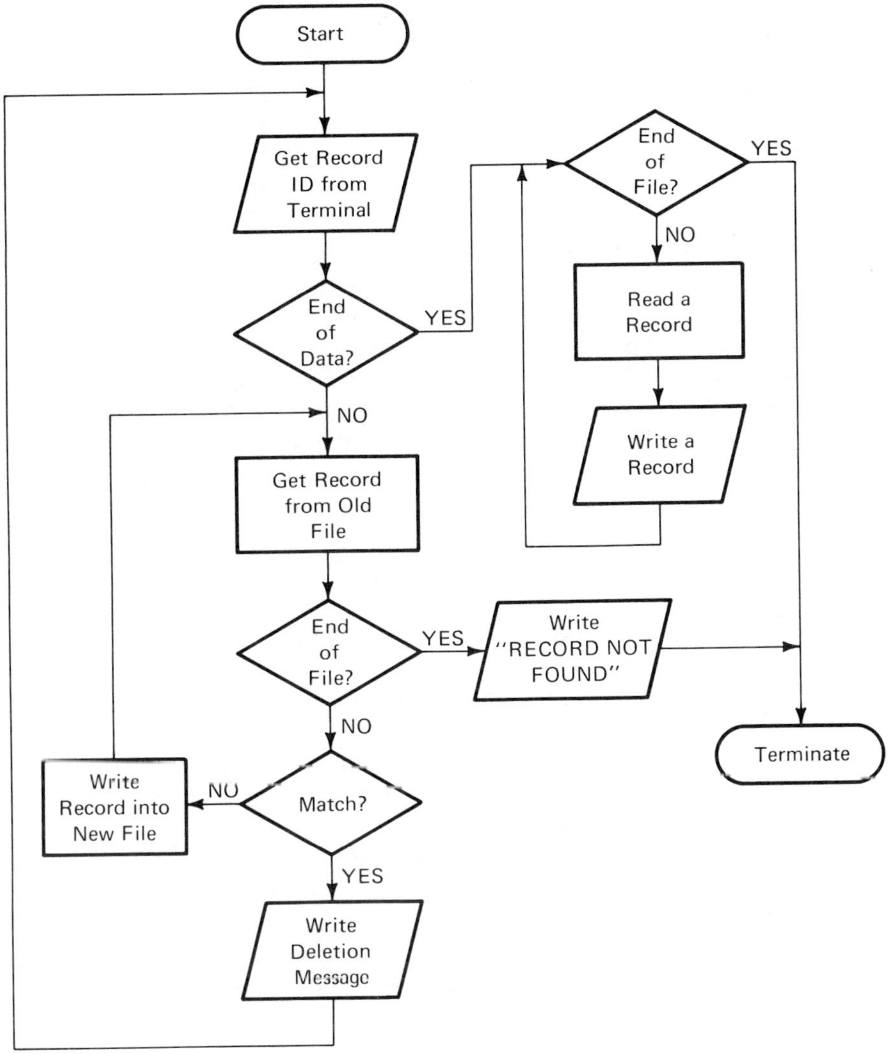

Flowchart for Deleting Records from a File

Figure 6–3

To determine whether the program worked, print the "EMPLO4" file. Modify your program that prints the "EMPLO3" file as follows and run it.

100 OPEN "EMPLO4" AS FILE #1

```
101  1    ADAMS       5       40    0
103  12   BAKER       5.6     40    4
108  16   COHEN       6.25    38    0
172  2    JOHNSON     3.75    40    0
198  1    TANNER      4.25    36    0
206  7    LESTER      5.25    40    0
255  12   SCHMIDT     5.6     40    4
281  12   MILLER      6       40    0
313  7    SMITH       4.25    40    4
347  12   GRAY        6       38    0
368  1    WEAVER      3.5     40    2
422  1    WILLIAMS    4       40    0
Stop at line 500
```

There are no new statements in this program. Just old instructions in a new arrangement. But what an arrangement! Three input statements, four decisions, two prints to a file, and many explanatory REM statements.

When we look at such a program, the mind boggles at the amount of detail. But let's look at it as a computer would see it–one instruction at a time. That way the whole process is simplified.

We start by getting the identification number of a record (employee number) to be deleted from the terminal:

If the data is not finished (ID number is not 99)
    Then
        We read a record from the old file
        If the file is empty
            Then print the record not found message and terminate
            Else (there are records in the file)
            If the terminal ID matches the record ID from the file
                Then the record deleted message is
                    printed and we go back to get another
                    record from the terminal
                Else (record ID does not match terminal ID)
                    The record is printed in the new file
                    and we go back to get another record
    Else (there are no more records to be deleted)
        If there are no more records in the file (we might have deleted the last record in the file)
            Then terminate
            Else Read a record from the file
                Print it in the new file
                Go back to check end of file (EOF) again.

Notice that when we look at the program from this viewpoint, we do not look forward. Rather, we work with the limited amount of data available at any particular time. By golly, the computer is abysmally ignorant; so, we need to be very precise and consider all possibilities in order to cover all bases in our programs–*before* they are written. Otherwise, if something is overlooked and that particular condition occurs, the program will not work.

Look at this program again. Then review the other examples provided. After that you can practice thinking logically by doing the exercises.

Example

Inventory Example: Delete from the new inventory file ("INVl") the records for Part Numbers 101, 219, and 300. Print the new file.

```
100 REM THIS PROGRAM DELETES  RECORDS FROM THE INVENTORY FILE
110 REM
120 REM OPEN FILES FOR INPUT AND OUTPUT
130 REM
140 OPEN "INV1" FOR INPUT AS FILE #1
150 OPEN "INV2" FOR OUTPUT AS FILE #2
160 REM
170 REM GET THE PART NUMBER FOR THE ITEM TO BE DELETED FROM THE TERMINAL
180 REM
190 PRINT "TYPE THE PART NUMBER OF RECORD TO BE DELETED"
200 PRINT "WHEN FINISHED --TYPE 99"
210 INPUT N1
220 IF N1=99 THEN 550
230 REM
240 REM READ A RECORD FROM THE EXISTING FILE
250 REM
260 INPUT #1 N,B,R1,R2,C
270 REM
280 REM CHECK FOR END OF FILE
290 REM
300 ON ERROR GO TO 480
310 REM
320 REM CHECK TO SEE IF THE RECORD SHOULD BE DELETED
330 REM
340 IF N1=N THEN 430
350 REM
360 REM ID NUMBERS NOT EQUAL--RECORD REMAINS IN THE FILE
365 REM PRINT RECORD IN THE FILE
370 REM
380 PRINT #2 N;",";B;",";R1;",";R2;",";C
383 REM
385 REM READ ANOTHER RECORD FROM THE FILE
390 GO TO 260
400 REM
410 REM ID NUMBERS EQUAL--RECORD NOT TRANSFERRED
420 REM
430 PRINT "RECORD REMOVED";N;B;R1,R2,C
432 REM
435 REM GET THE NEXT RECORD TO BE REMOVED FROM THE TERMINAL
440 GO TO 190
450 REM
460 REM END OF FILE FOUND WITH RECORD NOT FOUND
470 REM
480 PRINT "END OF FILE REACHED"
490 PRINT "RECORD"N1,"NOT FOUND"
500 GO TO 620
510 REM
520 REM NO MORE RECORDS TO BE DELETED
530 REM TRANSFER REMAINING RECORDS TO A NEW FILE
540 REM
550 ON ERROR GO TO 620
560 INPUT #1 N,B,R1,R2,C
570 PRINT #2 N;",";B;",";R1;",";R2;",";C
580 GO TO 560
590 REM
```

```
600 REM END OF PROGRAM
610 REM
620 CLOSE #1,#2
740 STOP
32767 END
```

```
TYPE THE PART NUMBER OF RECORD TO BE DELETED
WHEN FINISHED --TYPE 99
? 101
RECORD REMOVED 101   120   40                 45             5
TYPE THE PART NUMBER OF RECORD TO BE DELETED
WHEN FINISHED --TYPE 99
? 219
RECORD REMOVED 219   60   60    80            3.25
TYPE THE PART NUMBER OF RECORD TO BE DELETED
WHEN FINISHED --TYPE 99
? 300
RECORD REMOVED 300   0   150    70            6.85
TYPE THE PART NUMBER OF RECORD TO BE DELETED
WHEN FINISHED --TYPE 99
? 99
Stop at line 740
```

Modify your program that prints the "INV" file to print the "INV2" file.

```
 112          0            50           10           8.25
 226          5            110          90           2.95
 235          100          0            50           6.2
 347          0            50           20           4.6
Stop at line 500
```

Exercises

Account Balance Exercise: Delete from the new customer statement file ("CUST1") the records for customer numbers 2741, 2937, and 3426. Print the new file ("CUST2") with another program.

(Attach additional paper to complete your program.)

Sales Commission Exercise: Delete from the new sales file ("SALES1") the records for salesmen Bill, Tom, and Harry. Print the new file with another program.

(Attach additional paper to complete your program.)

SUMMARY

This chapter did not deal with BASIC statements; it dealt with how to use what you have already learned in order to solve two problems–deleting and adding records.

The use of sequential files, and some of their limitations, becomes apparent in these problems. Sequential files can only be read from the beginning. We cannot start anywhere in the middle. We must start with the first record in the file, and proceed record by record until the desired record is found. Then, and only then, can the operation be performed–adding a record or deleting a record.

If sequential files are so restricted, why then are they so common? The answer is simple–cost. Sequential file processing is efficient when large numbers of active records are involved. Such is the case for many business applications. We can collect a large amount of data and process it all together in a batch.

All of the records are processed in an identical way. The basic logic for sequential processing is simply input-process-output (and repeat the input-process-output sequence until finished). Each transaction receives identical treatment.

In this chapter you have learned more about how to handle sequential files:

- How to add records to the end and to the middle of a file
- How to remove records from a file

In the next chapter this added skill will become useful when you update sequential files.

PROBLEMS

1. Use the file "XKl" from Problem 1 in Chapter 4 (page 89) and add the following records:

ID	*Time 1*	*Time 2*
107	35	0
209	40	4
420	40	2

Call the new file "XK2". PRINT the new file.

2. Use the file "TOP" from Problem 3 in Chapter 4 (page 89) and add the following records:

ID	*Name*
250	Bong
263	Cabot
270	Walters
273	Beck

Call the new file "TOP1". Print the new file.

3. Use the file "XK2" from Problem 1 above and delete records with the following IDs: 101, 209, 281, 422. Call the new file "XK3". Print the new file.

4. Use the file "TOP1" from Problem 2 above and delete records with the following IDs: 247, 262, 263, 273. Call the new file "TOP2". Print the new file.

7 / Updating Sequential Files

Performance Objectives

At the end of this chapter you should be able to update sequential files with:

- One transaction record for each master record
- Transaction records missing
- Master records missing
- Multiple transaction records for each master record
- Coded transaction records

UPDATING FILES

So far, you have used one or two files in a program. The two files have generally had records with the same fields. When you have created files, the records have also contained the same fields. In this chapter, sequential files are used; however, the records of the different files will not contain the same number of fields. Updating is the term used to describe the processing and/or programs that take master files and transaction files and create new master files.

The programs in this chapter may appear to be long. Most of the statements in each program are remarks. The programs contain these remarks so that you may follow the logic in the programs more easily.

The payroll example has the file "EMPLOY" that contains records with the following fields: employee number, department number, name, hourly rate, regular hours worked, overtime hours worked. This file has been sufficient for our needs until now. In using this file, you may have thought that for each pay period (week), this file is input by a data entry operator with one record per employee. This is not the way it is done by businesses. If the "EMPLOY" file was prepared this way each week, there would be a great deal of duplication. To have to type employee number, department number, and hourly rate for each employee each week would be a great waste of time, especially if there were thousands of employees.

In order to avoid this duplication, master files and transaction files are used. A master file contains information that does not change often. A transaction file contains information that changes regularly. In the payroll example, the only information about an employee that may change regularly (with each payroll) will be regular and overtime hours worked. As a consequence of this, each employee may have two records in two different files. The first file will contain the information that does not change from pay period to pay period; this is the employee master file. The second file will contain the information that does change regularly; this is the employee transaction file.

An example of typical information contained in an employee master file and transaction file is given in Figure 7–1. The information that changes regularly, regular and overtime hours, appears in the transaction file along with the employee number (for identification of the record). The employee master file contains information that does not change often: department number, name, hourly rate, number of exemptions as well as some other information. The year-to-date information is kept in the master record and,

Employee Master File
- Employee Master Records
  - Employee Number
  - Department Number
  - Name
  - Marital Status
  - Hourly Rate
  - Number of Exemptions
  - Year-to-Date Gross Pay (YTD GROSS)
  - Year-to-Date Federal Income Tax Withheld (YTD FIT)
  - Year-to-Date Social Security Withheld (YTD FICA)

Employee Transaction File
- Employee Transaction Record
  - Employee Number
  - Regular Hours Worked
  - Overtime Hours Worked

Figure 7–1 Data in Employee Master and Transaction Files

obviously, these amounts will change with each payroll. So, the definition of a master record given above must be modified. A master record contains information that does not often change, as well as summary information. In this case the summary information is year-to-date data. In a business, an employee master record for payroll would contain many more fields, but for brevity, the record defined in Figure 7–1 will be sufficient to illustrate an update.

In programming terms, an update may be thought of as a program that matches transaction records with master records and updates the summary information in the master record. As an integral part of this procedure, a payroll can be prepared as well as any management reports concerning payroll. In this chapter, to compute the federal income tax (FIT), use 20% of gross pay; to compute the FICA amount, use 6.13% of gross pay. Emphasis is placed on the programming logic needed to deal with master and transaction files to perform an update. In a later chapter, the tax information will be given and you will be able to program the exact computations for taxes. There is no field for year-to-date net pay since it can easily be computed (YTD NET PAY = YTD GROSS PAY − YTD FIT − YTD FICA).

Table 7–1 shows the information in the employee master file, "EMPMAS", Table 7–2 shows the information in the employee transaction file, "EMPTRA". You can create the file "EMPMAS" by writing a program that will take the "EMPLOY" file and print on the records of the

Employee Master File

Table 7–1

Employee No.	*Dept. No.*	*Name*	*Marital Status*	*Hourly Rate*	*No. of Exemp.*	*YTD Gross*	*YTD FIT*	*YTD FICA*
101	1	Adams	2	5.00	3	1000.00	200.00	61.30
103	12	Baker	1	5.60	2	1288.00	257.60	78.95
104	17	Bravo	2	4.00	4	860.00	172.00	52.72
108	16	Cohen	2	6.25	4	1187.50	237.50	72.79
172	2	Johnson	1	3.75	0	750.00	150.00	45.98
198	1	Tanner	2	4.25	4	765.00	153.00	46.89
202	16	Wilson	2	4.00	5	800.00	160.00	49.04
206	7	Lester	2	5.25	3	1050.00	210.00	64.37
255	12	Schmidt	2	5.60	5	1288.00	257.60	78.95
281	12	Miller	2	6.00	4	1200.00	240.00	73.56
313	7	Smith	2	4.25	3	977.50	195.50	59.92
347	12	Gray	2	6.00	3	1140.00	228.00	69.88
368	1	Weaver	1	3.50	1	752.50	150.50	46.13
422	1	Williams	2	4.00	2	800.00	160.00	49.04

Employee Transaction File

Table 7–2

Employee Number	*Regular Hours*	*Overtime Hours*
101	40	0
103	40	4
104	40	2
108	38	0
172	40	0
198	36	0
202	40	0
206	40	0
255	40	4
281	40	0
313	40	4
347	38	0
368	40	2
422	40	0

"EMPMAS" file the following fields: employee number, department number, name, and hourly rate. Make sure that you leave space for the five missing fields. Then write another program or continue in the same program to input from the keyboard the missing fields—marital status, number of exemptions, year-to-date gross pay, year-to-date federal income tax withheld, and year-to-date social security withheld. Marital status is defined as follows: 1 = single, 2 = married. The alternative way to create the "EMPMAS" file is to input all of the data from the keyboard by writing a program as shown in Chapter 4, page 66.

The "EMPTRA" file may be created by writing a program that reads the "EMPLOY" file and places employee number, regular hours, and overtime hours in the "EMPTRA" file. Alternatively, you may write a program that will input the data from the keyboard. The transaction file data is found in Table 7–2.

A program that combines the creation of the "EMPMAS" and "EMPTRA" files is given below.:

```
100 REM THIS PROGRAM CREATES THE EMPLOYEE MASTER FILE
110 REM AND THE EMPLOYEE TRANSACTION FILE
120 ON ERROR GO TO 260
130 OPEN "EMPLOY" FOR INPUT AS FILE #1
140 OPEN "EMPMAS" FOR OUTPUT AS FILE #2
150 OPEN "EMPTRA" FOR OUTPUT AS FILE #3
160 INPUT #1 N,D,N$,H,R,V
170 PRINT "MARITAL STATUS (1 OR 2),EXEMPTIONS  FOR  ";N$
180 INPUT M,E
190 PRINT "YTD GROSS, YTD FIT, YTD FICA"
200 INPUT G,F,F1
230 PRINT #2 N;",";D;",";N$;",";M;",";H;",";E;",";G;",";F;",";F1
240 PRINT #3 N;",";R;",";V
250 GO TO 160
260 IF ERR=11 THEN RESUME 290
270 PRINT "UNUSUAL ERROR",ERR
280 STOP
290 CLOSE #1,#2,#3
300 STOP
32767 END
```

In the program, the transaction file with the weekly hours worked will be used to update the master file. Also a list of employees and their gross pay will be printed.

In order to understand the programming involved in an update, the following example illustrates what is required.

Problem Summary

Input

1. Employee master file, "EMPMAS"
2. Employee transaction file, "EMPTRA"

Processing

Match transaction records and master records by employee number. Calculate gross pay, taxes, and net pay.

Output

An updated master file with the new values for year to date fields. Print out a list of employee numbers, their names, their net pay, and the updated master file suitably labelled.

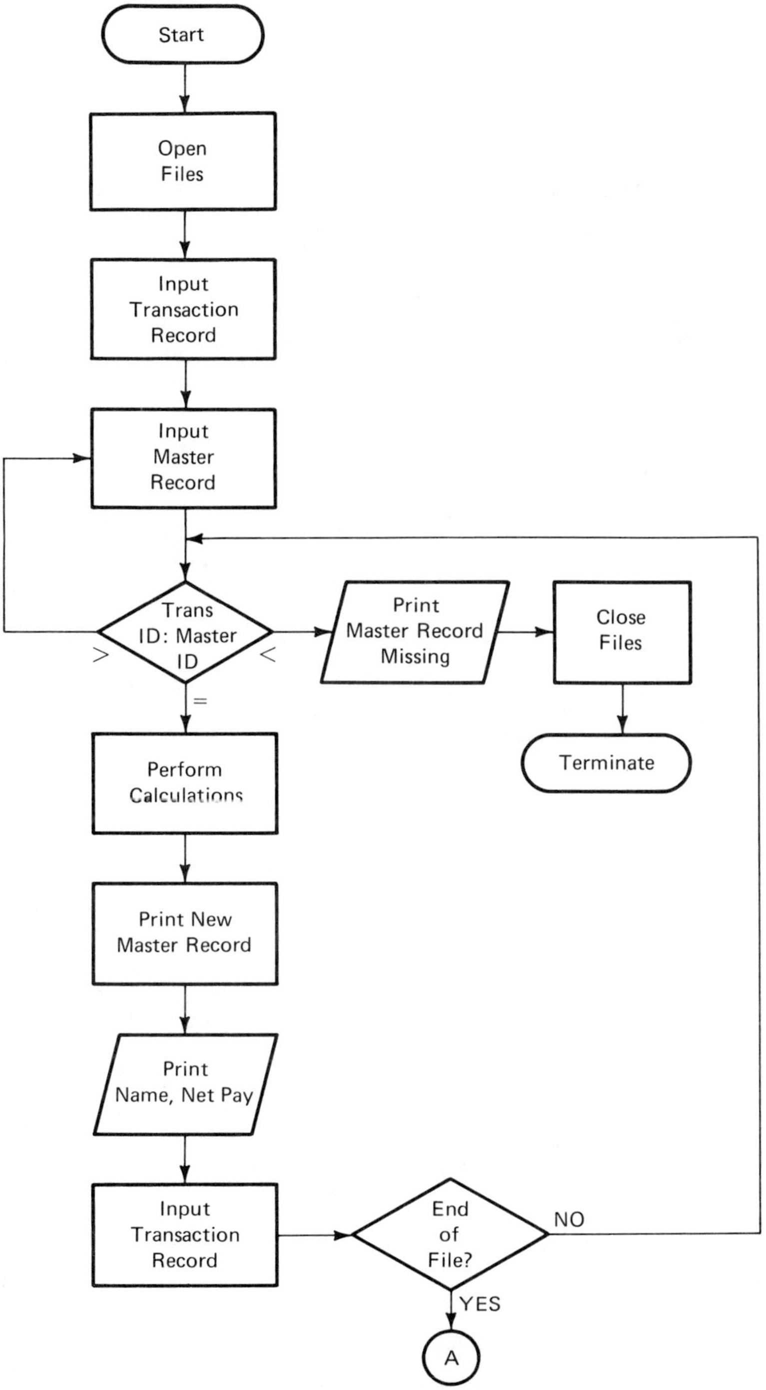

(a) Matching Logic

Flowchart of Update Program

Figure 7–2

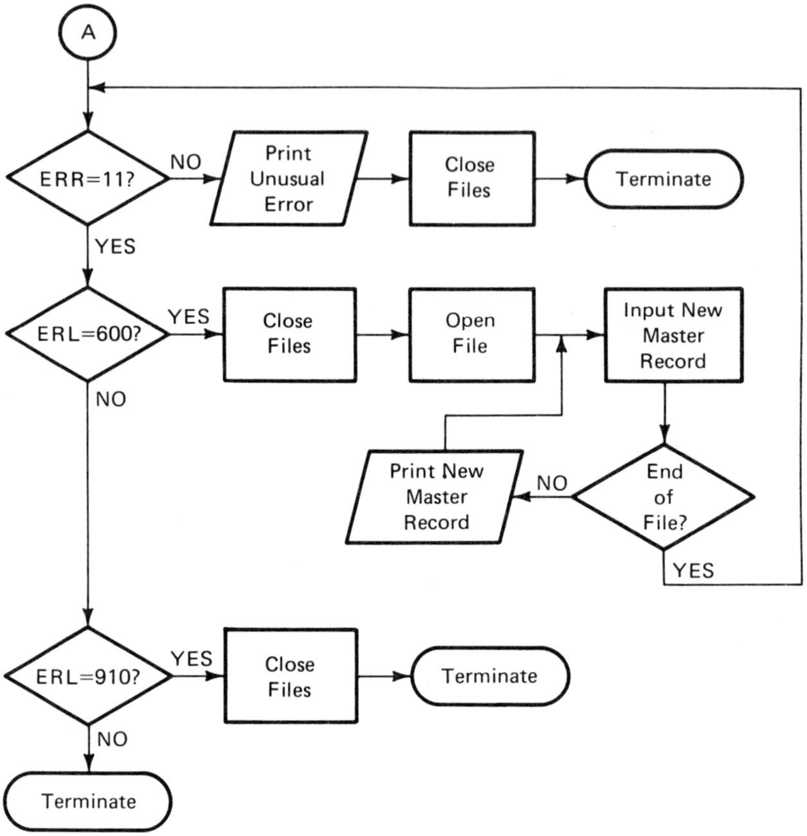

(b) Error Logic (Error Routines)

Figure 7–2 Flowchart of Update Program (cont'd)

The program therefore has to perform the following steps:

1. Establish a link to the transaction file, master file, and the new master file.
2. Read a transaction record and associated master record.
3. Calculate the taxes and print the employee number, name, and net pay.
4. Update the master record with the payroll data.
5. Write the updated master record into a new master file.
6. Go back to read more records while there is still data in the files.
7. Print out the updated master file.

A program is shown below:

```
100 REM          UPDATE OF MASTER FILE
110 ON ERROR GO TO 650
120 REM
130 REM          SET UP HEADINGS
140 REM
150 PRINT
160 PRINT "EMPLOYEE  NAME         NET"
170 PRINT "NUMBER                 PAY"
180 PRINT
190 REM
200 REM
210 OPEN "EMPMAS" FOR INPUT AS FILE #1
220 OPEN "EMPTRA" FOR INPUT AS FILE #2
230 OPEN "EMPMA1" FOR OUTPUT AS FILE #3
240 REM
250 REM          READ A TRANSACTION RECORD
260 REM
270 INPUT #2 I,R,V
280 REM
290 REM          READ A MASTER RECORD
300 REM
310 INPUT #1 N,D,N$,M,H,E,G,F,F1
320 REM
330 REM          COMPARE ID'S
340 REM
350 IF I=N THEN 410
360 IF I>N THEN 310
370 IF I<N THEN 750
380 REM
390 REM          ID'S MATCH -- DO COMPUTATIONS FOR UPDATE
400 REM
410 G1=(R*H)+(V*H*1.5)
420 F2=.2*G1
430 F3=.0613*G1
440 P=G1-F2-F3
450 G=G+G1
460 F=F+F2
470 F1=F1+F3
480 P1=P1+P
490 REM
500 REM          PRINT UPDATED MASTER RECORD
510 REM
520 PRINT #3 N;",";D;",";N$;",";M;",";H;",";E;",";G;",";F;",";F1
530 REM
540 REM          PRINT ID,NAME,NET PAY
550 REM
560 PRINT USING" ###     \        \  ####.##"N,N$,P
570 REM
580 REM          READ A TRANSACTION RECORD
590 REM
600 INPUT #2 I,R,V
610 GO TO 350
620 REM
630 REM          *** ERROR CHECK ***
640 REM
650 IF ERR=11 THEN RESUME 690
660 PRINT "UNUSUAL ERROR",ERR
670 CLOSE #1,#2,#3
680 STOP
690 IF ERL=600 THEN 780
700 IF ERL=910 THEN 940
710 STOP
720 REM
730 REM          MISSING MASTER RECORD
```

```
740 REM
750 PRINT "MASTER RECORD MISSING FOR EMPLOYEE NUMBER",I
760 CLOSE #1,#2,#3
770 STOP
780 CLOSE #1,#2,#3
790 REM
800 REM           PRINT OUT OF UPDATED MASTER FILE
810 REM
820 PRINT
830 PRINT
840 PRINT
850 PRINT
860 PRINT "                        UPDATED MASTER FILE"
870 PRINT
880 OPEN "EMPMA1" FOR INPUT AS FILE #4
890 PRINT "EMPLOYEE  DEPT  NAME     MARITAL   HOURLY  EX-   YTD       YT
D      YTD"
900 PRINT "NUMBER                   STATUS    RATE    EMP   GROSS     FI
T      FICA"
910 INPUT #4 N,D,N$,M,H,E,G,F,F1
920 PRINT USING " ###      ##    \         \ #       ##.##    #   #####.##
  ####.## ####.##"N,D,N$,M,H,E,G,F,F1
930 GO TO 910
940 CLOSE #4
950 STOP
32767 END
```

EMPLOYEE NUMBER	NAME	NET PAY
101	ADAMS	147.74
103	BAKER	190.29
104	BRAVO	127.06
108	COHEN	175.44
172	JOHNSON	110.81
198	TANNER	113.02
202	WILSON	118.19
206	LESTER	155.13
255	SCHMIDT	190.29
281	MILLER	177.29
313	SMITH	144.42
347	GRAY	168.42
368	WEAVER	111.17
422	WILLIAMS	118.19

UPDATED MASTER FILE

EMPLOYEE NUMBER	DEPT	NAME	MARITAL STATUS	HOURLY RATE	EX-EMP	YTD GROSS	YTD FIT	YTD FICA
101	1	ADAMS	2	5.00	3	1200.00	240.00	73.56
103	12	BAKER	1	5.60	2	1545.60	309.12	94.75
104	17	BRAVO	2	4.00	4	1032.00	206.40	63.26
108	16	COHEN	2	6.25	4	1425.00	285.00	87.35
172	2	JOHNSON	1	3.75	0	900.00	180.00	55.17
198	1	TANNER	2	4.25	4	918.00	183.60	56.27
202	16	WILSON	2	4.00	5	960.00	192.00	58.85
206	7	LESTER	2	5.25	3	1260.00	252.00	77.24
255	12	SCHMIDT	2	5.60	5	1545.60	309.12	94.75
281	12	MILLER	2	6.00	4	1440.00	288.00	88.27
313	7	SMITH	2	4.25	3	1173.00	234.60	71.90
347	12	GRAY	2	6.00	3	1368.00	273.60	83.86
368	1	WEAVER	1	3.50	1	903.00	180.60	55.35
422	1	WILLIAMS	2	4.00	2	960.00	192.00	58.85

Stop at line 950

The easiest way to understand the logic that is required for an update is to begin with the flowchart (Figure 7–2). This flowchart does not represent each line in the program with a box. It focuses on the logic of matching transaction records with master records in (a) and the logic of the error routines in (b). First, a record from the transaction file "EMPTRA" is input then a record from the master file "EMPMAS" is input. In matching the transaction record to the appropriate master record three conditions may occur. The employee number (ID) of the transaction record may be greater than, less than, or equal to the employee number (ID) of the master record.

- If the transaction record ID is greater than the master record ID: Then, there is no transaction and input the next master record. This should not occur since there is one transaction record for each master record.
- If the transaction record ID is equal to the master record ID: Then, perform the update calculations, print the updated (new) masterfile, and print the employee ID, name, net pay. Read the next transaction record.
- If the transaction record ID is less than the master record ID: Then, a master record is missing from the master file. If a master record is missing, a message is generated and the program is terminated.

Note: *Remember, the transaction and master files must be in ascending order of employee number (ID).*

If the flowchart does not help you understand the program, then let us perform the job (update) manually. There are two files "EMPMAS" and "EMPTRA", assume that they are in separate cabinets. Also assume that the data on each record in both files are on a separate sheet of paper, and that the files are organized in ascending employee number. In order to focus on the problem of matching master and transaction records only the first field, employee number (ID), is shown in Figure 7–3.

Record Number	Master File "EMPMAS" Employee Number	Transaction File "EMPTRA" Employee Number
1	101	101
2	103	103
3	104	104
4	108	108
5	172	172
6	198	198
7	202	202
8	206	206
9	255	255
10	281	281
11	313	313
12	347	347
13	368	368
14	422	422

Employee Number Fields for Master and Transaction Records Figure 7–3

Manually we would reach into the transaction file and read the first record. Remember, you can only read one record at a time! We then reach into the master file for a record. The IDs match (both are 101). We update the master record with the information on the transaction record and then read the second transaction record. Its ID is 103, the master record ID is still 101 so we read the next master record. Its ID is 103 and we have a match. We update and read the third transaction record—ID is 104. The master ID is still 103, so we read the next (third) master record and have a match. We update and proceed until there are no more records to be processed.

In the program the ON ERROR condition is reached after the last master record is updated. To be more specific, the ON ERROR is reached at line 600 where an attempt to read a transaction record encounters the end of file. Then the files are closed and the updated master file ("EMPMA1") is printed.

In the program, a new BASIC instruction appears in lines 690 and 700.

```
IF ERL = 600 THEN RESUME 780
IF ERL = 910 THEN RESUME 940
```

All of the programs that read files test for the end of a file (after the last record) with the ON ERROR instruction. In all of the prior programs, when the end of a file occurred the program would close the file and terminate. Or, a test value was set so that other functions could be performed before termination. The ERL instruction allows us to test for the line number in a program where an ERROR (in this case an end of file) occurs. It is similar to ERR. The computer determines the value when the program is executed. The logic of the program and a one to one correspondence between master and transaction records will result in the end of file occurring at line 600. ERL has a value equal to the line number at which the ERROR occurs. The test IF ERL = 600 will allow the execution of line 780 next, and result in a print out of the updated master file. When the end of file is reached, the ON ERROR will allow the execution of line 650 again and the program will test for ERL = 600 which is not the case. Then it will test for ERL = 910 which is the case. So file 4 will be closed and the program will terminate. A flowchart for the testing of the ERROR conditions is found in Figure 7–2(b).

You may be thinking at this point that all you have to do is read a transaction record and a master record and they will match. This is the case here where there is one, and only one, transaction record for each and every master record. It is rarely the situation!

UPDATING WITH MISSING TRANSACTIONS

The payroll example illustrates an update where there is one transaction record for each master record. There are many instances where there may be more than one transaction record for each master record or no transaction record for a master record. Common examples are credit card statements, sales, inventory, and customer statements.

For the next example, the sales file "SALES" will be used as the master file and the transaction file will be called "SALEST". The data in these files is given in Tables 7–3 and 7–4. If you have the "SALES" file saved, you can run the alphabetic sort given in Appendix B on this file or create a new "SALES" file with data shown in Table 7–3. The transaction file, "SALEST", must be created. The program should print out an error message if a master record is missing, but it should not terminate.

Sales Master File "SALES" Sorted Alphabetically By Salesman — Table 7–3

Department	*Salesman*	*Gross Sales Year-to-Date*	*Commission Rate*
1	Bill	12050	.05
3	Bob	14690	.05
3	Clyde	7340	.04
3	Harry	9460	.045
1	Joe	5270	.045
2	Phil	11200	.055
2	Tom	6940	.04

Sales Transaction File "SALEST" Sorted Alphabetically By Salesman — Table 7–4

Salesman	*Amount of Sale*
Bill	1050
Bill	275
Bill	390
Clyde	460
Clyde	290
Harry	1500
Joe	280
Joe	490

Problem Summary

Input

1. Sales commission master file, "SALES"
2. Sales transaction file, "SALEST"

Processing

Match transaction records and master record by salesman's name. Calculate the commissions for the salesmen due on the transaction data.

Output

A list of commissions for the salesmen for their latest sales, an updated master file with the new value of year to date sales, and print out the updated master file.

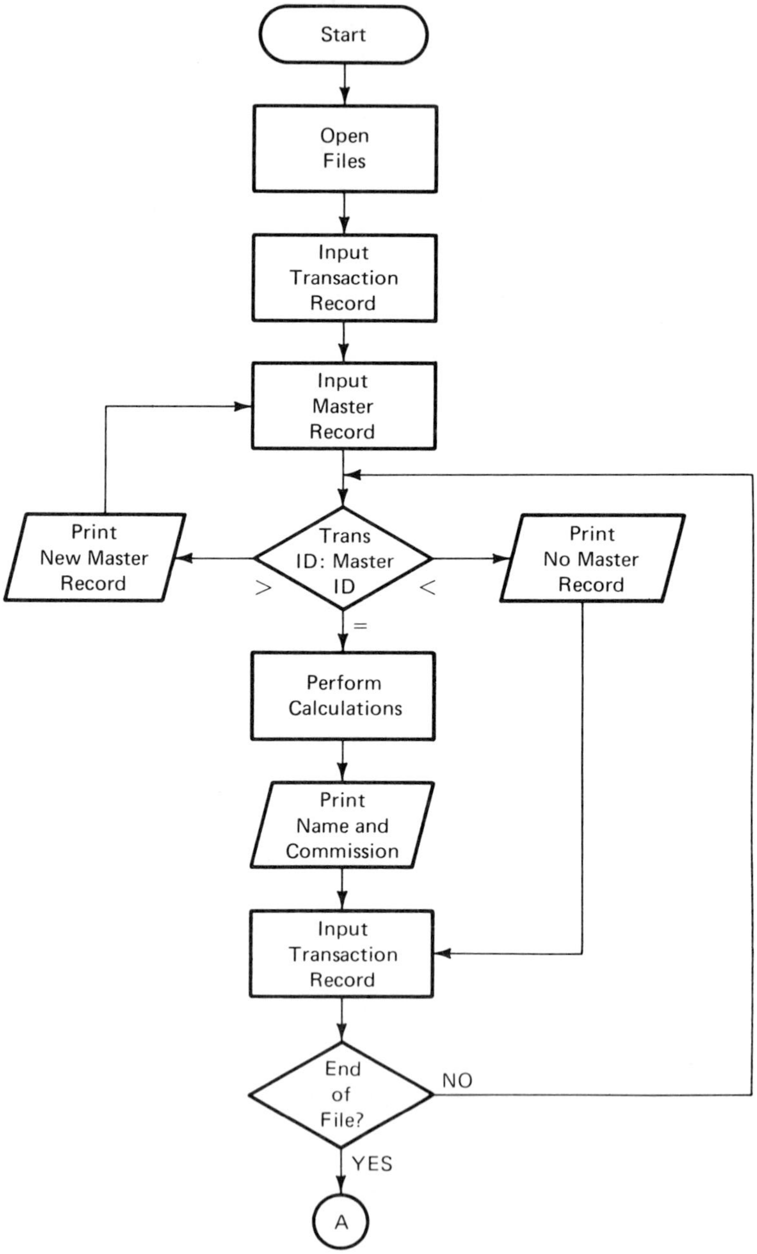

(a) Matching Logic

Figure 7–4 Flowchart of the Sales Update

The program therefore has to perform the following steps:

1. Establish a link to the transaction, master and new master files.
2. Read a transaction record and the associated master record.
3. Calculate the commissions for the latest sales.
4. Print the commissions for the salesmen.
5. Update the master record with the transaction data.
6. Write the updated master record into a new master file.
7. Go back to read more records while there is still data in the files.
8. Print out the updated master file.

See the flowchart (Fig. 7–4) and the program on the next page.

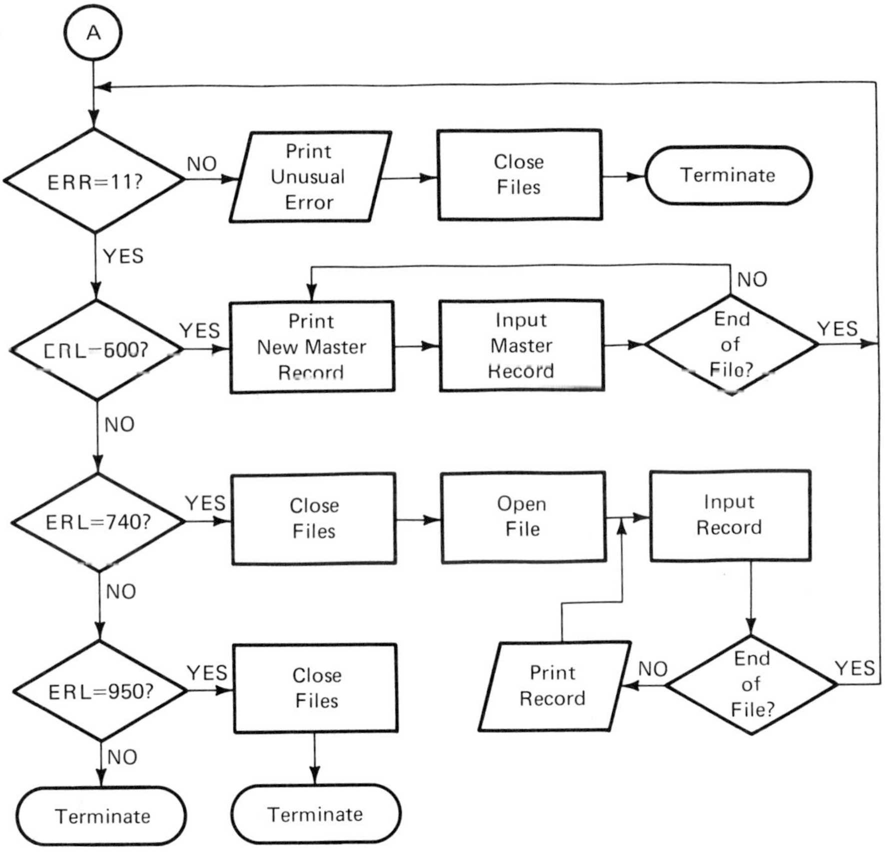

(b) Logic of Error Routines

Flowchart of the Sales Update (cont'd.) Figure 7–4

```
100 REM     PROGRAM TO UPDATE SALES
110 ON ERROR GO TO 1040
120 REM
130 REM          SET UP HEADINGS FOR OUTPUT
140 REM
150 PRINT "NAME","COMMISSION"
160 PRINT "--------------------------"
170 REM
180 REM          LINK TO FILES
190 REM
200 OPEN "SALEST" FOR INPUT AS FILE #1
210 OPEN "SALMAS" FOR INPUT AS FILE #2
220 OPEN "NSALES" FOR OUTPUT AS FILE #3
230 REM
240 REM          READ A TRANSACTION RECORD
250 REM
260 INPUT #1 N$,A
270 REM
280 REM          READ A MASTER RECORD
290 REM
300 INPUT #2 D,S$,G,C
310 REM
320 REM          COMPARE TRANSACTION WITH MASTER
330 REM
340 IF N$=S$ THEN 410
350 IF N$>S$ THEN 550
360 IF N$<S$ THEN 670
370 REM
380 REM          TRANSACTION EQUAL TO MASTER
390 REM              UPDATE THE MASTER
400 REM
410 G=G+A
420 C1=A*C
430 REM
440 REM           PRINT NAME AND COMMISSION
450 REM
460 PRINT USING"\          \      ###.##"S$,C1
470 REM
480 REM          READ NEXT TRANSACTION AND GO TO COMPARE
490 REM
500 INPUT #1 N$,A
510 GO TO 340
520 REM
530 REM          TRANSACTION GREATER THAN MASTER
540 REM                WRITE UPDATED MASTER
550 PRINT #3 D;",";S$;",";G;",";C
560 REM
570 REM   GO BACK AND GET ANOTHER MASTER
580 REM
590 GO TO 300
600 REM
610 REM          TRANSACTION LESS THAN MASTER
620 REM           ERROR -- NO MASTER IN FILE
630 REM           WRITE ERROR MESSAGE,  THEN
640 REM           READ ANOTHER TRANSACTION &
650 REM             CONTINUE PROCESSING.
660 REM
670 PRINT "***TRANSACTION WITHOUT MASTER***";N$;A
680 GO TO 500
690 REM
700 REM  NO MORE TRANSACTIONS -- WRITE REMAINING MASTER
710 REM                          RECORDS
720 REM
730 PRINT #3 D;",";S$,",";G;",";C
740 INPUT #2 D,S$,G,C
750 GO TO 730
760 REM
```

```
770 REM              UPDATE IS FINISHED -- PRINT THE
780 REM                                   UPDATED MASTER
790 CLOSE #1,#2,#3
800 OPEN "NSALES" FOR INPUT AS FILE #1
810 REM
820 REM              PRINT HEADINGS
830 REM
840 PRINT
850 PRINT
860 PRINT "UPDATED FILE --NSALES"
870 PRINT "---------------------"
880 PRINT
890 PRINT "TERRITORY","NAME","YTD","COMMISION"
900 PRINT " "," ","SALES","RATE"
910 PRINT "---------","---------","---------","---------"
920 REM
930 REM  READ A RECORD AND PRINT
940 REM
950 INPUT #1 D,S$,G,C
960 PRINT USING"   ##         \          \    ##,###.##      .###"D,S$,G,C
970 GO TO 950
980 REM
990 CLOSE #1
1000 GO TO 1110
1010 REM ********************************
1020 REM *** ERROR CHECKING ROUTINES ***
1030 REM ********************************
1040 IF ERR = 11 THEN RESUME 1080
1050 PRINT "UNUSUAL ERROR",ERR
1060 CLOSE #1,#2,#3
1070 STOP
1080 IF ERL = 500 THEN 730
1090 IF ERL = 740 THEN 790
1100 IF ERL = 950 THEN 990
1110 STOP
32767 END

Ready
```

```
NAME          COMMISSION
-------------------------
BILL             52.50
BILL             13.75
BILL             19.50
CLYDE            18.40
CLYDE            11.60
HARRY            67.50
JOE              12.60
JOE              22.05


UPDATED FILE --NSALES
---------------------

TERRITORY     NAME          YTD           COMMISION
                            SALES         RATE
---------     ---------     ---------     ---------
    1         BILL          13,765.00     .050
    3         BOB           14,690.00     .050
    3         CLYDE          8,090.00     .040
    3         HARRY         10,960.00     .045
    1         JOE            6,040.00     .045
    2         PHIL          11,200.00     .055
    2         TOM            6,940.00     .040
Stop at line 1110
```

The flowcharts and program are different from the payroll update in five ways:

1. Missing transaction records occur.
2. The new master record is printed on the file when the transaction record ID is greater than the master record ID.
3. The matching of IDs is on alphabetic data.
4. The program will not terminate when a master record is missing.
5. Multiple transaction records for each master record occur.

Missing transactions are accounted for in the logic in two places. First, new master records are printed on the file only when the transaction record ID is greater than the master record ID. Second, if the end of the transaction file has been read and master records remain to be processed, line 1080 IF ERL = 500 THEN 730 and the instructions that follow line 730 take care of this problem.

IDs that consist of alphabetic information (salesman name) are matched in this program. There is no essential difference between matching alphabetic as opposed to numeric IDs as far as the programming is concerned.

The program will not terminate if master records are missing. This problem is solved by printing the appropriate message and reading the next transaction record.

Finally, the program will handle the case where there is more than one transaction record for a master record. This is done by not printing a new master record until the transaction record ID is greater than the master record ID. Also, the accumulation of the gross sales in line 410, G = G + A, will update the gross sales on the master record correctly. The value of G is changed each time a master record is read, while the value of A will be added to it for each transaction record.

The program can best be understood by referring to the flowchart (Figure 7–4), Figure 7–5, and tracing the logic. The first transaction record is input followed by the first master record. The salesman for both these records is Bill. There is a match, the name and commission are printed and the second transaction record is input. The master record ID is Bill and the second transaction record ID is Bill. So the name and commission are printed using the data of the second transaction record. The third transaction record is read. There is another match and the printout of name and commission occurs again. The fourth transaction record is read (Clyde) and the transaction record ID is greater than the master record ID so the master record for Bill, now fully updated by three transaction records, is printed and the second master record is read (Bob). You may wonder how Clyde is greater than Bob. The answer is that the letter "C" is greater, or of higher value, than the letter "B". The alphabet from A to Z is viewed by the computer as just a series of increasing values. It is this fact that allows us to perform alphabetic sorts as in Appendix B, and compare alphabetic fields with IF statements.

Master File SALES		Transaction File SALEST
Record Number	Salesman	Salesman
1	Bill	Bill
2	Bob	Bill
3	Clyde	Bill
4	Harry	Clyde
5	Joe	Clyde
6	Phil	Harry
7	Tom	Joe
8		Joe

Salesman Fields For Master and Transaction Records

Figure 7–5

At this point, we have printed Bill's updated master record, input Bob's master record, and input Clyde's transaction record. Clyde is greater than Bob (TR>MR) so Bob's master record is printed. There were no transaction records for Bob; so his updated master record remains the same and the next master record is input (Clyde). There is a match, name and commission are printed, and the next transaction record is input (five). There is another match, name and commission are printed and the next transaction record is input (Harry). Harry is greater than Clyde, so Clyde's master record is printed and the next master record input (Harry). The logic continues in the above manner until the end of the master file is reached and the program is finished. Note, there are no transactions for Phil or Tom so that the end of file for the transaction file occurs at line 500. The statement ERL = 500 THEN 730 will direct the computer to line 730 and the remaining master records that do not have any transaction records will be printed on the new master file. The two other ERL statements are used to print out the updated master file and produce the required report.

UPDATING WITH CODED TRANSACTIONS

The final example of an update program will use exactly the same logic as the last program, but the transaction file will be more complex. This last example will be an inventory problem. It will use as the master file the file "INVMR". Table 7–5 gives the contents of the master file, Table 7–6 the transaction file, "INVTR".

Table 7–5

Inventory Master File

Part Number	*Units on Hand*	*Cost*
101	350	5.00
110	275	7.00
219	90	3.25
226	120	2.95
235	360	6.20
247	140	4.60

Table 7–6

Inventory Transaction File

Part Number	*Transaction Code*	*Quantity*
101	1	150
101	2	75
101	2	60
101	2	20
219	2	20
226	1	75
226	1	100
226	2	90
235	2	30
247	1	70

You will have to write programs to create both the transaction and master file. The transaction records have three fields: the part number (ID), a transaction code, and a quantity. The transaction code field has either the number 1 or 2 in it. A transaction code of 1 means that the transaction is a receipt to inventory. A transaction code of 2 means that the transaction is an issuance of goods from inventory. The first transaction record (101,1,150) means that 150 units of part 101 were received in inventory. The third transaction record (101,2,60) means that 60 units of part 101 were issued from inventory.

You may assume that the master file is updated at the end of each week and that the transactions were generated during this week. The files are sorted by part number and you have to write the program for the update. For the *updated* master file, the calculation is as follows:

Units on Hand = Units on Hand (in the old master file)
+ Units received (transaction code 1)
− Units issued (transaction code 2)

Besides updating the master file, one report is to be produced. The report is an "Inventory Valuation Report." It lists the part numbers and the amount of money that is tied up in inventory at the end of the week. It is produced from the updated master file.

Problem Summary

Input

1. Inventory master file, "INVMR"
2. Inventory transaction file, "INVTR"

Processing

Match transaction records and master records by part number. Calculate quantities received and issued by transaction code. Calculate units on hand.

Output

An updated master file, "INVSN", and an inventory valuation report.

The program therefore has to perform the following steps:

1. Establish a link to the transaction file and the master and new master files.
2. Read a transaction record and associated master record.
3. Determine from the transaction code whether the quantity is issued or received.
4. Update the master record.
5. Write the updated master record.
6. Go back to read more records while there is still data in the files.
7. Print out the new master file.
8. Produce the report from the updated master file.

The program follows:

```
100 REM PROGRAM TO UPDATE INVENTORY
110 REM
120 REM          LINK TO FILES
130 REM
140 OPEN "INVTR" FOR INPUT AS FILE #1
150 OPEN "INVMR" FOR INPUT AS FILE #2
160 OPEN "INVSN" FOR OUTPUT AS FILE #3
170 REM
180 REM          READ A TRANSACTION RECORD
190 REM
200 ON ERROR GO TO 1260
210 INPUT #1 P1,T1,Q1
220 REM
230 REM          READ A MASTER RECORD
240 REM
250 INPUT #2 P2,Q2,C2
```

```
260 REM
270 REM          COMPARE TRANSACTION WITH MASTER
280 REM
290 IF P1=P2 THEN 380
300 IF P1>P2 THEN 560
310 IF P1<P2 THEN 680
320 REM
330 REM          TRANSACTION EQUAL TO MASTER
340 REM              UPDATE THE MASTER
350 REM
360 REM          CHECK IF TRANSACTION IS RECEIPT OR ISSUE
370 REM
380 IF T1=2 THEN 470
390 REM
400 REM RECEIPT:  T1=1
410 REM
420 Q2 = Q2 + Q1
430 GO TO 510
440 REM
450 REM ISSUE:    T1=2
460 REM
470 Q2 = Q2 - Q1
480 REM
490 REM          READ NEXT TRANSACTION AND GO TO COMPARE
500 REM
510 INPUT #1 P1,T1,Q1
520 GO TO 290
530 REM
540 REM          TRANSACTION GREATER THAN MASTER
550 REM                WRITE UPDATED MASTER
560 PRINT #3 P2;",";Q2;",";C2
570 REM
580 REM    GO BACK AND GET ANOTHER MASTER
590 REM
600 GO TO 250
610 REM
620 REM          TRANSACTION LESS THAN MASTER
630 REM           ERROR -- NO MASTER IN FILE
640 REM           WRITE ERROR MESSAGE,  THEN
650 REM           READ ANOTHER TRANSACTION &
660 REM             CONTINUE PROCESSING.
670 REM
680 PRINT"***TRANSACTION WITHOUT MASTER***";P1;T1;Q1
690 GO TO 510
700 REM
710 REM  NO MORE TRANSACTIONS -- WRITE REMAINING MASTER
720 REM                             RECORDS
730 REM
740 PRINT #3 P2;",";Q2;",";C2
750 INPUT #2 P2,Q2,C2
760 GO TO 740
770 REM
780 REM          UPDATE IS FINISHED -- PRINT THE UPDATED
790 REM                 FILE AND THE REPORT
800 CLOSE #1,#2,#3
810 OPEN "INVSN" FOR INPUT AS FILE #1
820 REM
830 REM          HEADINGS FOR UPDATED FILE
840 REM
850 PRINT
860 PRINT "   NEW INVENTORY MASTER FILE"
870 PRINT "   -------------------------"
880 PRINT
890 PRINT "PART     UNITS     COST"
900 PRINT "NUMBER   ON HAND"
910 PRINT "------   -------   ----"
920 INPUT #1 P,Q,C
930 PRINT USING"###       ####      #.##"P,Q,C
940 GO TO 920
950 CLOSE #1
```

```
960 OPEN "INVSN" FOR INPUT AS FILE #1
970 REM          PRINT REPORT HEADINGS
980 REM
990 PRINT
1000 PRINT
1010 PRINT" INVENTORY VALUATION REPORT"
1020 PRINT" -------------------------"
1030 PRINT
1040 PRINT" PART","DOLLAR"
1050 PRINT"NUMBER","AMOUNT"
1060 PRINT"------","------"
1070 REM
1080 REM  READ A RECORD AND CALCULATE INVENTORY VALUES
1090 REM
1100 T = 0
1110 INPUT #1 P,Q,C
1120 D = Q*C
1130 T = T + D
1140 PRINT USING" ###          #,###.##"P,D
1150 GO TO 1110
1160 REM
1170 REM   END OF DATA -- PRINT TOTAL
1180 REM
1190 PRINT"------------------------"
1200 PRINT USING"\    \       ##,###.##""TOTAL",T
1210 CLOSE #1
1220 GO TO 1340
1230 REM ******************************
1240 REM *** ERROR CHECKING ROUTINES ***
1250 REM ******************************
1260 IF ERR = 11 THEN RESUME 1300
1270 PRINT "UNUSUAL ERROR",ERR
1280 CLOSE #1,#2,#3
1290 STOP
1300 IF ERL = 510 THEN 740
1310 IF ERL = 750 THEN 800
1320 IF ERL = 920 THEN 950
1330 IF ERL = 1110 THEN 1190
1340 STOP
32767 END
```

```
   NEW INVENTORY MASTER FILE
   -------------------------

PART      UNITS     COST
NUMBER    ON HAND
------    -------   ----
101        345      5.00
110        275      7.00
219         70      3.25
226        205      2.95
235        330      6.20
247        210      4.60
```

```
 INVENTORY VALUATION REPORT
 -------------------------

 PART          DOLLAR
NUMBER         AMOUNT
------         ------
 101          1,725.00
 110          1,925.00
 219            227.50
 226            604.75
 235          2,046.00
 247            966.00
------------------------
TOTAL         7,494.25
Stop at line 1340
```

The flowchart is the same as the flowchart of the sales update program (Figure 7–4) with one minor exception—the logic for handling the transaction codes. The flowchart for this portion of the program is Figure 7–6. Since the master record inputs the value of Q2, the two statements

$$Q2 = Q2 + Q1$$
$$Q2 = Q2 - Q1$$

will accumulate the value of Q2 updated by the transaction records until the new master record is printed and a new master record is input.

The data for the required report are obtained from the new master file and the report is the last part of the program.

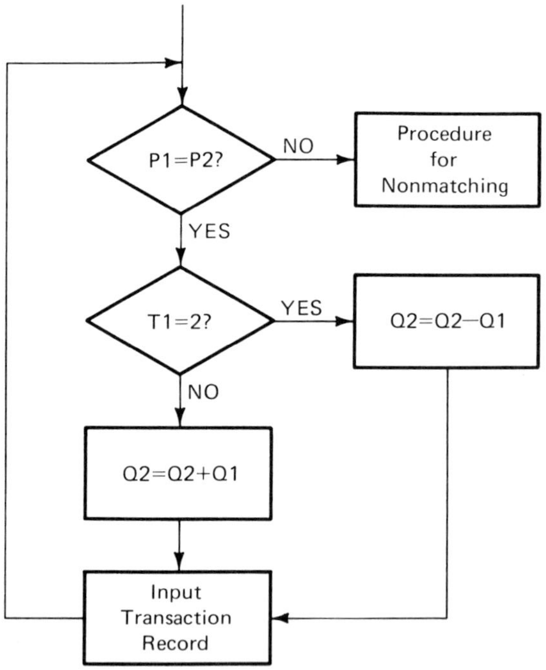

Figure 7–6 Flowchart of Transaction Code Logic

SUMMARY

This chapter covered the updating of sequential files. Descriptions of master files and transaction files to produce a new updated master file were given. Various conditions with respect to the correspondence of master and transaction records were handled by the programs. In each program the third IF statement used to match master and transaction records could have been replace by a GO TO statement. The IF statement was used to emphasize the logic of matching. The new instruction ERL was discussed and illustrated.

The objective of data processing in a business environment is achieved by the update. Through the update, customer statements, payrolls, accounts receivable, accounts payable and general ledgers are produced on some time cycle, usually once a month.

BASIC Instructions Introduced:

Instruction	*Explanation*
ERL	Gives the line number at which an ON ERROR condition took place.

PROBLEMS

1. Modify the first update program (payroll example) so that it will provide the logic required to:

   a. Handle a missing transaction record.

   b. Continue processing rather than stop after printing the error message "MASTER RECORD MISSING FOR EMPLOYEE NUMBER".

   Create and use the following transaction file to test the program.

Employee Number	*Regular Hours*	*Overtime Hours*
103	40	4
108	38	0
165	40	0
198	36	0
255	40	4
313	40	4
368	40	2

   Use "EMPMAS" as the master file.

   Print out the updated master file with suitable headings.

   Print out the employee numbers, names and their net pay. Remember some employees will receive no pay.

2. Modify the sales update program so that it will print out the total commission due to each salesman, rather than the commission for each sale. Also print out the total commission due to all salesmen.

3. Modify the inventory update to print out for each part number the total units issued and received.

4. Assume that the payroll transaction file can contain more than one record for an employee. Modify your program in Problem 1 so that it can use the following transaction file and perform the update.

Employee Number	*Regular Hours*	*Overtime Hours*
104	20	0
104	20	5
108	10	0
198	40	7
202	15	0
202	25	4

202	0	6
206	20	0
206	20	3
313	30	0
313	10	0
313	0	8

There should be a printout for every employee showing number, name, and net pay—even if it is zero. Use one line per employee. Also print out the new master file.

8 / Using Lists and Tables

Performance Objectives

At the end of this chapter you should be able to:

- Set up lists and tables
- Use lists to accumulate summary output
- Use tables to hold data for reference
- Use lists and tables to hold data for processing

All the transaction processing applications that we have discussed have basically the same pattern. The pattern consists of getting a transaction, doing the required computation for that transaction, outputting required results, and then looping back to get the next transaction. Such processing minimizes the amount of data required by the computer.

But business has problems that require a group of data to be entered at the beginning and used for all transactions. Tax tables come readily to mind. And business also has analytic problems, where all the data has to be available to solve a problem or where data is collected from all transactions and held for output until the end of all transactions. An example of the first type would be a linear programming problem (which is a management science method). An example of the second type would be analytic reports that classify data in categories.

To help solve these types of problems, BASIC provides lists and tables. A list is a series of items in a meaningful grouping or sequence. Employee names in alphabetic sequence would be an example of a list. Total sales in item number sequence might be another example. Any row or column of items constitutes a list.

A table is an arrangement of words, numbers, or signs in parallel columns. It is used to show a set of facts or relationships in a compact and comprehensive form. Income tax tables are a clear example of "an arrangement of . . . numbers . . . in parallel columns." A table is therefore a grouping of lists. A list is a one-dimensional (row or column, but not both) presentation of data; and a table is a two-dimensional (both rows and columns) presentation of data.

SUMMARY OUTPUT

Let's derive a problem from the payroll application to get a feel for the use of lists and tables. Assume that you need to summarize the payroll expense by department. As you recall, there are 20 departments—numbered consecutively from 1 to 20. But sorting the file is a time consuming process. Hence the "EMPLOY" file will not be sorted for this problem. A simple representation of this type of problem is shown in Figure 8–1.

Problem Summary

Input

"EMPLOY" file

Processing

Calculate gross pay and accumulate gross pay by department.

Output

Total gross pay by department

The program therefore has to:

1. Link to the "EMPLOY" file.
2. Read a record.
3. Calculate the gross pay.
4. Accumulate gross pay by department number.
5. When all records have been processed, print the departmental gross pay totals.
6. Terminate.

A flowchart (Fig. 8–1), a program to perform these tasks, and the output are shown below:

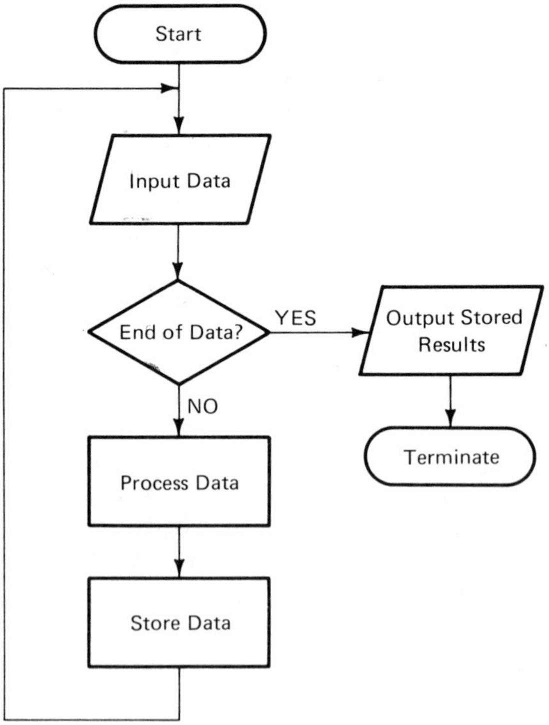

Figure 8–1 Flowchart for Summary Output

```
100 REM PROGRAM TO ACCUMULATE GROSS PAY BY DEPARTMENT
110 REM
120 REM OPEN FILE
130 REM
140 OPEN "EMPLOY" FOR INPUT AS FILE #1
150 REM
160 REM SET UP A LIST TO HOLD DEPARTMENTAL TOTALS
170 REM
180 DIM T(20)
190 REM
200 REM READ A RECORD, UNTIL OUT OF DATA
220 ON ERROR GO TO 360
230 INPUT #1 N, D, N$, H, R, V
240 REM
250 REM CALCULATE AMOUNT OF GROSS PAY
260 REM
270 G = H*R + H*V*1.5
280 REM
290 REM ACCUMULATE GROSS PAY BY DEPARTMENT NUMBER
300 REM
310 T(D) = T(D) + G
320 GO TO 230
330 REM
340 REM CHECK FOR END OF FILE AND PRINT RESULTS
350 REM
360 IF ERR = 11 THEN RESUME 420
370 PRINT "UNUSUAL ERROR", ERR
380 GO TO 520
390 REM
400 REM PRINT DEPARTMENTAL TOTALS WITH HEADINGS
410 REM
420 PRINT "DEPARTMENTAL GROSS PAY TOTALS"
430 PRINT
440 PRINT "DEPARTMENT", "GROSS PAY"
450 PRINT "----------", "---------"
460 FOR M = 1 TO 20
470 PRINT USING "   ###        ####.##"M,T(M)
480 NEXT M
490 REM
500 REM TERMINATE
510 REM
520 CLOSE #1
530 STOP
32767 END
```

```
DEPARTMENTAL GROSS PAY TOTALS

DEPARTMENT     GROSS PAY
----------     ---------
     1         663.50
     2         150.00
     3           0.00
     4           0.00
     5           0.00
     6           0.00
     7         405.50
     8           0.00
     9           0.00
    10           0.00
    11           0.00
    12         983.20
    13           0.00
    14           0.00
    15           0.00
    16         397.50
    17         172.00
    18           0.00
    19           0.00
    20           0.00
Stop at line 530
```

Now here is a program with some interesting new features:

- The DIM statement in line 180
- The summation in line 310 and the output in 470
- The FOR statement in line 460 and its associated NEXT statement in line 480

Let's look at each of these three items in turn. The DIM statement sets up a list, at least that is what the preceding remark in line 160 says. But what exactly does it do? In this case, line 180 tells the computer to reserve 20 consecutive positions all under the name "T." Previously, one field name served to identify one value. Here, one field name serves to identify many values.

If many values are identified by one name, how can you differentiate between the values? The answer is simple—by position. Line 180 sets up a list of 20 positions, thus:

T	1	2	3	4	5	6	7	13	14	15	16	17	18	19	20

To get any one item in the list, we need to specify its position (1–20). The value in the first position would be referred to as T(1). If we wanted the value from the second position, then T(2) is used. The location in the list is specified by enclosing a number, or a field name that has the position desired, in parentheses.

Line 310 refers to T(D). Here the "D" (enclosed in parentheses) specifies which position in T is involved. Hence the Dth position (whatever the department number D may be) of T is referenced. Similarly, in line 470, the reference is to position M (whatever value M may have) in T.

A new BASIC instruction in this program is found in lines 460 and 480. These two lines define a *loop*. A loop is a shorthand way of telling the computer to repeat a series of instructions a certain number of times. Line 460 sets up the loop and gives the loop parameters. The loop parameters tell the computer how often the statements in the loop are to be repeated. Line 480 closes the loop.

In general, the FOR-NEXT statements form loops. The statements within a loop are repeated the number of times specified in the FOR statement by the loop parameters. The loop parameters (in line 460), 1 TO 20, specify that the loop will be repeated twenty times. Each time the loop is repeated, the value of M will be increased by one. By this manner, when M reaches a value of 20, the loop will be repeated one more (final) time.

Line 460 tells the computer to repeat the statements between 460 and 480 (the NEXT M statement) twenty times. In this example, line 470 is performed for M values of 1, 2, 3, 4, 5, 6, 7, 8, 9, 10, 11, 12, 13, 14, 15, 16, 17, 18, 19 and 20 in turn.

Let us look closely at what the program does. First it opens a file for input. This is the file "EMPLOY" from past examples. The file contains employee records with six fields:

- Employee number
- Department number
- Employee name
- Hourly rate
- Regular hours
- Overtime hours

The department number is between 1 and 20. The range of department numbers is important because we want to accumulate gross pay by department. Next a list "T" with 20 positions: one for each of the departments, is set up. Then the program reads a record and calculates gross pay. The department number (D) is used to add the gross pay to that location in T. In other words, whenever the gross pay for a person in department 2 is calculated, it is added to the second position in T. Similarly if the department were 16, gross pay would be added to the sixteenth position in T.

After the end-of-file has been reached, the gross pay for each of the departments is printed in lines 460–480. Notice that line 470 will print M, which stands for the department number, as well as the Mth value of T (which is the departmental gross pay total).

REFERENCE TABLES

Many problems require the use of reference tables. Income tax tables are the most obvious example. But life insurance companies use actuarial tables; statisticians use statistical tables; and financial analysts use present value or annuity tables. If you look closely, you can see tables everywhere. Even this book has a table, a table of contents.

Tables hold data for reference. When the data is needed, we look it up in the appropriate table. One problem that requires table referencing is an income tax calculation. A simple representation of this type of problem is shown in Figure 8–2.

The income tax problem requires two tables: one for single people; another for married people. Both are shown in Table 8–1. But the tables pro-

Table 8–1

Percentage Withholding Tables

(a) SINGLE person—including head of household:

If the amount of wages is: / *The amount of income tax to be withheld shall be:*

Not over $27 0

Over—	But not over—		of excess over—
$27	—$63	.....15%	—$27
$63	—$131	....$5.40 plus 18%	—$63
$131	—$196	....$17.64 plus 21%	—$131
$196	—$273	....$31.29 plus 26%	—$196
$273	—$331	....$51.31 plus 30%	—$273
$331	—$433	....$68.71 plus 34%	—$331
$433		..............$103.39 plus 39%	—$433

(b) MARRIED person—

If the amount of wages is: / *The amount of income tax to be withheld shall be:*

Not over $46 0

Over—	But not over—		of excess over—
$46	—$127	....15%	—$46
$127	—$210	....$12.15 plus 18%	—$127
$210	—$288	....$27.09 plus 21%	—$210
$288	—$369	....$43.47 plus 24%	—$288
$369	—$454	....$62.91 plus 28%	—$369
$454	—$556	....$86.71 plus 32%	—$454
$556		..............$119.35 plus 37%	—$556

Table 8–2 Weekly Tax Tables

a. **Single person**—including head of household

Amount of Wages Lower and Upper End	*End*	*Amount to be Withheld*	*Percentage for Excess over Low End*
$ 0	$ 27	$ 0	0
27	63	0	.15
63	131	5.40	.18
131	196	17.64	.21
196	273	31.29	.26
273	331	51.31	.30
331	433	68.71	.34
433	999	103.39	.39

b. **Married person**

Amount of Wages Lower and Upper End	*End*	*Amount to be Withheld*	*Percentage for Excess over Low End*
$ 0	$ 46	$ 0	0
46	127	0	0.15
127	210	12.15	0.18
210	288	27.09	0.21
288	369	43.47	0.24
369	454	62.91	0.28
454	556	86.71	0.32
556	999	119.35	0.37

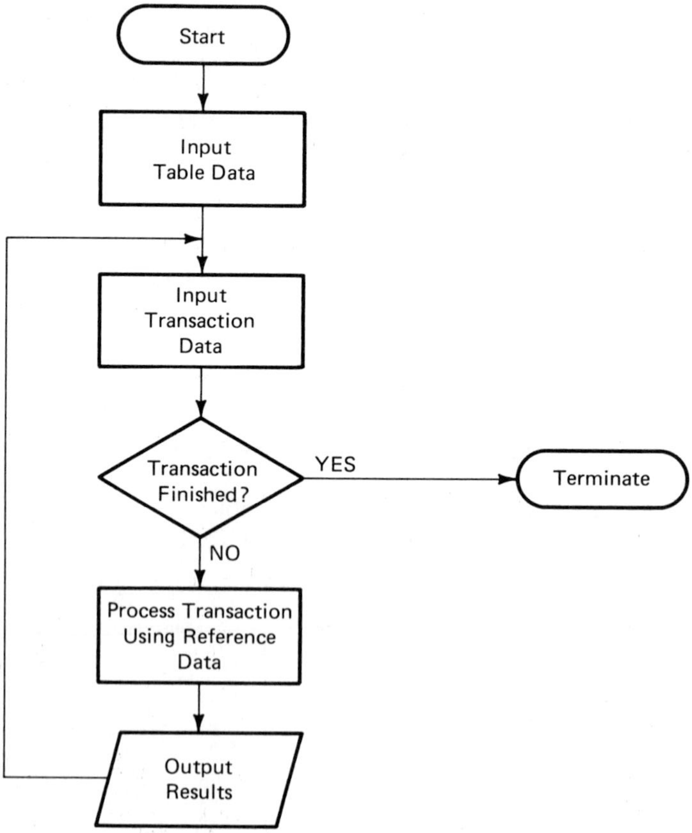

Figure 8–2 Flowchart for Reference Tables

vided by the Internal Revenue Service have to be changed to fit our requirements. The tables need to be consistent. Table 8–2 is the same IRS tables–made consistent by the addition of the first line.

Before the tables can be used in the weekly payroll calculation, they have to be set up. Since tax rates are liable to annual changes, the tax tables are stored in separate files: "SINGLE" for single people; and "MARRID" (note the spelling–file names are limited to six characters) for married people. The program to get the data into the "SINGLE" file is shown below.

```
100 REM PROGRAM TO SET UP TAX TABLE
110 REM
120 REM LINK TO FILE
130 REM
140 OPEN "SINGLE" FOR OUTPUT AS FILE #1
150 REM
160 REM SET UP A TABLE OF 8 ROWS AND 4 COLUMNS
170 REM
180 DIM T(8,4)
190 REM
200 REM FOR EACH ROW, GET DATA FROM TERMINAL
210 REM
220 FOR R=1 TO 8
230 PRINT "ENTER LOW AND HIGH WAGES, MINIMUM AND PERCENTAGE"
240 INPUT T(R,1),T(R,2),T(R,3),T(R,4)
250 NEXT R
260 REM
270 REM PRINT TABLE AND PLACE IT INTO FILE
280 REM
290 PRINT
300 PRINT
310 FOR L=1 TO 8
320 PRINT T(L,1),T(L,2),T(L,3),T(L,4)
330 PRINT #1, T(L,1);",";T(L,2);",";T(L,3);",";T(L,4)
340 NEXT L
350 CLOSE #1
360 STOP
32767 END
```

```
ENTER LOW AND HIGH WAGES, MINIMUM AND PERCENTAGE
? 0,27,0,0
ENTER LOW AND HIGH WAGES, MINIMUM AND PERCENTAGE
? 27,63,0,.15
ENTER LOW AND HIGH WAGES, MINIMUM AND PERCENTAGE
? 63,131,5.40,.18
ENTER LOW AND HIGH WAGES, MINIMUM AND PERCENTAGE
? 131,196,17.64,.21
ENTER LOW AND HIGH WAGES, MINIMUM AND PERCENTAGE
? 196,273,31.29,.26
ENTER LOW AND HIGH WAGES, MINIMUM AND PERCENTAGE
? 273,331,51.31,.30
ENTER LOW AND HIGH WAGES, MINIMUM AND PERCENTAGE
? 331,433,68.71,.34
ENTER LOW AND HIGH WAGES, MINIMUM AND PERCENTAGE
? 433,999,103.39,.39

 0              27             0              0
 27             63             0              .15
 63             131            5.4            .18
 131            196            17.64          .21
 196            273            31.29          .26
 273            331            51.31          .3
 331            433            68.71          .34
 433            999            103.39         .39
Stop at line 360
```

The program gets table data from the terminal and places it into the "SINGLE" file. The details of its operation deserve closer inspection.

Line 180 reserves the spaces for the table T. The dimensions of the table are given in parentheses as 8,4. These dimensions show that the table consists of 8 rows (first dimension) by 4 columns (second dimension). Therefore 32 positions are reserved for T.

The data is entered into the table by the loop in lines 220–250. The "FOR-NEXT" loops the computer through the statements in 230 and 240 eight times. The first time through the loop, R has the value 1. Therefore line 240 gets four values from the terminal and assigns them to row 1 (first dimension: R is 1), columns 1 through 4 in turn.

Then the NEXT R is encountered. The computer adds 1 to R and checks the R value against its limit (the 8 specified in the FOR statement). (Since R is less than 8, lines 230 and 240 are executed.) This time, the data are placed into row 2.

Every time the computer encounters the NEXT R (until R would exceed 8), it adds 1 to R and fills the next successive row of T. After the eighth row has been filled, the looping is finished. The computer continues with the next statement in the program.

Lines 310 through 340 print the data on the terminal and also place it into the SINGLE file. The FOR-NEXT loop sends the computer through the statements in 320 and 330 eight times. For each value of L (1 to 8), it prints that row of the table and places the row into the SINGLE file. Thus the eight rows of T are filed away for future use.

A similar program has to be written to place the data into "MARRID". You can use TABPGM if you change the file name from "SINGLE" to "MARRID".

These two tables are used in the calculation of the taxes for the employees in "EMPTRA". We will also need the master file "EMPMAS" to get the number of exemptions and the year-to-date social security (YTD FICA). Each exemption claimed by the employee deducts $19.23 from taxable wages. And social security deductions are 6.13% up to a limit of $22,900 gross pay.

The old UPDATE program from Chapter 7 serves as the basis for solving this problem. We have modified it to handle the tax tables and the social security calculations.

Problem Summary

Input

"SINGLE" and "MARRID" files for the tax tables
"EMPTRA" file for the weekly earnings
"EMPMAS" file for the deductions and year-to-date FICA

Processing

For each employee: Calculate gross pay, social security (FICA), federal income tax (FIT), and net pay (by subtracting FICA and FIT from gross pay).

Output

The results of the "pay check" calculations, giving employee name and number, gross pay, social security and income tax deductions, and net pay

The updated master file, "EMPMA1"

The program therefore has to

1. Link to the files.
2. Read and hold the tax tables.
3. Get an employee record from "EMPTRA".
4. Find the matching record from "EMPMAS".
5. Calculate gross pay.
6. Determine the amount of the social security deduction:
   a. If YTD gross pay plus weekly gross pay is less than $22,900, *then* all of weekly gross pay is subject to FICA.
   b. If YTD gross pay is less than $22,900, but weekly gross pay added to YTD gross pay makes it greater than $22,900, *then* only that portion of weekly gross pay that brings the YTD up to $22,900 is subject to FICA.
   c. If YTD gross pay is greater than $22,900, *then* no social security is withheld.
7. Calculate taxable income by subtracting deductions from gross pay.
8. Find the applicable tax in the tax tables.
9. Calculate net pay.
10. Update the master record and place it into "EMPMA1".
11. Print the output.
12. Repeat steps 3 through 12 for all other "EMPLOY" records.
13. Terminate.

A program to do all those tasks is shown on the following pages.

```
100 REM          UPDATE OF MASTER FILE
110 ON ERROR GO TO 650
120 REM
130 REM          SET UP HEADINGS
140 REM
150 PRINT
160 PRINT "EMPLOYEE  NAME         GROSS         FIT          FICA
 NET"
170 PRINT "NUMBER                 PAY"
180 PRINT
190 REM
200 REM
202 OPEN "SINGLE" FOR INPUT AS FILE #4
204 OPEN "MARRID" FOR INPUT AS FILE #5
210 OPEN "EMPMAS" FOR INPUT AS FILE #1
220 OPEN "EMPTRA" FOR INPUT AS FILE #2
230 OPEN "EMPMA1" FOR OUTPUT AS FILE #3
231 REM
232 REM TAX TABLES
233 REM
234 DIM S(8,4), M(8,4)
235 FOR L1 = 1 TO 8
236     INPUT #4 S(L1,1), S(L1,2), S(L1,3), S(L1,4)
237     INPUT #5 M(L1,1), M(L1,2), M(L1,3), M(L1,4)
238 NEXT L1
239 REM
240 REM
250 REM          READ A TRANSACTION RECORD
260 REM
270 INPUT #2 I,R,V
280 REM
290 REM          READ A MASTER RECORD
300 REM
310 INPUT #1 N,D,N$,M,H,E,G,F,F1
320 REM
330 REM          COMPARE ID'S
340 REM
350 IF I=N THEN 410
360 IF I>N THEN 310
370 IF I<N THEN 750
380 REM
390 REM          ID'S MATCH -- DO COMPUTATIONS FOR UPDATE
400 REM
405 REM CALCULATE GROSS PAY
406 REM
410 G1=(R*H)+(V*H*1.5)
411 REM
412 REM CALCULATE SOCIAL SECURITY
413 REM
414 F3 = 0
415 REM
416 REM SOCIAL SECURITY IS ZERO IF YTD GROSS OVER 22,900
417 REM
418 IF G > 22900 THEN 433
419 REM
420 REM SOCIAL SECURITY IS 0.0613 OF WEEKLY GROSS
421 REM IF YTD GROSS + WEEKLY GROSS LESS THAN 22900
422 REM
423 IF G+G1 > 22900 THEN 429
424 F3 = G1*0.0613
425 GO TO 433
426 REM SOCIAL SECURITY IS 0.0613 OF DIFFERENCE
427 REM BETWEEN 22,900 AND YTD GROSS
428 REM
429 F3 = (22900-G) * 0.0613
430 REM
431 REM CALCULATE TAXABLE INCOME BY SUBTRACTING EXEMPTIONS
432 REM
433 T = G1 - E*19.23
```

```
434 REM
435 REM DETERMINE TAX TABLE
436 REM
437 IF M =2 THEN 452
438 REM
439 REM M IS 1; FIND ROW IN SINGLE TABLE
440 REM
441 FOR R1 = 1 TO 8
442     IF T <= S(R1,2) THEN 447
443 NEXT R1
444 REM
445 REM CALCULATE TAX
446 REM
447 F2 = S(R1,3) + (T-S(R1,1))*S(R1,4)
448 GO TO 462
449 REM
450 REM M IS 2; FIND ROW IN MARRID TABLE
451 REM
452 FOR R1 = 1 TO 8
453     IF T <= M(R1,2) THEN 458
454 NEXT R1
455 REM
456 REM CALCULATE TAX
457 REM
458 F2 = M(R1,3) + (T-M(R1,1))*M(R1,4)
459 REM
460 REM CALCULATE NET PAY
461 REM
462 P = G1 - F2 - F3
463 REM
464 REM ADD WEEKLY GROSS, FIT AND FICA TO YTD TOTALS
465 REM
466 G = G + G1
467 F = F + F2
470 F1=F1+F3
480 P1=P1+P
490 REM
500 REM          PRINT UPDATED MASTER RECORD
510 REM
520 PRINT #3 N;",";D;",";N$;",";M;",";H;",";E;",";G;",";F;",";F1
530 REM
540 REM          PRINT ID,NAME,NET PAY
550 REM
560 PRINT USING"  ###     \          \ ####.##      ####.##      ####.##
    #####.##"N,N$,G1,F2,F3,P
570 REM
580 REM          READ A TRANSACTION RECORD
590 REM
600 INPUT #2 I,R,V
610 GO TO 350
620 REM
630 REM          *** ERROR CHECK ***
640 REM
650 IF ERR=11 THEN RESUME 690
660 PRINT "UNUSUAL ERROR",ERR
670 CLOSE #1,#2,#3,#4,#5
680 STOP
690 IF ERL=600 THEN 780
700 IF ERL=910 THEN 940
710 STOP
720 REM
730 REM          MISSING MASTER RECORD
740 REM
750 PRINT "MASTER RECORD MISSING FOR EMPLOYEE NUMBER",I
760 CLOSE #1,#2,#3
770 STOP
780 CLOSE #1,#2,#3
790 REM
800 REM          PRINT OUT OF UPDATED MASTER FILE
```

```
810 REM
820 PRINT
830 PRINT
840 PRINT
850 PRINT
860 PRINT "                                UPDATED MASTER FILE"
870 PRINT
880 OPEN "EMPMA1" FOR INPUT AS FILE #4
890 PRINT "EMPLOYEE   DEPT   NAME       MARITAL    HOURLY  EX-    YTD          YT
D       YTD"
900 PRINT "NUMBER                       STATUS     RATE    EMP    GROSS        FI
T       FICA"
910 INPUT #4 N,D,N$,M,H,E,G,F,F1
920 PRINT USING "  ###        ##   \          \ #        ##.##     #   #####.##
  ####.## ####.##"N,D,N$,M,H,E,G,F,F1
930 GO TO 910
940 CLOSE #4
950 STOP
32767 END
```

EMPLOYEE NUMBER	NAME	GROSS PAY	FIT	FICA	NET
101	ADAMS	200.00	14.91	12.26	172.83
103	BAKER	257.60	37.31	15.79	204.50
104	BRAVO	172.00	7.36	10.54	154.09
108	COHEN	237.50	18.19	14.56	204.75
172	JOHNSON	150.00	21.63	9.20	119.18
198	TANNER	153.00	4.51	9.38	139.11
202	WILSON	160.00	2.68	9.81	147.52
206	LESTER	210.00	16.71	12.87	180.42
255	SCHMIDT	257.60	18.35	15.79	223.46
281	MILLER	240.00	18.64	14.71	206.64
313	SMITH	195.50	14.10	11.98	169.42
347	GRAY	228.00	19.95	13.98	194.08
368	WEAVER	150.50	17.70	9.23	123.58
422	WILLIAMS	160.00	11.33	9.81	138.86

UPDATED MASTER FILE

EMPLOYEE NUMBER	DEPT	NAME	MARITAL STATUS	HOURLY RATE	EX-EMP	YTD GROSS	YTD FIT	YTD FICA
101	1	ADAMS	2	5.00	3	1200.00	214.91	73.56
103	12	BAKER	1	5.60	2	1545.60	294.91	94.75
104	17	BRAVO	2	4.00	4	1032.00	179.36	63.26
108	16	COHEN	2	6.25	4	1425.00	255.69	87.35
172	2	JOHNSON	1	3.75	0	900.00	171.63	55.17
198	1	TANNER	2	4.25	4	918.00	157.51	56.27
202	16	WILSON	2	4.00	5	960.00	162.68	58.85
206	7	LESTER	2	5.25	3	1260.00	226.71	77.24
255	12	SCHMIDT	2	5.60	5	1545.60	275.95	94.75
281	12	MILLER	2	6.00	4	1440.00	258.64	88.27
313	7	SMITH	2	4.25	3	1173.00	209.60	71.00
347	12	GRAY	2	6.00	3	1368.00	247.95	83.96
368	1	WEAVER	1	3.50	1	903.00	168.20	55.35
422	1	WILLIAMS	2	4.00	2	960.00	171.33	58.85

```
Stop at line 950
```

The key statements for the table reference are in lines 452–454 for married employees and in lines 441–443 for single employees, where the appropriate row of the table is found. But before we can discuss that, let's look at how the tables were set up in line 234–238.

First, line 234 reserves the space for two tables: S for single and M for married employees. Each table consists of eight rows and four columns. According to the tax tables of the Internal Revenue Service, each row corresponds to a range of income. The columns of the table are as follows:

- Column 1: the low end of the weekly income range
- Column 2: the upper end
- Column 3: the taxes up to the low end
- Column 4: the tax rate for anything above the low end (but below the high end of the range)

Then in lines 235–238 the tables are filled. The field L1 stands for the row number. It is assigned the values 1 through 8 successively by the FOR-NEXT statement. For each value of L1, the four columns of each table are input. So if L1 is 1, then the first row is filled. When L1 is two, the second row of the tables S and M is given values. Once all eight rows are filled, we exit from the loop and start to process the employee records.

Now we can see how to work with these tables. The taxable income has already been computed when we arrived at line 437. The statement in 437 checks whether the single person or married person tax table has to be used. Depending on this test, we go either to line 441 for a single person or to line 452 for a married person.

The taxable income tells us what row of the table is used for the tax calculation. Hence taxable income is compared to the upper end of an income range. Because the ranges are in ascending order, each row holds the data for a weekly income that is less than the upper end of that row, but greater than the upper end of the earlier rows. Since the rows are checked starting with the lowest income, as long as taxable income is greater than the upper end of a range, we have not yet reached the correct row of the table.

Once the right row has been found, then we can use the row number R1 to calculate the taxes. Line 458 calculates the tax for married employees and line 447 calculates the tax for single employees.

Besides the table reference, this program also contains one other complication—the social security calculation. Actually, there is nothing new in lines 414–429; it's just cumbersome because we have to follow the rules of the Internal Revenue Service. All the conditions make it awkward to follow the calculations. The program handles three conditions:

1. Year-to-date greater than $22,900; in which case no social security is calculated (determined in line 418).

2. Year-to-date plus weekly wages less than $22,900; where all of the weekly wages are subject to social security (calculated in line 424).

3. Year-to-date less than $22,900, but year-to-date plus weekly wages greater than $22,900; here the difference between $22,900 and the year-to-date is subject to a social security deduction. (That deduction is calculated in line 429.)

Of course, the actual payroll calculation for a real firm would have many more deductions. Not included in this example are deductions for health insurance, pension plans, payroll savings plans, state and local taxes where required, union dues, etc. But from this example you can appreciate what is needed to do payroll calculations.

Look at the other example that follows.

Example

Inventory Report: Some industries experience rapid price fluctuations. When prices fluctuate rapidly, it is often convenient to establish and maintain separate price tables for parts in inventory. Table 8–3 shows the price table for the parts in inventory.

Table 8–3

Inventory Price Table

Part Number	*Price*
101	5.25
110	7.00
219	3.25
226	3.10
235	6.20
247	4.85

Management has asked for a report that shows the dollar value of issues and receipts by part number. The issues and receipts are in the transaction file "INVTR".

Problem Summary

Input

"INVTR" file

Price table file, "INVPRC"

Processing

Accumulate subtotals and totals for the dollar amounts issued and received by part number and for the file as a whole.

Output

An inventory report, giving by part number the dollar amount of issues and the dollar amount of receipts.

```
100 REM  PROGRAM TO PRICE ISSUES AND RECEIPTS
101 REM
102 REM  HEADINGS FOR REPORT
103 PRINT
104 PRINT
105 PRINT "      RECEIPTS AND ISSUES REPORT"
106 PRINT
107 PRINT "  PART          RECEIPTS           ISSUES"
110 REM
120 REM          LINK TO FILES
```

```
130 REM
140 OPEN "INVTR" FOR INPUT AS FILE #1
150 OPEN "INVPRC" FOR INPUT AS FILE #2
160 REM
170 REM          SET UP PRICE TABLE AND GET DATA FROM INVPRC
180 REM
190 DIM P(6,2)
200 R=0
210 ON ERROR GO TO 770
220 INPUT #2, N,D
230 R=R+1
240 P(R,1) = N
250 P(R,2) = D
260 GO TO 220
270 REM
280 REM          READ AN INVENTORY TRANSACTION
290 REM
300 INPUT #1, P1, T1, Q1
310 REM
320 REM          SET P9 TO PART NUMBER FOR LATER COMPARISON
330 REM
340 P9 = P1
350 REM
360 REM          DETERMINE PRICE OF PART BY COMPARING P1 TO
370 REM          COLUMN 1 OF TABLE P
380 REM
390 FOR R = 1 TO 6
400 IF P1 = P(R,1) THEN 450
410 NEXT R
420 REM
430 REM          DETERMINE WHETHER TRANSACTION IS SHIPMENT OR RECEIPT
440 REM
450 IF T1 = 2 THEN 540
460 REM
470 REM          RECEIPT: T1 = 1
480 REM
490 R1 = R1 + Q1*P(R,2)
500 GO TO 580
510 REM
520 REM          SHIPMENT: T1 = 2
530 REM
540 S1 = S1 + Q1*P(R,2)
550 REM
560 REM          READ NEXT TRANSACTION
570 REM
580 INPUT #1, P1, T1, Q1
590 REM
600 REM          CHECK WHETHER IT'S THE SAME PART AS BEFORE
610 REM
620 IF P1 = P9 THEN 390
630 REM
640 REM          PRINT OUT OLD PART NUMBER, RECEIPTS, AND SHIPMENTS
650 REM
660 PRINT USING "  ###        #####.##          #####.##"P9,R1,S1
670 REM
680 REM          SET RECEIPT AND SHIPMENT ACCUMULATORS TO ZERO
690 REM          AND PROCESS TRANSACTION
700 REM
710 R1 = 0
720 S1 = 0
730 GO TO 340
740 REM
750 REM          ERROR CHECKING ROUTINE
760 REM
770 IF ERR = 11 THEN RESUME 780
780 IF ERL = 220 THEN 300
790 IF ERL = 580 THEN 800
800 CLOSE #1, #2
32767 END
```

```
RECEIPTS AND ISSUES REPORT

PART         RECEIPTS         ISSUES
101          787.50           813.75
219            0.00            65.00
226          542.50           279.00
235            0.00           186.00
```

The program INVREP generates a report of receipts and shipments by part number from the "INVTR" file. INVREP performs the following tasks:

1. It links to files "INVTR" and "INVPRC" (statements 140 and 150).
2. It reserves room for the price table (statement 190).
3. It gets a part number and a price from "INVPRC" and assigns it to the price table (statements 200–260).
4. It reads the first inventory transaction from "INVTR" (statement 300).
5. It "remembers" the part number (statement 340).
6. It processes the transaction:
   a. It determines which row of the price table has the same part number (statements 390–410).
   b. It determines whether the transaction is a shipment or a receipt (statement 450).
      (1) It accumulates the dollar amount of receipts (statement 490).
      (2) It accumulates the dollar amount of shipments (statement 540).
7. It reads the next transaction (statement 580).
8. If the part number of this transaction is the same as the part number on a prior transaction, then repeat steps 6 and 7 (statement 620).
9. If the part number of this transaction is not the same as the part number of a prior transaction, then print the prior part number receipts and shipments (statement 660); set accumulators for receipts and shipments to zero (statements 710 and 720) and perform steps 5, 6 and 7.
10. It terminates when out of transaction data.

The table reference in this example is in step 6. Let's look at it again to see the details of its operation. The price table P looks as follows:

	Column	
Row	*1*	*2*
1	101	5.25
2	110	7.00
3	219	3.35
4	226	3.10
5	235	6.20
6	247	4.85

Now let's take the first transaction:

Part Number	*Transaction Code*	*Quantity*
101	1	150

The FOR-NEXT loop starts R at 1. So in line 400 when we compare the part number (P1) to column 1 of the table, we have a match. Therefore we skip out of the loop (R is still 1 since it was not changed) and use this row number to calculate the dollar value of the receipt in line 490.

That example was too easy. Take another transaction:

Part Number	*Transaction Code*	*Quantity*
226	2	90

Again R starts at 1 in line 390. The comparison between P1 (the part number) and the table P (Row 1, Column 1) shows they are not equal. Therefore we come to the NEXT R statement in 410. A one is added to R: R is now 2; and the comparison in line 400 is between P1 (value of 226) and row 2, column 1 of table P (value of 110). Again, they are not equal.

Notice that as R is changed, from 1 to 2, to 3, to 4, the program skips down the first column of P. At each value of R the next row of the table is used in the comparison. Once the proper row has been found, the row number (R) is used with the second column of P to calculate the dollar value of a transaction, either in line 490 or in line 540.

SORTING LISTS AND TABLES

Sometimes we must change the order of a small amount of data. For example, we might want a listing of our employees by descending order of gross pay for labor negotiations. Or we might want product lines in ascending order of sales. Or we might want to rank our customers by volume of sales.

Sorting of files has already been mentioned. Appendix B has the sorts needed. But sometimes the data is in lists or tables, not on a file, and we need to sort it.

Let's assume that we need a list of employees in descending order of net pay. The net pay of the employees has already been calculated in the revised employee payroll program. But the output from that program is in employee number sequence. Our need is in descending order of net pay.

Problem Summary

Input

Employee number
Employee name
Weekly net pay

Processing

Store the fields in lists. Sort by weekly net pay (in descending order).

Output

Print employee name and number in descending order of pay.

The program therefore has to:

1. Get the employee data and put it into lists.
2. Sort the list into descending order of net pay.
3. Print the sorted data.
4. Terminate.

A program that performs these tasks is shown below:

```
100 REM PROGRAM TO SORT LISTS
110 REM
120 REM SET UP LISTS TO HOLD DATA
130 REM
140 DIM N(100),N$(100),P(100)
150 REM
160 REM GET THE DATA FROM THE TERMINAL AND PLACE IT INTO
170 REM THE LISTS
180 REM
190 L=0
200 PRINT "TYPE EMPLOYEE NUMBER, EMPLOYEE NAME"
210 PRINT "AND NET PAY - SEPARATED BY COMMAS"
220 PRINT "WHEN FINISHED - TYPE 99,AA,99"
230 INPUT N1,M$,P1
240 IF N1 = 99 THEN 340
260 L = L+1
270 N(L) = N1
280 N$(L) = M$
290 P(L) = P1
300 GO TO 230
310 REM
320 REM SORT THE DATA
330 REM
340 U = L-1
350 F = 0
360 FOR K = 1 TO U
370 REM COMPARE TWO CONSECUTIVE VALUES
380 REM IF THEY ARE NOT IN ORDER, THEN EXCHANGE
390 IF P(K) >= P(K+1) THEN 600
400 REM
410 REM VALUES OUT OF SEQUENCE, HENCE EXCHANGE
420 REM
430 T = P(K)
440 P(K) = P(K+1)
450 P(K+1) = T
460 REM
470 REM EXCHANGE NAME AND ID ALSO TO KEEP THEM
480 REM AND RATES TOGETHER
490 REM
500 T = N(K)
510 N(K) = N(K+1)
520 N(K+1) = T
530 T$=N$(K)
540 N$(K) = N$(K+1)
550 N$(K+1) = T$
560 REM
570 REM SET F TO INDICATE THAT AN EXCHANGE HAS OCCURRED
580 REM
```

```
590 F = 1
600 NEXT K
610 REM
620 REM CHECK IF ANY EXCHANGES HAVE OCCURRED
630 REM
640 IF F = 1 THEN 350
650 REM
660 REM END OF SORT
670 REM
680 REM PRINT OUT LISTS WITH HEADINGS
690 REM
700 PRINT "EMPLOYEE", "EMPLOYEE", "WEEKLY"
710 PRINT "NUMBER", "NAME", "PAY"
730 FOR K = 1 TO L
740 PRINT N(K), N$(K), P(K)
750 NEXT K
770 STOP
32767 END
```

```
TYPE EMPLOYEE NUMBER, EMPLOYEE NAME
AND NET PAY - SEPARATED BY COMMAS
WHEN FINISHED - TYPE 99,AA,99
? 101,ADAMS,172.70
? 103,BAKER,204.50
? 104,BRAVO,154.09
? 108,COHEN,204.44
? 172,JOHNSON,119.18
? 198,TANNER,139.11
? 202,WILSON,147.51
? 206,LESTER,180.19
? 255,SCHMIDT,223.15
? 281,MILLER,206.32
? 313,SMITH,169.32
? 347,GRAY,193.69
? 368,WEAVER,123.58
? 422,WILLIAMS,138.86
? 99,AA,99
EMPLOYEE        EMPLOYEE        WEEKLY
NUMBER          NAME            PAY
 255            SCHMIDT          223.15
 281            MILLER           206.32
 103            BAKER            204.5
 108            COHEN            204.44
 347            GRAY             193.69
 206            LESTER           180.19
 101            ADAMS            172.7
 313            SMITH            169.32
 104            BRAVO            154.09
 202            WILSON           147.51
 198            TANNER           139.11
 422            WILLIAMS         138.86
 368            WEAVER           123.58
 172            JOHNSON          119.18
Stop at line 770
```

This program puts data into lists in lines 190–300. Then it sorts the lists in lines 340 to 640. Finally, it prints out the lists in lines 700 to 750. Let's look at each of these actions in turn.

The storage of data starts by setting the field L to zero. L will be used in lines 270 through 290 to indicate the location in a list. Notice that the lists have 100 spaces each (the dimension is set in line 140), although fewer spaces will be needed for our data.

Then line 230 gets the first record for the file. The program adds 1 to L in line 260. L is now 1. Hence in lines 270–290, the first (L value of 1) location of N, N$, and P is filled with the values of N1, M$ and P1 respectively.

Line 300 takes us back to the input of data. As long as there are records in the file, the program reads the data; adds one to L; and places the desired fields into successive locations in the lists. At the end of the data input, L will contain the number of records; L is also the highest position in the lists that has been filled with data.

Lines 340 to 640 sort the data into descending order of weekly pay. The sort is finished when all items are in order. It works by comparing two adjacent positions in the pay list. If they are in sequence, we compare the next two positions. But if two adjacent positions are out of sequence, they are first placed in the proper sequence before the next two positions are compared.

We know that all items are in their proper sequence if we do not have to interchange any items. Whether an interchange has occurred is shown by an indicator (a "flag" called F in the program). The indicator is set to zero at the beginning of each pass through the array. When an interchange occurs, it is set to one. Therefore if the indicator is one, we don't know yet that the lists are in their desired sequence. Line 640 tests F, and if F is one, we repeat the process.

We can see the operations of this sort by looking at the first five records of the lists. These records would be in the lists N, N$ and P as follows:

	List		
Position	*N*	*N$*	*P*
1	101	Adams	172.83
2	103	Baker	204.50
3	104	Bravo	154.09
4	108	Cohen	204.75
5	172	Johnson	119.18

Now let's start through the steps of the sort. First, U, a field to hold the upper limit for the comparisons, will be 4. Therefore K, the loop index, will take on values 1 to 4 in turn. Line 350 sets F to zero, because at this stage no exchanges have occurred. Then K is set to 1, and we compare the K (first) position and K + 1 (second) position in the net pay list. They are out of sequence. P(2) is $204.50, and P(1) is $172.83. To put them in proper order, Baker should come before Adams. Hence lines 430 to 450 interchange the values.

Notice that an interchange is a three-step process. If we tried it in two steps, it wouldn't work:

```
P (K) = P (K + 1)
P (K + 1) = P (K)
```

Why not? Because the computer is a sequential machine. For a K value of 1, the following would happen in the two-step process: Step 1: P (K) = P (K + 1). This means P (1) = P (2) and after the assignment the first two positions of P would look as follows:

Position 1	204.50
Position 2	204.50

Because we put the value from position 2 into the first position, they are both identical. The value in the first position is lost, wiped out, erased. And the second step would put a 204.50 into position 2 again.

The three-step process works, because it puts the value for the first position temporarily somewhere else–in T. Now when a value is placed into P (K), we still have its old value in T as shown below:

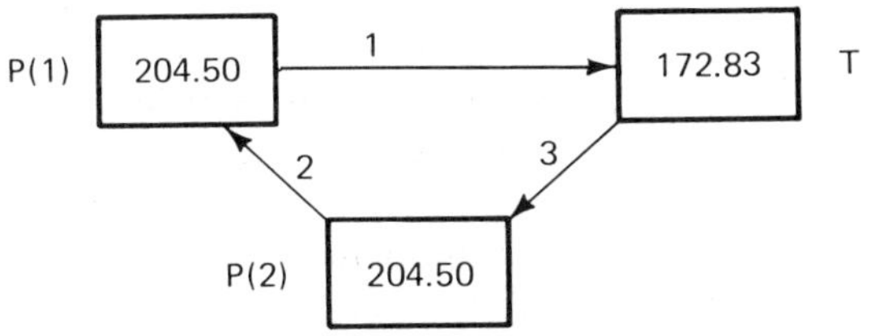

The numbers on the arrows give the sequence in which the assignments have to occur to do the exchange.

At the end of line 450, our lists would look as follows:

N	*N$*	*P*
101	Adams	204.50
103	Baker	172.83
104	Bravo	154.09
108	Cohen	204.75
172	Johnson	119.18

As you can see the net pays are in order, but they are not with the right employee name and number. Lines 500–550 interchange the names and ID numbers so that the list will look like this:

N	*N$*	*P*
103	Baker	204.50
101	Adams	172.83
104	Bravo	154.09
108	Cohen	204.75
172	Johnson	119.18

Then line 590 sets F to 1 because an interchange has occurred and we are ready for the next K value.

When K is 2, the second (Kth) and third positions of P are compared. They are already in sequence. Therefore we go to the next K value.

When K is 3, we compare the third and fourth position. They are out of sequence. Therefore we interchange and our list would look as follows before the next K value is executed:

N	*N$*	*P*
103	Baker	204.50
101	Adams	172.83
108	Cohen	204.75
104	Bravo	154.09
172	Johnson	119.18

When K is 4, the comparison between the fourth (Kth) and fifth (K + 1) values of P shows that they are in sequence.

Since K has now reached its upper limit (the value of U), the looping is finished. But a check with F (in line 640) shows that at least one exchange has occurred. Since the lists may not be in sequence, the program sends us back to 350 for another pass through the data.

At the end of the second pass (K value of 1, 2, 3 and 4), the lists would look as follows:

N	*N$*	*P*
103	Baker	204.50
108	Cohen	204.75
101	Adams	172.83
104	Bravo	154.09
172	Johnson	119.18

It takes one more pass to get the data in order and another to assure us that no more interchanges are needed. Then we know that the lists are in the desired sequence.

Notice that the sequence of the items is basically defined by the test in line 390. In this example, the contents of two adjacent positions in the list are compared to see if they are in descending sequence.

It is important that two equal values *not* be exchanged. If the test in 390 was just *greater than* (as opposed to the actual *greater than or equal*), then two values that were equal would be exchanged. And they would be exchanged again in the next pass. And the next. And the next. And the next. In fact, the exchanges would never end.

A situation like that, called an infinite loop, can cost you a lot in computer time. Therefore care must be taken to avoid infinite loops. In this case, the test must be a *greater than or equal,* or *less than or equal,* so that an infinite loop is not generated.

SUMMARY

This chapter has discussed the use of lists and tables. Lists and tables are convenient ways to hold data either for subsequent processing or for output after processing.

In the first example, a list was used to accumulate departmental totals. To use the list, space for the list had to be reserved and labelled. To access individual elements of the list, subscripts giving the location of a position in a list had to be used.

Tables are different from lists, because two subscripts are needed—a row indicator and a column indicator. Two tables were used to determine income taxes for the employees.

Besides lists and tables, this chapter also presented a way to perform looping. The FOR-NEXT construction lets you control how often a set of BASIC statements would be executed.

BASIC Instructions Introduced:

Statement	*Explanation*
DIM Y(X),Z(Q,R)	Sets the lists Y (represented by a letter) to X positions. Defines that Z (represented by a letter) has Q rows and R columns. Individual elements of lists and tables are identified by their location: the position number in a list or the row number *and* column number in a table.
FOR Y = N TO M : NEXT Y	Sets up a loop. The FOR statement begins the loop. It sets Y to N (beginning value); the loop will continue until Y has a value greater than M (the upper bound). The NEXT statement closes the loop.

PROBLEMS

1. Write a program that will generate a summary report of inventory by department from the "INV" file (see Chapter 5). Use a list to hold the inventory cost by department.

2. A machine shop has seven machines. When an order for a part arrives, the sequence in which any of the seven machines will be used is determined. To make a part requires four of the seven machines. The time in minutes for each machine to make a part is shown below:

Machine	*Time*
1	20
2	30
3	12
4	26
5	32
6	17
7	14

   a. Write a program to store the data as a table in the "MCHTM" file.
   b. The data regarding orders will be input from a terminal. Order data consists of an order number and the numbers of the machines in the required sequence to make the part. The following orders have arrived:

Order Number	*Machine Sequence*
7442	2,4,5,6
7443	1,5,3,7
7444	1,6,5,4
7445	1,3,6,7

   Write a program that will input the "MCHTM" file and the order data; then print the order number and the total time required to process that order.

3. In Problem 2, the time required to transport the orders from one machine to another has been neglected. Modify your program to take transportation times into account in determining the total time to process an order. The transportation times in minutes are as follows:

		To Machine						
		1	*2*	*3*	*4*	*5*	*6*	*7*
	1	0	15	23	7	16	5	19
	2	12	0	16	9	12	17	5
From	*3*	25	14	0	12	17	12	18
Machine	*4*	8	12	13	0	9	8	14
	5	19	14	15	11	0	12	10
	6	7	15	10	10	15	0	9
	7	17	8	14	18	12	13	0

Write a program to store the transportation times as a table in the "TRTM" file and modify your program in Problem 2 to include transportation time. Use the same order data as in Problem 2.

4. Change the sort program in this chapter (page 194) so that it will sort in ascending order. Use the net pay data to test the program.

9 / Using Direct Access Files

Performance Objectives

At the end of this chapter you should be able to:

- Create virtual files
- Read and print virtual files
- Change field values in a virtual record
- Update master records in a virtual file
- Query records in a virtual file

So far, sequential files have been used exclusively for all problems, exercises, and examples. There is one major drawback in using sequential files—every time you want to read any record in a file you must start with the first record and read each record until the desired record is reached. If a file has 20,000 records, and you want to print the 19,995th record, 19,995 records would have to be read to reach the record to be printed. A great deal of time would be wasted reading and testing every record until the one to be printed is reached. The time to reach a record in a sequential file is proportional to the position of the record (first, middle, last) in the file.

You may still wonder why a few seconds may be important. A sequential file of 20,000 records with the same fields as "EMPLOY" was created to test the time required to find and print a record. It took less than a second to read and print the first record. It took over six minutes to read and print the 19,995th record!

In the early days of computers, only sequential files were available. But to reduce the time required to find a record, direct access files were developed. All direct access files share one characteristic—the time to find any record in a file is constant. With direct access files, there is a method to find a record without reading from the beginning of a file.

CREATING A VIRTUAL FILE

There is more than one way to create and use direct access files in BASIC. The simplest method is called virtual core. It follows the techniques of Chapter 8 where lists and tables were discussed. We shall create a virtual file in almost the same manner as a table is created. An inventory example will be used throughout this chapter to illustrate the use of virtual (direct access) files.

The data for the inventory master file are found in Table 9–1. Note that the part number and the record number are the same! In an actual business, the part number would be a multi-digit number within which the record number would exist or be added to the existing part number after a dash. For example, part number 27364–001 could indicate that part 27364 is record number one. There are other more sophisticated ways of obtaining record numbers from part numbers; but they are beyond the introductory level of this book.

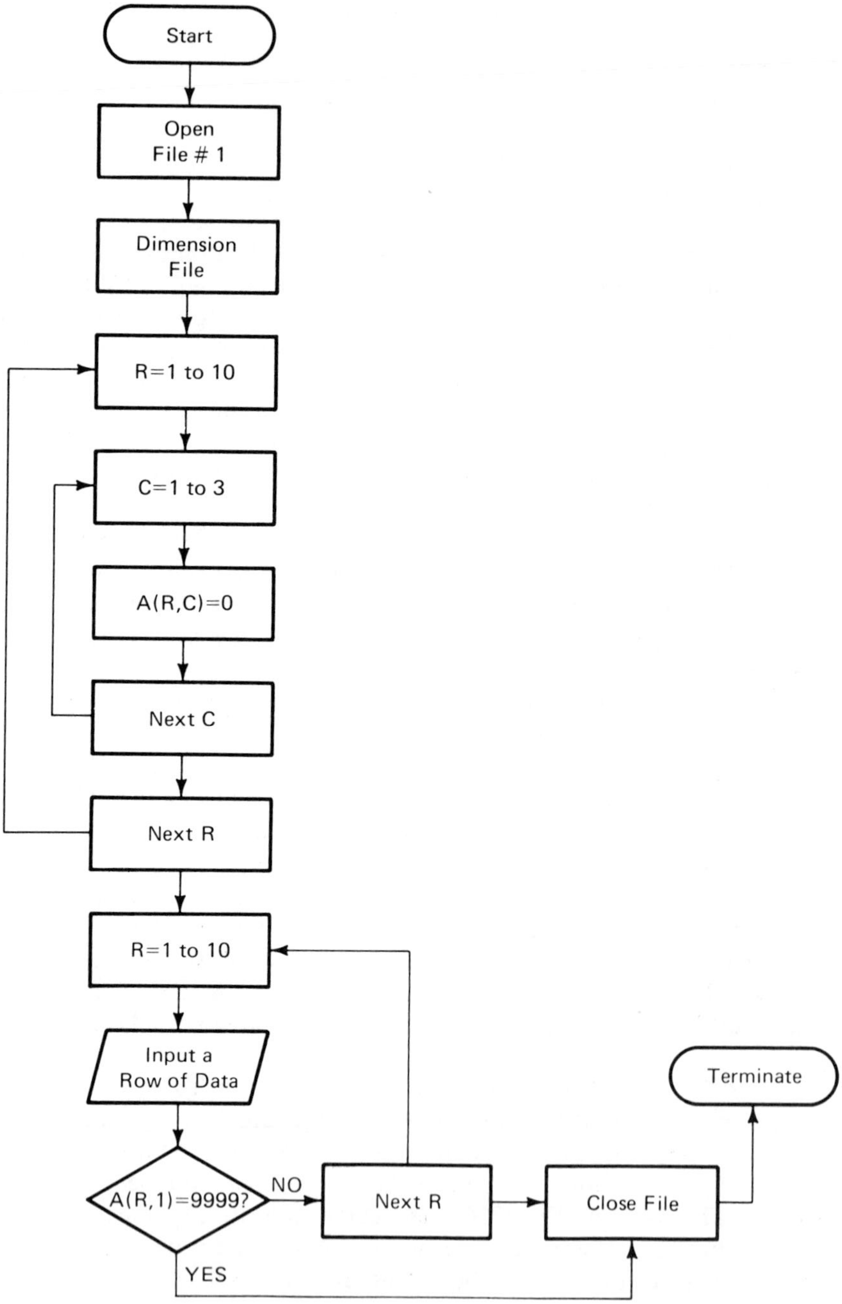

Figure 9–1 Flowchart to Create a Virtual File

Table 9–1

Inventory Master File—"INVMST"

Part Number	Stock on Hand	Unit Cost
1	590	1.50
2	750	2.75
3	231	1.39
4	395	5.96
5	674	7.23
6	279	6.79
7	942	4.26
8	27	5.49
9	152	1.26
10	420	3.74

Problem Summary

Input
Inventory master file.

Processing
Input the data at execution time.

Output
Instructions for input and a virtual file, "INVMST".

The program consists of the following steps:

1. Link to the virtual file.
2. Dimension the virtual file.
3. Initialize all the fields in the virtual file.
4. Input the data.
5. Stop when all the data has been entered.

See the flowchart (Fig. 9–1). A program to perform all of these steps is below:

```
100 REM          THIS PROGRAM CREATES A VIRTUAL FILE
110 REM          AND INPUTS THE DATA
120 REM
130 REM
140 REM          OPEN THE VIRTUAL FILE
150 REM
160 OPEN "INVMST" AS FILE #1
170 REM
180 REM          DIMENSION VIRTUAL FILE AND SET LAST ELEMENT TO ZERO
190 REM
200 DIM #1, A(10,3)=0
210 REM
220 REM          SET ALL VALUES TO ZERO
230 REM             R INDEX IS ROW NUMBER
240 REM             C INDEX IS COLUMN NUMBER
250 REM
```

```
260 FOR R=1 TO 10
270 FOR C=1 TO 3
280 A(R,C)=0
290 NEXT C
300 NEXT R
310 REM
320 REM          INPUT THE FILE (TABLE) VALUES ROW BY ROW
330 REM
340 FOR R=1 TO 10
350 PRINT "TYPE PART NUMBER,STOCK ON HAND,UNIT COST,TO END TYPE 9999,0,0
"
360 INPUT A(R,1),A(R,2),A(R,3)
370 IF A(R,1)=9999 GO TO 420
380 NEXT R
390 REM
400 REM          FINISH
410 REM
420 CLOSE #1
430 STOP
32767 END
```

Before discussing the program, there is a very important concept that must be understood. The creation of a virtual file results in a table. The rows of the table correspond to records in a file. The columns of the table correspond to fields in a record. In the explanations that follow, the terms virtual file and table may be interchanged. The virtual file is a direct access file because the value in any field may be retrieved by a row and column number without any read or input statement. It is exactly the same as retrieving values from a table.

In line 160 the file is opened using the usual OPEN instruction. The dimension statement in line 200 is different from prior dimension statements. The file number follows DIM, then the Table A is defined as ten rows and three columns and at the same time, the last element of Table A (row ten, column 3) is assigned the value zero. This is done in order to reserve all the space necessary for Table A. In a virtual file, unless the last is given a value upon dimensioning, all of the space necessary will not be reserved until data is put into all the elements. In lines 260 through 300 every element in Table A is assigned the value zero. This is done to eliminate any other data that may exist in the space assigned to A.

	Column		
Row	1	2	3
1	1	590	1.50
2	2	750	2.75
3	3	231	1.39
4	4	395	5.96
5	5	674	7.23
6	6	279	6.79
7	7	942	4.26
8	8	27	5.49
9	9	152	1.26
10	10	420	3.74

Table A (10,3)

Figure 9–2 The Virtual File—"INVMST"

Next the data is input and tested for the end of data input in lines 340 through 380. The data is entered one row (record) at a time. Finally, the file is closed and the program ends.

Upon completion of the data input, you have set up and stored the virtual file "INVMST" as if it were a table. The terms virtual file and virtual table are interchangeable. The file looks like Figure 9–2.

READING AND PRINTING A VIRTUAL FILE

The program to read and print out the inventory master file is given below. It is a very simple program.

```
100 REM
110 REM          THIS PROGRAM READS AND PRINTS THE VIRTUAL FILE INVMST
120 REM
130 REM
140 REM          PRINT HEADINGS FOR PRINTOUT
150 REM
160 PRINT "PART      STOCK     UNIT"
170 PRINT "NUMBER    ON HAND   COST"
180 REM
190 REM          DIMENSION VIRTUAL FILE
200 REM
210 DIM #1,A(10,3)
220 REM
230 REM          OPEN VIRTUAL FILE
240 REM
250 OPEN "INVMST" AS FILE #1
260 REM
270 REM          PRINT OUT VIRTUAL FILE
280 REM            L INDEX IS ROW NUMBER
290 REM
300 FOR L=1 TO 10
310 PRINT USING "###      ####      ##.##"A(L,1),A(L,2),A(L,3)
320 NEXT L
330 REM
340 REM          FINISH
350 REM
360 CLOSE #1
32767 END
```

In lines 160 and 170 the headings for the output are printed. In line 210 the table is dimensioned. The last element of the table is *not* assigned the value zero. A zero value is assigned *only* for the creation of the file. Next, the file is opened. The DIM and OPEN statements need not be in any order (either may appear first), but they should precede any operations on the data in the file. Lines 300 through 320 print the file, row by row. You may wonder why no read or input statement is necessary, as when you read and print a sequential file. The answer is that you have implicitly read all the data in the file when you opened it. This is one of the features of a virtual file.

CHANGING VALUES IN A VIRTUAL FILE

It is necessary to change values in an inventory master record due to price changes and adjustments. The stock on hand has to be adjusted because a manual count of stock on hand just took place. The following records have to be adjusted for stock on hand or cost.

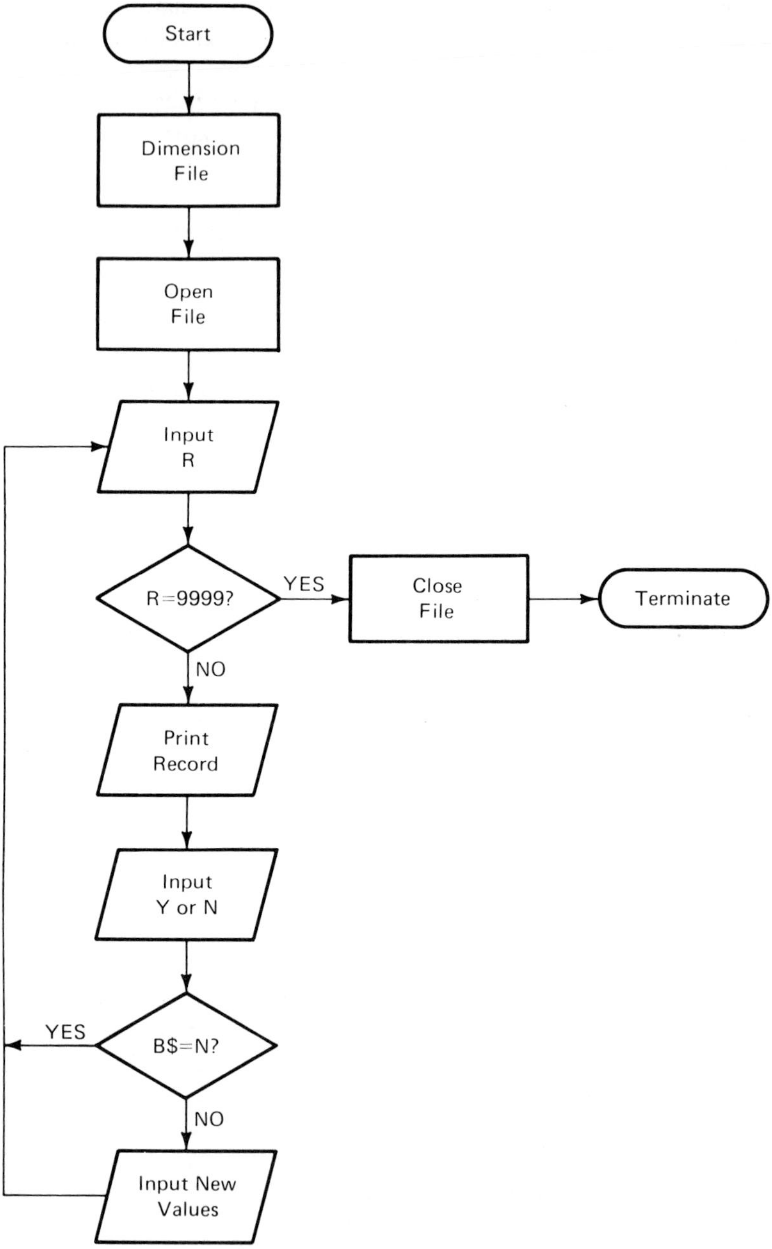

Figure 9–3 Flowchart for Changing a Record

Changes to the Inventory Master File

Table 9–2

Part Number	*Stock on Hand*	*Unit Cost*
1	600	2.00
9	152	1.40
6	230	7.00
3	231	1.50
10	500	4.00
5	674	7.25

Since "INVMST" is a direct access file, you do not have to order the changes by record (part) number.

Problem Summary

Input

Inventory master file, "INVMST"

Processing

Find the record to be changed. Input the new values.

Output

The inventory master file, "INVMST", with the appropriate records changed.

See the flowchart (Fig 9–3). A program follows:

```
100 REM
110 REM THIS PROGRAM CHANGES VALUES IN A RECORD
120 REM
130 REM           DIMENSION VIRTUAL FILE
140 REM
150 DIM #1,A(10,3)
160 REM
170 REM           OPEN VIRTUAL FILE
180 REM
190 OPEN "INVMST" AS FILE #1
200 REM
210 REM           INPUT RECORD NUMBER (PART NUMBER)
220 REM
230 PRINT "WHAT IS THE RECORD NUMBER? TYPE 9999 TO END"
240 INPUT R
250 REM
260 REM           TEST FOR END OF INPUT
270 REM
280 IF R=9999 GO TO 550
290 REM
300 REM           PRINT OUT RECORD
310 REM
320 PRINT "IS THIS THE RECORD TO BE CHANGED?
330 PRINT USING "###     ####     ##.##"A(R,1),A(R,2),A(R,3)
340 REM
350 REM           IS THIS THE CORRECT RECORD?
360 REM
370 PRINT "TYPE Y IF YES, N IF NO"
380 INPUT B$
390 REM
400 REM           IF NOT CORRECT RECORD GO BACK TO INPUT
```

```
410 REM
420 IF B$="N" GO TO 230
430 REM
440 REM          CORRECT RECORD -- INPUT NEW VALUES
450 REM
460 PRINT "TYPE THE NEW VALUES: STOCK ON HAND, UNIT COST"
470 INPUT A(R,2),A(R,3)
480 REM
490 REM          GO BACK FOR MORE INPUT DATA
500 REM
510 GO TO 230
520 REM
530 REM          FINISH
540 REM
550 CLOSE #1
560 STOP
32767 END
```

The program dimensions A and opens "INVMST" as usual in lines 150 and 190. Next, the record (part) number is input in line 240. A test for the end of data input is on line 280. It is important to check that the record to be changed is the one found. It is printed out in line 330. Note that this line prints out the entire record—the appropriate row of Table A. Then a Y or an N is input to verify that the record printed out is the record to be changed. The Y or N is tested in line 420. If the input is Y, then the new values for stock on hand and price are input. Upon input, the values in the "INVMST" file (Table A) are changed. That is all that is necessary. Next, the record number is requested. The end of the program is signalled by input of 9999 for record number. The file is closed and the program ends.

You should notice that the time required to print out a record after the record (part) number is given, is the same for all records. There is no need to read from the beginning of the file to reach any record. After you have input the changes given in Table 9–2, run the program that prints out "INVMST". The file should look like Table 9–3 after the changes:

Table 9–3 Inventory Master File After Changes

Part Number	*Stock on Hand*	*Unit Cost*
1	600	2.00
2	750	2.75
3	231	1.50
4	395	5.96
5	674	7.25
6	230	7.00
7	942	4.26
8	27	5.49
9	152	1.40
10	500	4.00

UPDATING MASTER RECORDS IN A VIRTUAL FILE

The next logical step, after you have mastered changing records in a virtual file, is to update a virtual file. The update described below produces an instantaneously updated master file. There is no transaction file. Each transaction record updates its appropriate master record as soon as it is entered. In order to add a touch of realism to the update of the inventory master file "INVMST", assume that there are two computer terminals in the area where inventory is kept. The first terminal is located at the unloading area where shipments are received from suppliers. The second terminal is located by the loading area where items are shipped (issued) to the company's customers.

The first terminal is used to enter any receipts to inventory as soon as they are placed in inventory. The second terminal is used to enter any shipments (issues) from inventory.

The update program to handle direct access (virtual) files is much simpler than the inventory update program in Chapter 7. A transaction code will be used to indicate a receipt to inventory (code = 1) and a shipment from inventory (code = 2). A transaction consists of three fields: the code, part number, and amount. If a shipment transaction (code = 2) has an amount greater than the stock on hand, the order cannot be filled. The program should cancel the shipment and keep the old value of the stock on hand. The transaction data can be found in Table 9–4.

Table 9–4

Transaction Data to Update "INVMST"

Transaction Code	*Part (Record) Number*	*Quantity*
1	9	50
2	2	500
1	10	200
1	5	75
2	9	50
1	1	40
1	2	100
2	8	50

Problem Summary

Input

Inventory master file, "INVMST" (Table 9–3)
Transactions

Processing

Determine the transaction code and update the appropriate master record.

Output

An updated master file.

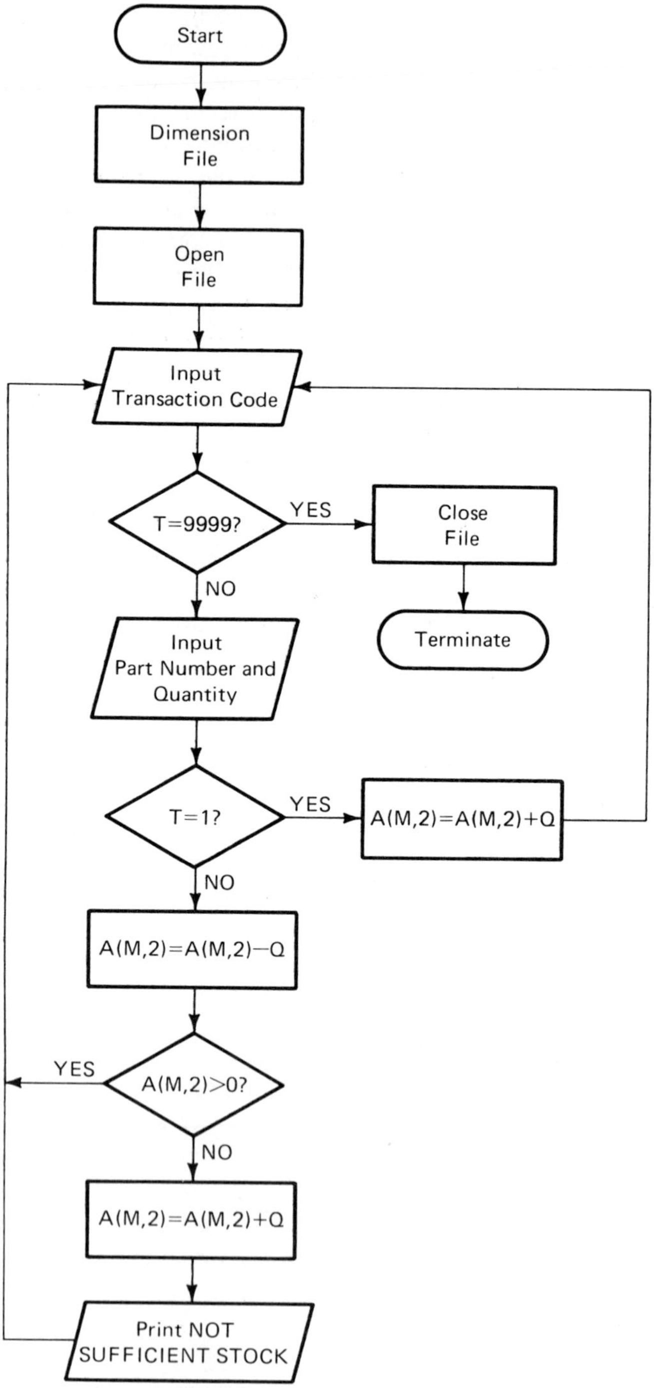

Figure 9–4 Flowchart of Direct Access Update

See the flowchart (Fig 9–4). A program appears below:

```
100  REM THIS PROGRAM UPDATES THE VIRTUAL FILE INVMST IN REAL TIME
110 REM
120 REM
130 REM           DIMENSION VIRTUAL FILE
140 REM
150 DIM #2,A(10,3)
160 REM
170 REM           OPEN VIRTUAL FILE
180 REM
190 OPEN "INVMST" AS FILE #2
200 REM
210 REM           INPUT TRANSACTION CODE
220 REM
230 PRINT "TYPE THE TRANSACTION CODE:
240 PRINT "  1 IS A RECEIPT TO INVENTORY"
250 PRINT "  2 IS A SHIPMENT FROM INVENTORY"
260 PRINT "TYPE 9999 TO END"
270 INPUT T
280 REM
290 REM           TEST TO END DATA INPUT
300 REM
310 IF T=9999 THEN 690
320 PRINT "TYPE THE PART NUMBER,QUANTITY"
330 REM
340 REM           INPUT TRANSACTION DATA
350 REM
360 INPUT M,Q
370 REM
380 REM           TEST FOR A RECEIPT TO INVENTORY
390 REM
400 IF T=1 THEN 610
410 REM
420 REM           SHIPMENT FROM INVENTORY
430 REM
440 A(M,2)=A(M,2)-Q
450 REM
460 REM           TEST FOR POSITIVE STOCK ON HAND
470 REM
480 IF A(M,2)>0 GO TO 230
490 REM
500 REM           NOT ENOUGH STOCK ON HAND TO SHIP,
510 REM              CANCELL ORDER AND REPLACE OLD STOCK
520 REM              ON HAND VALUE
530 REM
540 A(M,2)=A(M,2)+Q
550 PRINT "*** NOT SUFFICIENT STOCK *** ONLY ";A(M,2);" UNITS ON HAND **
*"
560 PRINT "****** SHIPMENT CANCELLED --- NOTIFY CUSTOMER ********"
570 GO TO 230
580 REM
590 REM           RECEIPT TRANSACTION: ADD QUANTITY TO STOCK ON HAND
600 REM
610 A(M,2)=A(M,2)+Q
620 REM
630 REM           GO BACK FOR MORE DATA
640 REM
650 GO TO 230
660 REM
670 REM           FINISH
680 REM
690 CLOSE #2
700 STOP
32767 END
```

In the program, A is dimensioned and “INVMST” is opened. In line 270 the transaction code is input, followed by the test to end data input. The transaction part (record) number and quantity are input next in line

360. The test on the transaction code is at line 400. If the transaction is a shipment from inventory (code = 2), then lines 440 through 570 are executed. If there is enough stock on hand, A(M,2), to make the required shipment, then the stock on hand is adjusted for the shipment in line 440: A(M,2) = A(M,2) − Q. If Q is greater than the stock on hand, A(M,2), then the newly assigned value of A(M,2) in line 440 will be negative. For example, the stock on hand is 20 and you wish to ship 30 units, there would be − 10 units in stock on hand. Line 480 tests for this condition. If the condition (stock on hand is less than zero) exists, then the old value of stock on hand is replaced in line 540, A(M,2) = A(M,2) + Q, and the shipment is cancelled (lines 550 and 560).

If the transaction is a receipt to inventory (code = 1), then in line 610 the quantity received is added to the stock on hand, A(M,2) = A(M,2) + Q. Then another transaction is entered.

The update of the master record occurs at lines 440, 540 or 610 where A(M,2) is assigned a value contingent upon the transaction code and other tests. The update program uses the same concept as the program to change a record. As soon as a transaction is entered, the master record is updated. The last transaction will result in a shipment being cancelled.

After the update program is run with the transactions given in Table 9–4, run the program that prints the "INVMST" file. The file should look like Table 9–5.

Table 9–5

The "INVMST" File After Updating

Part Number	*Stock on Hand*	*Unit Cost*
1	640	2.00
2	350	2.75
3	231	1.50
4	395	5.96
5	749	7.25
6	230	7.00
7	942	4.26
8	27	5.49
9	152	1.40
10	700	4.00

A virtual master file is organized by ascending record number. The transactions may be entered in any order. The time required to update a master record is the same, regardless of its location in the file, because virtual files are one form of direct access files.

If transactions are entered from the two terminals in the inventory area as stock is received and shipped, then the master file is updated in real-time. Real-time updating means the master files contain the latest up-to-the-second information. This is especially important when dealing with inventory.

In order to have real-time updating, direct access files must be used. Real-time updating may be contrasted with batch updating, which has a time cycle (a day, a week, or a month) for the running of the update program. The update programs in Chapter 7 were examples of batch updating. The transactions were accumulated in a file during the time cycle. Then they were sorted and the update program was run at the end of the cycle.

QUERYING RECORDS IN A VIRTUAL FILE

If the update is in real-time, then any time you retrieve and print a record of the master file, it contains the latest stock on hand. This is very useful when you consider that a company has a sales department. Salesmen need to know the latest inventory levels in order to give customers reasonable delivery dates. Assume, in our inventory example, that there is a third terminal in the sales department. When a salesman writes an order for a customer, he phones the sales department to determine whether sufficient stock is on hand to fill the order. The program that retrieves and prints master records is called a query program. "Query" is a short form for "inquiry". The program is the same as the first part of the program for changing a record.

Problem Summary

Input

Part (record) number
Inventory master file, "INVMST"

Processing

Retrieve a master record.

Output

Print the appropriate master record.

```
100 REM
110 REM QUERY PROGRAM
120 REM
130 REM
140 REM          DIMENSION VIRTUAL FILE
150 REM
160 DIM #1,A(10,3)
170 REM
180 REM          OPEN VIRTUAL FILE
190 REM
200 OPEN "INVMST" AS FILE #1
210 PRINT "WHAT IS THE PART NUMBER? TYPE 9999 TO END"
220 REM
230 REM          INPUT PART NUMBER (RECORD NUMBER)
240 REM
250 INPUT R
260 REM
270 REM          TEST FOR END OF DATA INPUT
280 REM
290 IF R=9999 GO TO 430
300 REM
310 REM          PRINT OUT RECORD
320 REM
330 PRINT "PART    STOCK      UNIT"
340 PRINT "NUMBER  ON HAND    COST"
```

```
350 PRINT USING "###      ####      ##.##"A(R,1),A(R,2),A(R,3)
360 REM
370 REM            GO BACK FOR MORE INPUT
380 REM
390 GO TO 210
400 REM
410 REM            FINISH
420 REM
430 CLOSE #1
440 STOP
32767 END
```

```
WHAT IS THE PART NUMBER? TYPE 9999 TO END
? 9
PART     STOCK       UNIT
NUMBER   ON HAND     COST
  9        152       1.40
WHAT IS THE PART NUMBER? TYPE 9999 TO END
? 1
PART     STOCK       UNIT
NUMBER   ON HAND     COST
  1        640       2.00
WHAT IS THE PART NUMBER? TYPE 9999 TO END
? 5
PART     STOCK       UNIT
NUMBER   ON HAND     COST
  5        749       7.25
WHAT IS THE PART NUMBER? TYPE 9999 TO END
? 10
PART     STOCK       UNIT
NUMBER   ON HAND     COST
 10        700       4.00
WHAT IS THE PART NUMBER? TYPE 9999 TO END
? 9999
Stop at line 440
```

The sales department would run this program to see if a customer's order could be filled. In a sophisticated company, the salesman would have portable terminals that use a telephone to reach the computer. Also the programs would be more complex in order to allow a salesman to reserve stock and to ship partial orders.

SUMMARY

In this chapter one type of direct access file is introduced. The programs necessary to handle a virtual file were given. In essence, a virtual file can be treated as a table where the rows represent records and the columns represent fields. The example throughout this chapter was inventory, not payroll. Inventory was selected because it represents a good example of the requirement for real-time updating. The real-time example was illustrated by an update where, as soon as a transaction was generated, the master file was updated. The final section dealt with an inquiry program that reads and prints records from a virtual file.

BASIC Instructions Introduced:

Instruction	*Explanation*
DIM #1,A(10,3) = 0	Dimensions a virtual file (table) and sets the last element value to zero

PROBLEMS

1. Modify the first program in this chapter so that you can stop an input session and continue entering the data at any point in the file without having to re-enter all the earlier records. To test your program, create a file "I11".

2. Create a virtual file, "CUMST", with eight records as follows:

Customer Number	*Current Balance*
1	$257.26
2	194.40
3	276.00
4	0.00
5	51.27
6	29.32
7	426.25
8	972.36

3. Write a program that will print the "CUMST" file as described in Problem 2.

4. Write a program that will update the "CUMST" file. There are three types of transactions: payments, purchases, and returns. Payments should be subtracted from the current balance (Transaction code = 1). Purchases should be added to the current balance (TR CODE = 2). Returns should be subtracted from the current balance (TR CODE = 3). If customers have a current balance less than zero, a message should be printed to issue a refund check to the customer. Use the following transactions to test your program:

Transaction Code	*Customer Number*	*Amount*
1	5	51.27
1	1	200.00
2	4	57.26
1	3	250.00
2	8	320.21
3	5	23.27
1	2	194.40
2	1	72.73
3	7	157.29

5. Write an inquiry program for the "CUMST" file, so that customers may call and be given their latest balance.

10 / Use and Design of Complex Programs

Performance Objectives

At the end of this chapter you should be able to:

- Use "canned" programs
- Recognize the role of structured programming

Programming is the expensive aspect of computer systems. It is also the most time-consuming. Without programs the computer cannot solve problems. However, once a program has been written and debugged (i.e., the errors have been removed), then using these programs to help solve recurring problems is simple.

In progressing through this book, you have built a program library. If a problem should develop that is similar to those you've already solved, you don't have to write a brand new program. Merely modify the appropriate program to meet the new requirements and it can aid in arriving at a solution. In effect, your program library is a toolbox. Simple changes to your tools allow you to solve most data processing problems.

You may have access to programs other than those you've written. Any number of sources may have contributed skills and energies to fill your toolbox: the vendor of your computer system, an independent consultant, other people in your organization, or other organizations in your industry.

At times it is difficult to transfer programs from one system to another. The procedures and problems of one organization may not match the procedures and problems of another organization. In other cases the transfer of programs is easy. Statistical, scientific, and engineering programs transfer easily from one organization to another. No matter what organization uses them, the rules for performing statistical computations remain the same. The programming of natural laws is not affected by the organization involved. And mathematical calculations are not a matter of opinion or preference ($2 + 2 = 4$ no matter who is involved, where the calculation is performed, or what we wish the result to be). Therefore once a statistical, scientific, or engineering program has been written, it can be copied and used by many organizations.

This chapter discusses how to use programs that have been written elsewhere. A statistical program serves as an example of a "canned" program. The chapter also discusses some elements of style that make a program easier to read and modify.

USING CANNED PROGRAMS

Programs developed by one organization that are transferred as a whole to another organization are called "canned" or "packaged" programs. No modification of the program logic is involved, although some statements may have to be changed to fit your system.

Once the program has been changed so that it will run on another system, it can be used by anybody with access to that system. A person provides the problem context and the data, runs the appropriate program, and interprets the output. Problem specification, data collection, selection of an appropriate program for solution, and interpretation of output are the key elements for the successful use of canned programs. But these elements are beyond the scope of this book. Here we shall focus on how to enter the data and run a canned program.

Linear regression is a statistical technique for determining the relationship between two variables. (Regression analysis is covered in statistical textbooks.) LINREG is a program that performs linear regression. A copy of this program is shown below:

```
LINREG
1 GO TO 630
200 DATA 7E22, 5E22
205 READ Q1
210 DIM D(250,2)
215 PRINT
220 LET I = 0
225 LET I = I + 1
230 READ D(I,1), D(I,2)
235 IF D(I,1) <> 7E22 THEN 225
240 LET Q2 = I-1
245 LET S9 = 0
250 IF Q1 = 1 THEN 270
255 IF Q1 = 2 THEN 325
260 IF Q1 = 3 THEN 395
265 GO TO 220
270 LET S9 = 1
275 GOSUB 490
280 PRINT "LINEAR:    Y=A+B*X    WITH  A=";Q8;" AND B=";Q9
285 GOSUB 565
290 FOR J = 1 TO Q2
295 LET W7 = Q8 + Q9*D(J,1)
300 LET Z7 = W7 - D(J,2)
305 LET Q4 = 100*Z7/D(J,2)
310 PRINT D(J,1), D(J,2), W7, Z7, Q4
315 NEXT J
320 GO TO 999
325 FOR J = 1 TO Q2
330 LET D(J,2) = LOG(D(J,2))
335 NEXT J
340 GOSUB 490
345 PRINT "EXPONENTIAL:    Y = A*EXP(B*X)    WITH A=";EXP(Q8);" AND B=";Q9
350 GOSUB 565
355 FOR J=1 TO Q2
360 LET W7 = EXP(Q8+Q9*D(J,1))
365 LET W8 = EXP(D(J,2))
370 LET Z7 = W7-W8
375 LET Q4 = 100*Z7/W8
380 PRINT D(J,1), W8, W7, Z7, Q4
385 NEXT J
390 GO TO 999
395 FOR J = 1 TO Q2
400 LET D(J,1) = LOG(D(J,1))
405 LET D(J,2) = LOG(D(J,2))
410 NEXT J
415 GOSUB 490
420 PRINT "POWER:    Y=A*(X**B)    WITH A=";EXP(Q8);" AND B="Q9
425 GOSUB 565
430 FOR J = 1 TO Q2
435 LET W7 = EXP(D(J,1))
440 LET W8 = EXP(D(J,2))
445 LET W9 = EXP(Q8)*W7**Q9
```

```
450 LET Q4 = W9/W8-1
451 LET Z7 = W9-W8
455 IF Q4 < 0 THEN 470
460 LET Q4 = INT(1000*Q4+0.5)/10
465 GO TO 475
470 LET Q4 = INT(1000*Q4-0.5)/10
475 PRINT W7, W8, W9, Z7, Q4
480 NEXT J
485 GO TO 999
490 LET Q3 = 0
495 LET Q4 = 0
500 LET Q5 = 0
505 LET Q6 = 0
510 LET Q7 = 0
515 FOR J = 1 TO Q2
520 LET Q3 = Q3+D(J,1)
525 LET Q4 = Q4+D(J,2)
530 LET Q5 = Q5+D(J,1)*D(J,2)
535 LET Q6 = Q6+(D(J,1))**2
540 LET Q7 = Q7+(D(J,2))**2
545 NEXT J
550 LET Q9 = (Q2*Q5-Q3*Q4)/(Q2*Q6-Q3**2)
555 LET Q8 = (Q4-Q3*Q9)/Q2
560 RETURN
565 LET Q0 = (Q2*Q5-Q3*Q4)/SQR((Q2*Q6-Q3**2)*(Q2*Q7-Q4**2))
570 PRINT
575 IF S9 = 0 THEN 590
580 PRINT "COEFFICIENTS;  ";
585 GOTO 595
590 PRINT "INDICIES:  ";
595 PRINT "CORREL = ";Q0;"    DETERM = ";Q0**2
600 PRINT
605 PRINT "COMPARISON OF ACTUAL Y'S WITH Y'S ESTIMATED FROM EQUATION: "
610 PRINT
615 PRINT "X-ACTUAL","Y-ACTUAL","Y-ESTIM","DIFFER","PCT-DIFF"
620 PRINT
625 RETURN
630 PRINT
635 PRINT "THIS IS A LINEAR REGRESSION PROGRAM FOR DATA IN TWO"
640 PRINT "VARIABLES, X AND Y.  FROM INPUT POINTS, DESCRIBED BY"
645 PRINT "THEIR X AND Y COORDINATES, AN EQUATION IS PRODUCED THAT"
650 PRINT "BEST FITS THESE POINTS IN THE LEAST-SQUARES SENSE.  TO"
655 PRINT "USE THE PROGRAM, TYPE THE FOLLOWING:"
660 PRINT
665 PRINT "      1 DATA K"
670 PRINT "              (WHERE K = 1 FOR LINEAR, 2 FOR EXPONENTIAL,"
675 PRINT "              AND 3 FOR POWER FUNCTION TO BE FITTED.)"
680 PRINT "      2 DATA X(1),Y(1),X(2),Y(2),.....,X(N),Y(N)"
685 PRINT "              (WHERE X(1),Y(1) IS THE FIRST POINT, X(2),"
690 PRINT "              Y(2) IS THE SECOND, AND SO ON UNTIL ALL"
695 PRINT "              POINTS HAVE BEEN ENTERED.  ADDITIONAL DATA"
700 PRINT "              STATEMENTS 3-199 MAY BE USED AS NEEDED)."
705 PRINT
710 PRINT "THEN TYPE 'RUN'."
999 STOP
32767 END
```

You can use LINREG by calling it up (OLD LINREG), entering your data, and typing RUN. But data entry for LINREG, as well as many similar programs, is different from how it was handled in earlier parts of this book. Data is entered with DATA statements that are part of the program. LINREG provides instructions for entering data:

```
OLD LINREG

Ready

RUN
LINREG

THIS IS A LINEAR REGRESSION PROGRAM FOR DATA IN TWO
VARIABLES, X AND Y.  FROM INPUT POINTS, DESCRIBED BY
THEIR X AND Y COORDINATES, AN EQUATION IS PRODUCED THAT
BEST FITS THESE POINTS IN THE LEAST-SQUARES SENSE.  TO
USE THE PROGRAM, TYPE THE FOLLOWING:

        1 DATA K
                (WHERE K = 1 FOR LINEAR, 2 FOR EXPONENTIAL,
                AND 3 FOR POWER FUNCTION TO BE FITTED.)
        2 DATA X(1),Y(1),X(2),Y(2),.....,X(N),Y(N)
                (WHERE X(1),Y(1) IS THE FIRST POINT, X(2),
                Y(2) IS THE SECOND, AND SO ON UNTIL ALL
                POINTS HAVE BEEN ENTERED.  ADDITIONAL DATA
                STATEMENTS 3-199 MAY BE USED AS NEEDED).

THEN TYPE 'RUN'.

Ready
```

This RUN shows what has to be entered in DATA statements. A DATA statement is a non-executable BASIC instruction that holds data for a program. It starts with a line number, the word DATA, and then the individual data values separated by commas. For example:

1 DATA 3.7,4.2,3.9,2.5,6

The DATA statement holds five values. They may be the values for five fields of a record, or they may be five values for one field. Either way, DATA statements hold a stream of values that are used one after another.

Data values in DATA statements are assigned to fields by READ statements. Look at LINREG, line 205 and line 230. Both contain the BASIC instruction READ. Line 205, READ Q1, being the first READ, assigns the first value found in any DATA statements to Q1. Line 230, READ D(I,1),D(I,2), assigns the next data value to D(I,1) and the following value to D(I,2).

Once an item of data has been assigned, the next READ uses the item of data that follows. Every READ "uses up" data values. Although data can be distributed over many DATA statements, they must follow the *order* of the READ statements. The READ statements follow the stream of data, using up data values in sequence.

Now we can run LINREG. First, call up the program. Then enter the data as specified by the instructions:

```
1 DATA 1
2 DATA 719,3756
3 DATA 1384,5100
4 DATA  995,4950
5 DATA 231,894
6 DATA 462,480
7 DATA 486,1908
```

```
8 DATA 1299,5388
9 DATA 233,240
10 DATA 189,468
11 DATA 759,1662
12 DATA 112,96
13 DATA 1252,5334
14 DATA 677,786
15 DATA 295,648
```

Then type the word "RUN", and it generates the output.

```
LINEAR:    Y=A+B*X    WITH  A=-562.488  AND B= 4.50729

COEFFICIENTS;  CORREL =  .927247    DETERM =  .859787

COMPARISON OF ACTUAL Y"S WITH Y"S ESTIMATED FROM EQUATION:

X-ACTUAL       Y-ACTUAL       Y-ESTIM        DIFFER         PCT-DIFF

 719            3756           2578.26       -1177.74       -31.3563
 1384           5100           5575.61        475.608        9.32564
 995            4950           3822.27       -1127.73       -22.7824
 231            894            378.697       -515.303       -57.6401
 462            480            1419.88        939.882        195.809
 485            1908           1528.06       -379.943       -19.9131
 1299           5388           5192.49       -195.512       -3.62866
 233            240            387.712        147.712        61.5466
 189            468            189.391       -278.609       -59.5318
 759            1662           2758.55        1096.55        65.9777
 112            96            -157.671       -253.671       -264.24
 1252           5334           4980.64       -353.355       -6.62458
 677            786            2388.95        1602.95        203.938
 295            648            667.164        19.1642        2.95744
Stop at line 999
```

The interpretation of this output and its use in decision making will determine the value of LINREG. But that aspect is peripheral to our focus. Notice how easy it is to use the program: Enter the data, type run, and the program can generate reams upon reams of output.

Other statistical programs are just as easy to use. Just enter the data and the program does the rest. It is not necessary to know anything about statistics or about computer programming to use these programs for analysis. Therein lies the power, as well as the danger, of using computers. Anybody, whether knowledgeable in the technique used or not, has the technique available if he can enter data and type RUN. But knowledge of the problem context, of the validity of the data, and of the technique of analysis is required to derive the proper conclusions from such use of canned programs.

Other examples of canned programs are the file sorts in Appendix B. Again, the detailed instructions of the program are unimportant. What is important is knowing how to use it properly to do the desired job.

Similar to canned programs, but at a much lower level, are functions. Functions perform one specific task in a program. For example, the INT function used in Chapter 6, gives the integer portion of a number. Functions are usually indicated by a three-letter keyword. Table 10-1 lists the mathematical functions available in BASIC.

Table 10–1 Mathematical Functions

*Function**	*Explanation*
Y = ABS(X)	Assigns to Y the absolute value of X.
Y = ATN(X)	Assigns to Y the arc tangent of X; X is expressed in radians.
Y = COS(X)	Assigns to Y the cosine of X; X is in radians.
Y = EXP(X)	Assigns to Y the value of e raised to the X power; where e is 2.71828.
Y = FIX(X)	Assigns to Y the truncated value of X; equal to Y = SGN(X) *INT(ABS(X)).
Y = INT(X)	Assigns to Y the greatest integer in X which is less than or equal to X.
Y = LOG(X)	Assigns to Y the natural logarithm of X.
Y = LOG10(X)	Assigns to Y the common logarithm of X.
Y = PI	Assigns to Y the value of π (3.14159).
Y = RND(X) or Y = RND	Assigns to Y a random number uniformly distributed between 0 and 1.
Y = SGN(X)	Assigns to Y the value 1 preceded by the sign of X.
Y = SIN(X)	Assigns to Y the sine of X; X is in radians.
Y = SQR(X)	Assigns to Y the square root of X.
Y = TAN(X)	Assigns to Y the tangent of X; X is in radians.

* Y stands for the name of any field; and X can be a field or a formula, but must be enclosed in parentheses.

STRUCTURED PROGRAMMING

Structured programming is a systematic way of designing a program. It is a philosophy of design to make a program readable and easy to change.

Structured programming breaks a program into a number of pieces, called modules. Each module performs one task. Since the modules are smaller than the whole program, each piece is easier to understand, easier to code, and easier to change. But breaking a program into modules requires planning. Structured programming emphasizes planning of what a program does and how its modules are related. All modules should be clearly specified before coding. All variables should be clearly defined and their roles in the various modules identified. Obviously this planning is not cheap and requires careful coordination between programmers.

Structured programming recognizes three types of sequences of instructions—simple sequence, selection, and looping. Any program can be composed using one or a combination of these elementary types. For example:

Simple sequence	100 LET R = 3.00 110 LET H = 40 120 LET P = R*H 130 PRINT P
Selection	100 IF T = 2 THEN 300
Alternative 1 (false)	200 Q2 = Q2 + Q1 210 GO TO 400
Alternative 2 (true)	300 Q2 = Q2 − Q1 400 . . . .
Loop	100 FOR R1 = 1 TO 8 : 200 NEXT R1

A simple sequence has no GO TO. Each statement follows the preceding statement until the sequence is finished.

A selection consists of an IF–THEN and its two possible groups of instructions. One of these two possible groups is selected when the IF–THEN is true. The other is selected when the IF–THEN is false.

A loop repeats a group of instructions until a specified condition has been met.

Of course the alternatives of a selection or the group of instructions in a loop may contain subsidiary selections or loops. Ideally each type of module should have one entry and one exit with no backtracking. The flow of a program should be top to bottom (except for loops.) GO TO's that jump back to previously executed code should be eliminated.

To clarify the relationship between the elements of a program, structured programming uses indentations and additional comments (REM statements) to highlight the structure of a program. Indentation shows which elements fit together. Comments aid in understanding both the logic (what the program does) and the structure (how the program is organized.)

Let's look at some examples to clarify these ideas. First, look at the SORT program in Chapter 8. It performs three major tasks that can be diagrammed as follows in Figure 10–1.

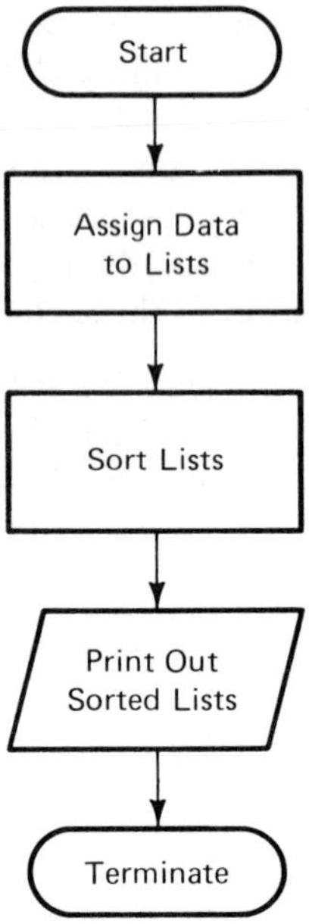

Figure 10–1 SORT Program

This program can be rewritten to make the structure stand out. A rewritten version follows:

```
100 REM *************************************************************
110 REM * PROGRAM NAME: LIST SORT                                   *
120 REM *                                                           *
130 REM * THIS PROGRAM --                                           *
140 REM *   1. GETS DATA FROM A TERMINAL AND STORES THEM IN         *
150 REM *      LISTS                                                *
160 REM *   2. SORTS THE LISTS IN DESCENDING ORDER OF NET PAY       *
170 REM *   3. PRINTS THE SORTED LISTS                              *
180 REM *                                                           *
190 REM * PROGRAMMER NAME: A. N. LYST                               *
200 REM * DATE: 1 APRIL 1979                                        *
210 REM *                                                           *
220 REM * FIELD NAMES:                                              *
230 REM *   F......EXCHANGE FLAG -- SET TO 1 WHEN AN                *
240 REM *          EXCHANGE HAS OCCURRED; 0 OTHERWISE               *
250 REM *   K......INDEX OF FOR-NEXT LOOP                           *
260 REM *   L......POINTER TO A LOCATION IN A LIST DURING           *
270 REM *          DATA ENTRY; THE NUMBER OF ITEMS IN A LIST        *
280 REM *          AFTER DATA ENTRY                                 *
290 REM *   M$.....EMPLOYEE NAME ENTERED FROM TERMINAL              *
300 REM *   N()....LIST TO HOLD EMPLOYEE NUMBER                     *
310 REM *   N1.....EMPLOYEE NUMBER ENTERED FROM TERMINAL            *
320 REM *   N$()...LIST TO HOLD EMPLOYEE NAME                       *
330 REM *   P()....LIST TO HOLD EMPLOYEE NET PAY                    *
340 REM *   P1.....EMPLOYEE NET PAY ENTERED FROM TERMINAL           *
350 REM *   T......TEMPORARY STORAGE OF A NUMERIC VALUE             *
360 REM *          DURING AN EXCHANGE                               *
370 REM *   T$.....TEMPORARY STORAGE OF EMPLOYEE NAME               *
380 REM *          DURING AN EXCHANGE                               *
390 REM *************************************************************
```

```
400 REM
410      DIM N(100), N$(100), P(100)
420 REM
430 REM GET DATA FROM TERMINAL AND PUT THEM INTO THE LISTS
440 REM
450      L = 0
460 REM *** BEGIN DATA ENTRY LOOP
470     PRINT "TYPE EMPLOYEE NUMBER, EMPLOYEE NAME,"
480     PRINT "AND NET PAY -- SEPARATED BY COMMAS."
490     PRINT "WHEN FINISHED -- TYPE   99,AA,99"
500     INPUT N1,M$,P1
510    REM -----> EXIT FROM LOOP WHEN DATA ENTRY FINISHED
520     IF  N1 = 99                                        THEN 640
530 REM ASSIGN DATA TO ARRAYS
540      L  = L + 1
550      N(L) = N1
560      N$(L) = M$
570      P(L) = P1
580 REM *** ENDIF 520
590                                                 GOTO 470
600 REM *** END DATA ENTRY LOOP
610 REM
620 REM  SORT THE LISTS INTO DESCENDING NET PAY ORDER
630 REM
640      U = L - 1
650 REM *** BEGIN SORT LOOP
660      F = 0
670      FOR K = 1 TO U
680 REM
690 REM  COMPARE TWO ADJACENT VALUES OF NET PAY
700 REM  IF THEY ARE NOT IN ORDER, EXCHANGE THEM
710 REM
720         IF P(K) >= P(K+1)                          THEN 900
730 REM
740 REM     NET PAY VALUES OUT OF SEQUENCE, HENCE EXCHANGE
750 REM
760           T = P(K)
770           P(K) = P(K+1)
780           P(K+1) = T
790           T = N(K)
800           N(K) = N(K+1)
810           N(K+1) = T
820           T$ = N$(K)
830           N$(K) = N$(K+1)
840           N$(K+1) = T$
850 REM
860 REM       SET EXCHANGE FLAG (F) TO 1
870 REM
880            F = 1
890 REM   *** ENDIF 720
900       NEXT K
910 REM -----> EXIT FROM SORT LOOP WHEN F = 0
920       IF  F = 1                                      THEN 660
930 REM *** END SORT LOOP
940 REM
950 REM PRINT HEADINGS AND SORTED LISTS
960 REM
970        PRINT "EMPLOYEE", "EMPLOYEE", "WEEKLY"
980        PRINT " NUMBER ", "  NAME  ", "  PAY "
990        PRINT "--------", "--------", "------"
1000 REM *** BEGIN PRINT LOOP
1010       FOR K = 1 TO L
1020           PRINT N(K), N$(K), P(K)
1030       NEXT K
1040 REM *** END PRINT LOOP
1050 END
```

As another example, compare the inventory update in Chapter 7 on page 167 with the structured version of the same program shown below.

```
100     REM ***********************************************************
110     REM * PROGRAM NAME: INVENTORY UPDATE                          *
120     REM *                                                         *
130     REM * THIS PROGRAM --                                         *
140     REM *    1. UPDATES THE OLD INVENTORY MASTERFILE:             *
150     REM *          READS INVENTORY TRANSACTION RECORDS            *
160     REM *          READS OLD INVENTORY MASTER RECORDS             *
170     REM *          UPDATES MASTER RECORDS WITH TRANSACTIONS       *
180     REM *          WRITES NEW (UPDATED) MASTER RECORDS            *
190     REM *    2. PRINTS THE NEW (UPDATED) MASTERFILE               *
200     REM *    3. PRINTS AN INVENTORY VALUATION REPORT              *
210     REM *                                                         *
220     REM * PROGRAMMER NAME: P. GRAMMER                             *
230     REM * DATE: 1 APRIL 1980                                      *
240     REM *                                                         *
250     REM * FIELD NAMES:                                            *
260     REM *    C....UNIT COST OF PART INPUT FROM UPDATED MASTER     *
270     REM *    C2...UNIT COST OF PART INPUT FROM OLD MASTERFILE     *
280     REM *    D....DOLLAR VALUE OF PART                            *
290     REM *    P....PART NUMBER INPUT FROM UPDATED MASTERFILE       *
300     REM *    P1...PART NUMBER INPUT FROM TRANSACTION FILE         *
310     REM *    P2...PART NUMBER INPUT FROM OLD MASTERFILE           *
320     REM *    Q....QUANTITY ON HAND INPUT FROM UPDATED MASTER      *
330     REM *    Q1...QUANTITY OF TRANSACTION INPUT FROM              *
340     REM *         TRANSACTION FILE                                *
350     REM *    Q2...QUANTITY ON HAND INPUT FROM OLD MASTERFILE      *
360     REM *    T....TOTAL DOLLAR VALUE OF INVENTORY                 *
370     REM *    T1...TRANSACTION CODE INPUT FROM TRANSACTION FILE    *
380     REM *         CODE VALUES:  1 = RECEIPT                       *
390     REM *                       2 = ISSUE                         *
400     REM ***********************************************************
410     REM
420     REM SET ERROR CONDITION
430     REM
440         ON ERROR GO TO 1710
450     REM
460     REM LINK TO FILES
470     REM
480         OPEN "INVTR" FOR INPUT AS FILE #1
490         OPEN "INVMR" FOR INPUT AS FILE #2
500         OPEN "INVSN" FOR OUTPUT AS FILE #3
510     REM
520     REM READ A TRANSACTION RECORD
530     REM
540         INPUT #1 P1, T1, Q1
550     REM
560     REM READ A MASTER RECORD
570     REM
580         INPUT #2 P2, Q2, C2
590     REM *** BEGIN UPDATE LOOP
600     REM
610     REM IF TRANSACTION EQUALS MASTER
620     REM
630         IF  P1 = P2                                       THEN 670
640                                                           GOTO 820
650     REM     THEN  UPDATE MASTER
660     REM     IF TRANSACTION IS A RECEIPT
670             IF T1 = 1                                     THEN 700
680                                                           GOTO 730
690     REM        THEN ADD TRANSACTION QUANTITY TO QUANT ON HAND
700                Q2 = Q2 + Q1
710                                                           GOTO 780
720     REM        ELSE SUBTRACT QUANTITY FROM QUANTITY ON HAND
730                Q2 = Q2 - Q1
740     REM     ***ENDIF 670
```

```
750     REM
760     REM     READ A TRANSACTION RECORD
770     REM
780             INPUT #1 P1, T1, Q1
790     REM ----->EXIT WHEN OUT OF TRANSACTION RECORDS
800                                                         GOTO 630
810     REM     ELSE IF TRANSACTION GREATER THAN MASTER
820             IF P1 > P2                                  THEN 850
830                                                         GOTO 960
840     REM     THEN WRITE UPDATED MASTER
850             PRINT #3 P2;",";Q2;",";C2
860     REM
870     REM     READ A MASTER RECORD
880     REM
890             INPUT #2 P2, Q2, C2
900     REM ----> EXIT WHEN OUT OF MASTER RECORDS
910                                                         GOTO 630
920     REM     ELSE TRANSACTION LESS THAN MASTER
930     REM
940     REM     WRITE ERROR MESSAGE -- NO MASTER IN FILE
950     REM
960             PRINT"***TRANSACTION WITHOUT MASTER***";P1;T1;Q1
970     REM
980     REM     READ A TRANSACTION RECORD
990     REM
1000            INPUT #1 P1, T1, Q1
1010    REM     *** ENDIF 820
1020    REM ------> EXIT WHEN OUT OF TRANSACTION RECORDS
1030                                                        GOTO 630
1040    REM *** END UPDATE LOOP
1050    REM
1060    REM TRANSFER REMAINING RECORDS FROM OLD TO NEW MASTER
1070    REM
1080    REM *** BEGIN TRANSFER LOOP
1090        PRINT #3 P2;",";Q2;",";C2
1100        INPUT #2 P2, Q2, C2
1110    REM -----> EXIT WHEN OUT OF MASTER RECORDS
1120                                                        GOTO 1090
1130    REM *** END TRANSFER LOOP
1140    REM
1150    REM PRINT THE UPDATED MASTERFILE
1160    REM
1170        CLOSE #1, #2, #3
1180        OPEN "INVSN" FOR INPUT AS FILE #1
1190    REM
1200    REM HEADINGS FOR UPDATED FILE
1210    REM
1220        PRINT
1230        PRINT "    NEW INVENTORY MASTER FILE"
1240        PRINT "    -------------------------"
1250        PRINT
1260        PRINT "PART     UNITS     COST"
1270        PRINT "NUMBER   ON HAND"
1280        PRINT "------   -------   ----"
1290    REM *** BEGIN PRINT LOOP
1300            INPUT #1 P, Q, C
1310            PRINT USING"###       ####      #.##"P,Q,C
1320    REM -----> EXIT WHEN OUT OF NEW MASTER RECORDS
1330                                                        GOTO 1300
1340    REM *** END PRINT LOOP
1350    REM
1360    REM PRINT INVENTORY VALUATION REPORT
1370    REM
1380        CLOSE #1
1390        OPEN "INVSN" FOR INPUT AS FILE #1
1400    REM
1410    REM HEADINGS FOR VALUATION REPORT
1420    REM
1430        PRINT
1440        PRINT
```

```
1450        PRINT " INVENTORY VALUATION REPORT"
1460        PRINT " --------------------------"
1470        PRINT
1480        PRINT " PART ", "DOLLAR"
1490        PRINT "NUMBER", "AMOUNT"
1500        PRINT "------", "------"
1510    REM
1520        T = 0
1530    REM *** BEGIN INVENTORY VALUATION LOOP
1540        INPUT #1 P, Q, C
1550        D = Q * C
1560        T = T + D
1570        PRINT USING"###          #,###.##"P,D
1580    REM---> EXIT WHEN OUT OF DATA
1590                                                              GOTO 154
0
1600    REM *** END INVENTORY VALUATION LOOP
1610    REM
1620    REM PRINT TOTAL VALUATION
1630    REM
1640        PRINT"------------------------"
1650        PRINT USING"\    \       ##,###.##" "TOTAL",T
1660        CLOSE #1
1670                                                      GOTO 1800
1680    REM*******************************
1690    REM*** ERROR CHECKING ROUTINES ***
1700    REM*******************************
1710        IF ERR = 11 THEN RESUME 1760
1720           PRINT "UNUSUAL ERROR",ERR
1730           CLOSE #1, #2, #3
1740           STOP
1750    REM
1760        IF ERL =  780 THEN 1090
1770        IF ERL = 1100 THEN 1170
1780        IF ERL = 1300 THEN 1380
1790        IF ERL = 1540 THEN 1640
1800    STOP
32767   END
```

Now make your evaluations. Which of the two versions of a program did you find easier to understand? In your opinion, which was easier to write? Since REM statements make a program larger and take time to write and enter (they only exist for the benefit of the reader—the computer ignores them), consider the following: Is the cost in time, effort, and added storage requirements less than, equal to, or greater than the benefit of readability? Only you can make that decision for yourself and your organization.

SUMMARY

BASIC Instructions Introduced:

Instruction	*Explanation*
READ X,Y,Z	Assigns values to fields from DATA statements (X,Y,Z are arbitrary field names)
DATA 5,2,7	Used to hold data for fields in READ statements

11 / Conclusion

Performance Objectives

At the end of this chapter you should be able to:

- Recognize the differences between batch, on-line, and real-time
- Understand the problems of a first-time user
- Understand trends in software and hardware for small business computer systems

In this concluding chapter, the payroll program that has been the main example throughout the book will be discussed and put in perspective with regard to other programs that are commonly found in business. The concepts of batch versus real-time programs will be discussed, as well as first-time user organizations. As a conclusion, we present an article that focuses, from the management perspective, on the first-time user and his dilemmas regarding computers.

The Payroll Programs

One of the vehicles for teaching programming in each chapter has been the payroll program. It has grown from a very elementary program to a program that has most of the elements found in an actual payroll program that a business might use. In its present form it is still missing some major elements. For example, it will not write paychecks, nor keep track of some data needed for quarterly tax payments by the employer. The intent of the authors in using payroll as the major example throughout was simple—to pick an application that everyone either is, or can become, familiar with.

BATCH, ON-LINE AND REAL-TIME PROCESSING

All of the programs that appear in this book, with the exception of Chapter 9, are for batch processing. In its simplest terms, batch processing means that transactions are allowed to accumulate before they are used to update master records. Batch processing implies a time cycle—how often the master file is updated. Transactions will accumulate until the update. Batch processing also implies the use of sequential files.

On-line processing is something you have been doing throughout this book. When you type a program at a terminal, you are on-line. The computer accepts or makes comments each time you enter a command or a line of a program. This interaction between a computer and user is referred to as on-line. Other examples of on-line processing are all of the programs that require data entry. The data is entered by you or a data entry operator in an on-line mode.

Files may be considered on-line or off-line. When a file is not being used, it can be stored outside the computer system. When files in computer readable form are removed from the system, they are off-line. They are brought on-line when they need to be used.

The final type of processing is real-time. In real-time, as soon as any transaction occurs, it is entered into the computer system, and the transaction updates the appropriate master record. In Chapter 9, the inventory example illustrated real-time processing. It is necessary to have real-time processing when there is a limited supply or a need for up-to-the-second information. Airline reservation systems were among the first and largest real-time applications.

ROUTINE BUSINESS APPLICATIONS

Payroll was one of the first manual systems to be computerized. After payroll, most accounting systems were computerized. These include invoicing, accounts receivable, accounts payable, general ledger, and financial statements. After the accounting area was computerized, the other functional areas of business proceeded with applications. Marketing, production, inventory, distribution, and finance are areas that have large numbers of computer applications. The accounting area was computerized first because it was the easiest. The rules by which bookkeeping is performed are explicit and relatively simple. These characteristics lend themselves to relatively easy computerization.

In simple terms, you have performed two distinct functions in producing the programs in this book. The two functions are: systems analysis and programming.

Systems analysis deals with defining a problem (application). Most of the systems analysis was done for you in defining the program requirements. However, you had to perform some of this function in designing and writing your programs. It is the systems analysis component that is the most difficult in converting from manual to computer systems.

As indicated above, the systems analysis function for accounting applications is simple compared to other areas in a business. As a result, the accounting area was the first highly affected by computers. This is why most of the programs in this book are accounting oriented. In contrast, the systems analysis function for a production/control system is very difficult.

FIRST-TIME USERS

With the price of computers decreasing dramatically, more and more organizations are using computers. Organizations that have never used computers are called first-time users. There are thousands of horror stories about computers and first-time users. This is not to say that organizations experienced with computers do not also have horror stories; but, first-time users are a special case.

Most first-time users rely on different computer manufacturers' salesmen to provide them with the information they need to choose a computer. Usually, no one in the organization has had any experience with computers. A situation that can be considered analogous to this is as follows: Assume that a cardiologist has recommended that a pacemaker be implanted in a patient. The patient then calls the various manufacturers' representatives for presentations. The patient then selects a model.

It is obvious in the previous analogy that the patient cannot make a rational choice. The same is true of a first-time user selecting a computer based on the sales presentations of manufacturers' representatives. The newspapers are full of reports of trials where users are suing manufacturers, or vice versa, because of basic misunderstandings regarding the computer hardware, software, or both. The best route for a first-time user is to hire someone with computer expertise–either as an employee or consultant. By not choosing either of these alternatives, the use of the computer in an organization might result in greater trauma than necessary.

Computer Price Trends and First-Time User Organizations

The price of computers has dropped dramatically. No longer are large sums required to get the benefits of computer power. Small computer systems can be bought for as little as $25,000 or $10,000. Alternatively, you can rent a small computer system for less than $1,000 per month. The small price tag lets small organizations, with three to 25 employees, obtain their first computer. And it lets large organizations distribute their data processing capabilities throughout the organization. Therefore, the number of computers in use by business firms is expected to increase considerably.

But both cases (first-time use in small business and distributed processing in large organizations) represent the introduction of computers to people who before had little or no contact with computers. Therein lies a danger. Unless managers prepare themselves and their people now, they may not be ready to meet the challenge when it comes.

Technical Background: Computers have been around for over 30 years. They've been commercially used since the mid-fifties. However, their cost, at that time, limited them to large-scale operations. This is no longer the case. With the advent of minicomputers in the '60s and microcomputers in the '70s, the cost of computers has fallen. Now even small organizations can afford computers.

Furthermore, the trend of smaller, cheaper, more powerful computers is expected to continue. New equipment is continually being developed and introduced to the market. The technological cauldron continues to bubble. New devices will continue to be developed. The cost of computers will drop even further.

But the cost of computers is *not* the cost of computer systems. Similarly, the cost of computation is *not* the cost of problem solving. The computer is a small essential part of a computer system. And computation is a small part of problem solving.

Computer systems are needed to help in solving problems. Computer systems consist of people, of hardware, and of software. Equipment is required for the input, storage, manipulation, and output of data and instructions. Software is required to specify how the equipment should do its work. The hardware is the tool, the software is the logic for using the tool. Both aspects, hardware and software, are discussed in the following two sections.

Hardware: Managers are faced with a wide variety of choices when they consider hardware. The market is flooded with alternatives. For example, the August 1978 issue of *Datamation*[1] contained a survey covering 57 systems from 46 manufacturers. But that is only a small fraction of what is available. More extensive and comprehensive listings are available in *Auerbach Reports* and *Datapro Reports.*

The equipment itself presents a wide spectrum of alternatives. From the TRS–80 from Radio Shack to the PDP 11/70, a whole range of price/performance options are available. Which options to choose depends on the needs of an organization.

The low end of the cost spectrum, such as the computer from Radio Shack, offers systems which are too small for most businesses. They have a CRT (cathode ray tube, a TV screen), a keyboard for entering commands, and a cassette tape recorder to store data and instructions. But these facilities are not enough. Business systems need more main storage, more auxiliary storage, and most important, hardcopy output.

Main storage for microcomputers ranges from 16KB–64KB (KB = kilobyte, roughly one thousand characters—used as a measure of storage capacity for a computer system). Larger main storage capacity is expected to be available in the near future. But useable operating systems facilities require from 20–25KB of main storage. And the application programs will need additional space for efficient operations. Therefore, 48KB of main storage should be considered a minimum for a business system.

Floppy disks provide economic auxiliary storage.[2] Each regular floppy disk holds about 250,000 characters. But at least two (and possibly four) floppy disk drives will be needed to hold the data and instructions. Multiple disk drives are also necessary to provide back up for files and programs.

A printing device is needed for the output of invoices, reports, etc. Although 15 cps (characters per second) printers are available, that equipment is too slow for most business applications. Typical requirements are better served by a line printer capable of printing at least 50 lines per minute. Otherwise the output from the system will be inordinately delayed. But even at 50 lines per minute, the printer can be exasperatingly slow.

Considering these additions and their associated programs, a small computer useable by a small business will cost between $15,000 and $25,000.[3] Although smaller systems can be configured for less money, their lack of capacity should preclude them from consideration.

---

[1] Nancy Krottek, "Mini and Micro Computer Survey," *Datamation,* Vol. 24, No. 8 (Aug. 1978), pp. 113–130.

[2] M. Steifel, "Floppy Disk Systems," *Mini-Micro Systems,* Vol. 11, No. 10 (Nov. 1978), pp. 37–51.

[3] Richard G. Canning and Barbara McNurtin, "MICROS Invade the Business World," *Datamation,* Vol. 24, No. 8 (Aug. 1978), pp. 93–95; and Neil D. Kelley, "Small Business Computers: Some New Options for Uses," *Infosystems,* Vol. 25, No. 10 (Oct. 1978), pp. 59–69.

The described configuration (48–64KB main storage, 500KB–1000KB floppy disk auxiliary storage, keyboard-CRT, and 50 lpm printer) is toward the low end of the spectrum for small computer systems. Depending on the needs of an organization, larger systems may be necessary.

Software: Software is the set of programs that makes a computer work. Without software a computer system is merely a knick-knack that eats electricity. A computer system needs two types of software–systems software and applications software. Systems software is the programs that operate the computer. Applications software uses systems software in the solution of business problems.

Every computer vendor provides systems software to operate their machine. The software includes operating systems, assemblers, compilers, interpreters, and various utilities, such as sort/merge. In general, the systems software provided with a machine is adequate, although software support continues to be a problem area.[4]

However, application software is another story. Application software, unlike systems software, does not deal directly with the computer. It uses the computer (and its systems software) for business data processing and for generating management reports. Application software requires an understanding of business problems, not of computers. Hence, computer vendors have been able to provide systems software that does the required job; but there is a dearth of applications software.

To be sure, most of the standard accounting applications are generally available. Such applications include programs for general ledger, payroll, accounts receivable (both open item and balance forward), accounts payable, and fixed asset accounting. But other application areas are less well developed. Order entry, sales analysis, sales forecasting, inventories, materials requirements planning, and master production scheduling, are currently available only for some computer systems. But independent program development is filling the void. Within the next two to three years, adequate application software should become widely available.

In the meantime, an organization will have to satisfy its needs for application software in other ways. The organization can develop its own specialized applications or contract for them. In either case, higher level programming languages speed the development of business applications. Currently, two languages, BASIC and FORTRAN, are generally available on small business computers.

BASIC is the most widely supported higher level programming language. BASIC (Beginners All-Purpose Symbolic Instruction Code) has the advantage of being easy to learn and use. It is interactive: This means that instructions can be entered and changed instantly. The immediate response

[4] "The Small Systems Market: A Survey," *Datamation,* Vol. 24, No. 12 (Nov. 1978), pp. 108–132.

of interactive systems eases the program development process. BASIC is interpretive: Each instruction is immediately changed into machine code. Interpreters typically require less main storage than compilers; therefore, less hardware is needed.

The other major, higher-level language that is extensively supported is FORTRAN. FORTRAN (FORmula TRANslator) requires a compiler and hence more main storage than a BASIC interpreter. It is excellent for analytic applications (engineering, scientific and management science problems).

COBOL (COmmon Business Oriented Language) and RPG (Report Program Generator) compilers are available on some systems. Support of other languages, such as PASCAL, APL, ALGOL, etc., is sporadic. Therefore, only BASIC and FORTRAN can be considered for generalized application development.

Success of a small computer system is not determined by the choice of hardware and software alone. Success takes a plan and people to unlock the power inherent in small computer systems.

Plan for Computers

The low price of computer systems tempts many managers. They have heard about the speed and accuracy of computers. They have heard about the prodigious storage capacity of computers. And they have heard about the almost miraculous way of providing information.

At the same time, managers have heard about bad experiences with computers. These horror stories deal with the inflexibility of computerized systems. They tell of problems in understanding computer professionals. And they tell of wasted effort, money, and manpower.

But the truth in either case, the glowing success story and the abysmal horror story, does not lie with the equipment. The computer is merely a tool. It can support either success or failure. Which will result depends on how it is used and what it is used for.

Management control of computer use determines whether or not a computer system supports organizational objectives. Hence, managers must know what the organizational objectives are before they can set the objectives for computer use. Then actual usage can be compared to the stated objectives to see if the system is effective.

Setting objectives for the use of computers is an important step. It should be done before an organization gets a system. But that requires identifying not only where the organization wants to go, but also where the organization is at present. Analysis of current operations identifies the areas where computers can be used to greatest benefit.[5]

[5] H. Bromberg, "The Consequences of Minicomputers," *Datamation,* Vol 24, No. 12 (Nov. 1978), pp. 98–103; Canning and McNurtin, loc. cit.; W. A. Saxon and Morris Edwards, "Decision Model for Distributed Processing," *Infosystems,* Vol 25, No. 9 (Sept. 1978), pp. 88–91; W. A. Saxon and Morris Edwards, "Inside the Distributed DP Model," *Infosystems,* Vol. 25, No. 10 (Oct. 1978), pp. 112–224; and Donald T. Winski, "Distributed Systems–Is Your Organization Ready?" *Infosystems,* Vol 25, No. 9 (Sept. 1978), pp. 38–42.

In the analysis, two types of questions need to be asked:

1. What are the data processing needs of the organization?
2. What are the information needs of management?

While the computer system can be designed to perform data processing efficiently and while it can answer management's cry for information, the ability of the computer system to respond to either need is only as good as the clarity and precision of the questions that it is asked. An ambiguous question will result in an amorphous design that leaves everybody dissatisfied. And such dissatisfaction perpetuates the horror stories.

Therefore, the organization must determine its data processing needs. Ask where computers can make a contribution to organizational operations. Are there problems in responding to customer questions? On-line inquiry systems should be able to speed up the answers. Are there problems with the accuracy of inventory records? Computers are noted for their accuracy. (Once a program has been debugged, all calculations will be consistent.) Have you inadvertently missed discount periods on vendor invoices? Set up a computerized tickling file so the system won't let you *accidentally* overlook a payment due date. Do you have too many stockouts? Delayed billings? Reports two to three weeks after the end of a period? Administrative people snowed by a blizzard of paper? Clerical people devoted solely to compiling reports for regulatory agencies? All of these problems, when carefully addressed, can be solved with the use of computer systems.

But these questions need to be addressed in detail. For each problem area detailed questions have to be asked, to provide the needed precision for computerized processing. What reports and documents have to be generated? How often? And how many? What are the input data? What is their volume and frequency? How much data has to be stored? How many files, what size, frequency of access, etc. These questions focus on the details of analysis. But these details are needed to explore a prospective problem area. A thorough description of the problem ensures that your organization adds to the number of success stories, not to the horror stories.

The use of computers is a business decision.[6] The low price of computer systems makes computer power available to small organizations and to individual departments in large organizations. To obtain the full benefits of computerized speed, accuracy and memory, an organization needs to plan. The plan should consider where and how the computer can be put to use. And in order to plan, an organization must know what its needs are. Therefore, a foundation for the use of a computer system has to exist before the computer system can be used successfully.

Prepare your People

The introduction of a computer system into an organizational unit is a dramatic change. The computer system changes the nature of the work performed by people. It changes the flow of work through an organizational

[6] Winski, loc. cit.

unit. And therefore the relationships between people are changed.

Even small changes in procedures can be traumatic for some people. But first-time computerization has more impact than a small change in procedures. Therefore, people have to be prepared through orientation and training sessions for the new system. Don't limit the sessions to clerical people. Management also needs to know what it can and cannot expect from a new computer system.

Once the requirements have been defined, once a plan for computer use has been established, once a commitment for hardware and software acquisition has been made, once a specific system has been chosen and purchased, then intensive preparation for the upcoming change can start. (Note that we are recommending training and orientation sessions prior to the actual delivery of the computer system.) At this time the organization knows the details of the system to be delivered and how it will be used. Therefore, it can focus its training where it will do the most good.

Small business computers are generally easy to operate and use. Hence, in most cases it will not be necessary to hire computer professionals. In larger organizations an adequate staff exists already to support the needs of management. In small organizations, managers will have to do some of the work themselves and contract outside the organization for the more technical aspects. But in either case, the training and orientation sessions should prepare the people for interaction with computer systems professionals. Hence, some understanding of the terminology and capabilities of computers in general has to be provided by these sessions.

The low cost of small computer systems has led to predictions of almost exponential growth in the number of organizations using them. Rather than being a matter of *whether,* it becomes a matter of *when.* When will your workplace have a computer system? Given this inevitability, then preparation now will pay off in the future. Getting your people prepared now makes the path of transition to a new system smoother.

Of course, with the passage of time, more and more people will already be familiar with computers. Business schools require introductory courses in data processing or information systems for their graduates. They learn the terminology of computers. They learn about the capabilities and limitations of hardware. And they learn how to program computers in BASIC. Since BASIC is so widely supported on small business computer systems, the students will be ready to make a contribution to any organization that is contemplating the use of a small business computer.

CONCLUSION

Low cost computer systems are a reality. But a manager should not be hypnotized by the cost of hardware. To make a computer system successful takes more than computing equipment. Success takes software, tailored to the needs of a business. It takes people who are trained to operate the hardware and people who are trained to use it. But most of all, it takes management—managers who are committed to planning for computerization, managers who set objectives and control computer usage, and managers who are willing to devote themselves to the successful introduction of change.

Appendices

SUMMARY OF BASIC COMMANDS AND INSTRUCTIONS

APPENDIX A

Summary of BASIC Commands:

CAT	Lists the names of programs in the user save area (catalogue).
LIST	Gives a printout (listing) of the program.
NEW	Tells the system that the operator is about to type in a new program; the system will ask for a program name.
OLD	Asks for a copy of a program from the user save area; the system will ask for the name of the program that should be retrieved.
RENAME	Gives a new name to the program that the user is working on.
REPLACE	Puts a copy of the program into the user save area under the program name; used when a copy of the program with the current program name already exists in the user save area.
RUN	Executes a program, i.e., commands a computer to do what the program instructions tell it to do.
SAVE	Puts a copy of the program into the user save area under the current program name.
UNSAVE	Eliminates a program from the system.

Summary of BASIC Instructions:

CLOSE #n	Closes file n and stores it in the user save area.
DATA 5,2,7	Used to hold data for fields in READ statements.
DIM #1,A(10,3) = 0	Dimensions a virtual file (table) and sets the last element value to zero.

DIM Y(X),Z(Q,R)	Sets the lists Y (represented by a letter) to X positions; defines that Z (represented by a letter) has Q rows and R columns; individual elements of lists and tables are identified by their location: position number in a list; row number *and* column number in a table.
END	Indicates the physical end of a program.
ERL	Gives the line number at which an ON ERROR condition took place
FOR Y = N TO M ⋮ NEXT Y	Sets up a loop; the FOR statement begins the loop; it sets Y to M (beginning value); the loop will continue until Y has a value greater than M (the upper bound); the NEXT statement loses the loop.
GO TO nnn	Tells the system to go to line number nnn for the next instruction.
IF ERR = n THEN RESUME line number	Tells the computer that if the error encountered is n, then processing should resume at the line number given.
IF x THEN nnn	If x is true then go to line nnn for the next instruction, otherwise (if x is false) go to the next line in sequence.
INPUT #n fieldnames	Reads a record from file number n; the file is identified by its file number. Records are separated by their fieldnames.
INPUT X,Y	Takes numeric values for fields X and Y from the keyboard.
INPUT X$, Y$	Gets alphabetic values for fields X$ and Y$ from the keyboard.
INT(X)	Makes the value X into an integer (whole number).
LET X = Y	Places the value of Y into the memory location X.

ON ERROR GO TO line number
Tells the computer to go to *line number* when an error is encountered.

OPEN "filename" AS FILE #n
Opens the file identified by the filename and gives it an identifying number; the filename can be from 1 to 6 characters; the file number can be from 1 to 12.

PRINT #n fieldnamel; ",";fieldname2;",";etc.
Writes a record on file n; the fields of the record will be separated by commas.

PRINT USING	Prints columns of data in a manner that they may be easily read.
PRINT X,Y	Displays the values of X and Y.
PRINT "XYZ"	Displays the alphabetic information XYZ.
READ X,Y,Z	Assigns values to fields from DATA Statements (X,Y,Z are arbitrary field names).
REM	Prints remarks for programmer; ignored by the computer.
STOP	Tells the system to stop.

Arithmetic operations:

X + Y	Add X to Y
X − Y	Subtract Y from X
X*Y	Multiply X by Y
X/Y	Divide X by Y
X**Y	Raise X to the Y power

Comparison operators:

X = Y	Equal (if X equals Y, this comparison is true).

$X<Y$	Less than (if X is strictly less than Y, this comparison is true).
$X< = Y$	Less than or equal to (if X is less than *or* equal to Y, this comparison is true).
$X>Y$	Greater than (if X is strictly greater than Y, this comparison is true).
$X> = Y$	Greater than or equal to (if X is greater than *or* equal to Y, this comparison is true).
$X<>Y$	Not equal to (if X is greater than or less than—that is, not equal to—Y, this expression is true).

APPENDIX B SORTING

Records may be sorted either alphabetically or numerically from many applications. In order to use both sort programs given in this appendix, it is important to understand something about the programs:

1. The file to be sorted is unchanged at the end of the sort.
2. The sorted file, at the conclusion of the program is called "SORT.FIL".
3. You must rename the "SORT.FIL" with the NAME command as soon as the sort is finished. It will automatically be saved. You can not use the RENAME command since "SORT.FIL" is a data file.
4. You must type the command EXTEND before you enter or use these programs.

In the chapter on totals and subtotals, it is necessary to sort the "EMPLOY" file by department number; then it becomes the "EMPLDP" file.

A listing of the numeric sorting program, an example running the program, and a program to rename "SORT.FIL" follow:

```
LIST
SORT4
1  PRINT "THIS PROGRAM SORTS RECORDS ON NUMERIC FIELDS'
05 ON ERROR GO TO 9000
10 REM       BUBBLE SORT
20 REM      BY FLOYD EUGENE PITTMAN
25 DIM KY$(100%,3%)
30 PRINT CHR$(126%) + CHR$(28%)
35 PRINT CHR$(7%)
40 PRINT "THIS PROGRAM SORTS DISK FILES"
45 PRINT 'TO BUILD A SEQUENTIALLY SORTED FILE'
50 PRINT\PRINT
```

```
60 INPUT'POSITION OF FIELD TO BE SORTED;1,2,3,ETC.';FLDPOS%
80 !*****  MAIN ROUTINE
90 DIM SRTFIL$(255%)
100 SRTFIL$(I%) = STRING$(LENG%,127%) FOR I% = 1% TO 255%
210 INPUT 'ENTER FILE NAME';FILE$

    \OPEN FILE$ FOR INPUT AS FILE #5%
235 OPEN 'SORT.FIL' FOR OUTPUT AS FILE #1%
240 GO SUB 300 !*****  LOADING FILE
250 GO SUB 400 !*****  SORTING FILE
260 GO SUB 500 !*****  LIST SORTED FILE
270 CLOSE #1%,#5%
280 GO TO 32767
300 !*****  LOADING FILE
309 PRINT '***********  LOADING  ***********'
310 FOR I% = 1% UNTIL EOF$ = 'YES'
315 CNT% = CNT% + 1%
320 INPUT LINE #5% SRTFIL$(I%)
321 SRTFIL$(I%) = CVT$$(SRTFIL$(I%),6%)
322 LOC%  = 1%\FDKY% = 0%
324 GO SUB 600 UNTIL FDKY% = FLDPOS%
326 KY$(I%,1%) = NUM$(OLOC%)
327 KY$(I%,3%) = NUM$((LOC% - OLOC%) - 1%)
328 KY$(I%,2%) = MID(SRTFIL$(I%),VAL(KY$(I%,1%)),VAL(KY$(I%,3%)))
330 NEXT I%
399 RETURN



400 !*****  SORTING FILE
410 PRINT '***********  SORTING FILE  ***********'
415 I% = 1%
420 GO SUB 430 UNTIL SRTFIL$(I% + 1%) = STRING$(LENG%,127%)
429 RETURN


430 HA=VAL(MID(SRTFIL$(I%),VAL(KY$(I%,1%)),VAL(KY$(I%,3%))))
433 HB=VAL(MID(SRTFIL$(I%+1%),VAL(KY$(I%+1%,1%)),VAL(KY$(I%+1%,3%))))
435 IF HA <HB THEN I% = I% + 1%

     ELSE

          HI% = I% + 1%

        \GO SUB 450 UNTIL HA < HB

        \I% = HI%
440 RETURN


450 HOLD$ = SRTFIL$(I% + 1%)

      \SRTFIL$(I% + 1%) = SRTFIL$(I%)

      \SRTFIL$(I%) = HOLD$
452 HKY1$ = KY$(I% + 1%,1%)

      \HKY2$ = KY$(I% + 1%,3%)

      \KY$(I% + 1%,1%) = KY$(I%,1%)

      \KY$(I% + 1%,3%) = KY$(I%,3%)
454 KY$(I%,1%) = HKY1$

      \KY$(I%,3%) = HKY2$
455 I% = I% - 1%
456 HA=VAL(MID(SRTFIL$(I%),VAL(KY$(I%,1%)),VAL(KY$(I%,3%))))
457 HB=VAL(MID(SRTFIL$(I%+1%),VAL(KY$(I%+1%,1%)),VAL(KY$(I%+1%,3%)))
499 RETURN
```

```
500 !*****  LISTING SORTED FILE
503 PRINT CHR$(126%) + CHR$(28%)
507 PRINT CHR$(7%)
510 PRINT '**********  SORTED FILE  **********'
515 FOR I% = 1% UNTIL SRTFIL$(I%) = STRING$(LENG%,127%)
519 PRINT #1% SRTFIL$(I%)
520 PRINT SRTFIL$(I%)
540 NEXT I%
599 RETURN



600 !*****  FIND KEY FIELD
605 OLOC% = LOC%
610 FD = INSTR(LOC%,SRTFIL$(I%),',')
620 LOC% = FD + 1
630 FDKY% = FDKY% + 1%
699 RETURN
9000 !*****  ERROR ROUTINE
9005 IF ERR = 11 AND SRTFIL$(I%) = STRING$(LENG%,127%) THEN RESUME 599
9010 IF ERR = 11 THEN EOF$ = 'YES'

      \RESUME 330
9020 IF ERR = 8 THEN PRINT 'READER IN USE - - PLEASE WAIT'

      \SLEEP 5%\RESUME
9030 IF ERR  = 14 THEN PRINT 'TURN ON READER'

      \SLEEP 5%\RESUME
9040  IF ERR = 5 THEN PRINT 'FILE DOES NOT EXIST - - PLEASE TRY AGAIN'

          \RESUME 210
9999 ON ERROR GO TO 0
32767 END

RUN
SORT4
THIS PROGRAM SORTS RECORDS ON NUMERIC FIELDS'
~^\

THIS PROGRAM SORTS DISK FILES
TO BUILD A SEQUENTIALLY SORTED FILE


POSITION OF FIELD TO BE SORTED;1,2,3,ETC.? 2
ENTER FILE NAME? EMPLOY
**********  LOADING  **********
**********  SORTING FILE  **********
~^\

**********  SORTED FILE  **********
422,1,WILLIAMS,4,40,0
368,1,WEAVER,3.5,40,2
198,1,TANNER,4.25,36,0
101,1,ADAMS,5,40,0
172,2,JOHNSON,3.75,40,0
313,7,SMITH,4.25,40,4
206,7,LESTER,5.25,40,0
347,12,GRAY,6,38,0
281,12,MILLER,6,40,0
255,12,SCHMIDT,5.6,40,4
103,12,BAKER,5.6,40,4
202,16,WILSON,4,40,0
108,16,COHEN,6.25,38,0
104,17,BRAVO,4,40,2

Ready

NAME "SORT.FIL" AS "EMPLDP"

Ready
```

In the update chapter, the "SALES" file had to be sorted alphabetically by salesman name. A listing of the alphabetic sorting program, an example running the program, and the renaming of "SORT.FIL" follow:

```
LIST
SORT3
1   PRINT 'THIS PROGRAM SORTS RECORDS ON ALPHABETIC FIELDS'
05 ON ERROR GO TO 9000
10 REM        BUBBLE SORT
20 REM      BY FLOYD EUGENE PITTMAN
25 DIM KY$(100%,3%)
30 PRINT CHR$(126%) + CHR$(28%)
35 PRINT CHR$(7%)
40 PRINT "THIS PROGRAM SORTS DISK FILES"
45 PRINT 'TO BUILD A SEQUENTIALLY SORTED FILE'
50 PRINT\PRINT
60 INPUT'POSITION OF FIELD TO BE SORTED;1,2,3,ETC.';FLDPOS%
80 !*****  MAIN ROUTINE
90 DIM SRTFIL$(255%)
100 SRTFIL$(I%) = STRING$(LENG%,127%) FOR I% = 1% TO 255%
210 INPUT 'ENTER FILE NAME';FILE$

    \OPEN FILE$ FOR INPUT AS FILE #5%
235 OPEN 'SORT.FIL' FOR OUTPUT AS FILE #1%
240 GO SUB 300 !*****  LOADING FILE
250 GO SUB 400 !*****  SORTING FILE
260 GO SUB 500 !*****  LIST SORTED FILE
270 CLOSE #1%,#5%
280 GO TO 32767
300 !*****  LOADING FILE
309 PRINT '**********  LOADING  **********'
310 FOR I% = 1% UNTIL EOF$ = 'YES'
315 CNT% = CNT% + 1%
320 INPUT LINE #5% SRTFIL$(I%)
321 SRTFIL$(I%) = CVT$$(SRTFIL$(I%),6%)
322 LOC%  = 1%\FDKY% = 0%
324 GO SUB 600 UNTIL FDKY% = FLDPOS%
326 KY$(I%,1%) = NUM$(OLOC%)
327 KY$(I%,3%) = NUM$((LOC% - OLOC%) - 1%)
328 KY$(I%,2%) = MID(SRTFIL$(I%),VAL(KY$(I%,1%)),VAL(KY$(I%,3%)))
330 NEXT I%
399 RETURN


400 !*****  SORTING FILE
410 PRINT '**********  SORTING FILE  **********'
415 I% = 1%
420 GO SUB 430 UNTIL SRTFIL$(I% + 1%) = STRING$(LENG%,127%)
429 RETURN


430 HA$ = MID(SRTFIL$(I%),VAL(KY$(I%,1%)),VAL(KY$(I%,3%)))
433 HB$ = MID(SRTFIL$(I% + 1%),VAL(KY$(I% + 1%,1%)),VAL(KY$(I% + 1%,3%))
)
435 IF HA$ < HB$ THEN I% = I% + 1%

      ELSE

         HI% = I% + 1%

         \GO SUB 450 UNTIL HA$ < HB$

         \I% = HI%
440 RETURN
```

```
450 HOLD$ = SRTFIL$(I% + 1%)

     \SRTFIL$(I% + 1%) = SRTFIL$(I%)

     \SRTFIL$(I%) = HOLD$
452 HKY1$ = KY$(I% + 1%,1%)

     \HKY2$ = KY$(I% + 1%,3%)

     \KY$(I% + 1%,1%) = KY$(I%,1%)

     \KY$(I% + 1%,3%) = KY$(I%,3%)
454 KY$(I%,1%) = HKY1$

     \KY$(I%,3%) = HKY2$
455 I% = I% - 1%
456 HA$ = MID(SRTFIL$(I%),VAL(KY$(I%,1%)),VAL(KY$(I%,3%)))
457 HB$ = MID(SRTFIL$(I% + 1%),VAL(KY$(I% + 1%,1%)),VAL(KY$(I% + 1%,3%))
)
499 RETURN



500 !*****  LISTING SORTED FILE
503 PRINT CHR$(126%) + CHR$(28%)
507 PRINT CHR$(7%)
510 PRINT '**********  SORTED FILE  **********'
515 FOR I% = 1% UNTIL SRTFIL$(I%) = STRING$(LENG%,127%)
519 PRINT #1% SRTFIL$(I%)
520 PRINT SRTFIL$(I%)
540 NEXT I%
599 RETURN



600 !*****  FIND KEY FIELD
605 OLOC% = LOC%
610 FD = INSTR(LOC%,SRTFIL$(I%),',')
620 LOC% = FD + 1
630 FDKY% = FDKY% + 1%
699 RETURN
9000 !*****  ERROR ROUTINE
9005 IF ERR = 11 AND SRTFIL$(I%) = STRING$(LENG%,127%) THEN RESUME 599
9010 IF ERR = 11 THEN EOF$ = 'YES'

      \RESUME 330
9020 IF ERR = 8 THEN PRINT 'READER IN USE - - PLEASE WAIT'

     \SLEEP 5%\RESUME
9030 IF ERR  = 14 THEN PRINT 'TURN ON READER'

     \SLEEP 5%\RESUME
9040  IF ERR = 5 THEN PRINT 'FILE DOES NOT EXIST - - PLEASE TRY AGAIN'

          \RESUME 210
9999 ON ERROR GO TO 0
32767 END

Ready


RUN
SORT3
THIS PROGRAM SORTS RECORDS ON ALPHABETIC FIELDS
~^\

THIS PROGRAM SORTS DISK FILES
TO BUILD A SEQUENTIALLY SORTED FILE
```

```
POSITION OF FIELD TO BE SORTED;1,2,3,ETC.? 2
ENTER FILE NAME? SALES
**********  LOADING  **********
**********  SORTING FILE  **********
~^\

**********  SORTED FILE  **********
1,BILL,12050,.05
3,BOB,14690,.05
3,CLYDE,7340,.04
3,HARRY,9460,.045
1,JOE,5270,.045
2,PHIL,11200,.055
2,TOM,6940,.04

Ready

NAME "SORT.FIL" AS "SALESS"

Ready
```

SELECTED ERROR MESSAGES

APPENDIX C

In the ON ERROR statement, the error that is usually tested for is error number 11 (ERR = 11). If another error should occur, the statement PRINT "UNUSUAL ERROR" ERR will be printed with an error number (ERR). The following is an abbreviated list of error numbers and an interpretation of their meaning:

Error Number	*Interpretation*
2	The filename specified is not acceptable. It contains unacceptable characters or it has been specified incorrectly.
4	Storage space allowed for the current user on the device specified has been used or the device as a whole is too full to accept further data.
5	The file or account number specified was not found.
6	Attempt to use an illegal or nonexistent device specification.
7	An attempt was made to open one of the twelve I/O channels which had already been opened by the program.
9	Attempt to perform I/O on one of the twelve channels which has not been previously opened in the program.
10	The user was prohibited from performing the requested operation because the kind of operation was illegal (such as input from a line printer) or because the user did not have the privileges necessary (such as attempting to delete a protected file).

11 Attempt to perform input beyond the end of a data file; or a BASIC program is called into memory and is found to contain no END statement.

12 An I/O error has occurred on the system level. The user has no guarantee that the last operation has been performed.

13 One or more characters may have been transmitted incorrectly due to a parity error, bad punch combination on a card, or similar error.

16 An attempt was made to rename a file with the name of a file which already exists, or an attempt was made by the system manager to insert an account number which is already within the system.

17 Only one open DECtape output file is permitted per DECtape drive. Only one open file per magtape drive is permitted.

24 The current user does not have access to the specified private disk pack.

38 A parity error was detected in the memory occupied by this job.

42 Virtual core buffers must be 512 bytes long.

43 A non-disk device is open on the channel upon which the virtual array is referenced.

44 In-core array size is too large.

45 An attempt was made to use a virtual array before opening the corresponding disk file.

46 Attempt was made to open a file on an I/O channel outside the range of the integer numbers 1 to 12.

50 A READ or INPUT statement detected data in an illegal format. For example, 1..2 is an improperly formed number, and 1.3 is an improperly formed integer.

51 Attempt to use a computed integer outside the range $-32767 \leq n \leq 32767$. If no transfer to an error handling routine is made, zero is returned as the integer value.

52 Integer or floating point overflow or underflow.

55 Attempt to reference an array element beyond the number of elements created for the array when it was dimensioned.

57 The DATA list was exhausted and a READ requested additional data.

58 The index value in an ON-GOTO or ON-GOSUB statement is less than one or greater than the number of line numbers in the list.

59 An INPUT statement did not find enough data in one line to satisfy all the specified variables.

60 The integer index in a FOR loop attempted to go beyond 32766 or below − 32766.

61 Attempt by the user program to divide some quantity by zero. If no transfer is made to an error handler routine, a Ø is returned as the result.

APPENDIX D

HOW TO . . .

Problem	*Solution*
Stop a printout on the terminal or printer	Depress the C key while pressing CTRL
Stop execution of a program if nothing seems to be happening	Depress the C key while pressing CTRL
Renumber lines in a BASIC program	Your computer may have a resequence program. Try typing RUN RESEQ or RUN RESEQ$. If the program exists, it will ask for beginning line number and interval. Input of 100,10 will result in the program being renumbered so that the first statement is 100 and lines are numbered consecutively 100, 110, 120, etc. All GO TO and other statements that contain line numbers are automatically changed.
Delete programs from the catalog	UNSAVE PROGRAMNAME
Delete data files from the catalog	KILL "FILENAME"
Delete lines from a program	DELETE 180–270: This will cause lines 180–270 of the program in your work space to be deleted DELETE 120, 270,390: Lines 120, 270, and 390 will be deleted.
List a data file	Write a program that reads and prints it.

Index